Get Updates and More on Nolo.com

Go to this book's companion page at:

www.nolo.com/back-of-book/RENT.html

When there's an important change to the law affecting this book, we'll post updates. You'll also find articles and other related materials.

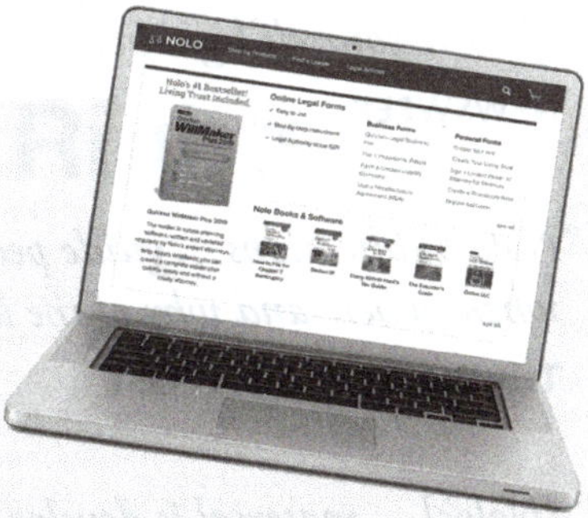

More Resources from Nolo.com

Legal Forms, Books, & Software
Hundreds of do-it-yourself products—all written in plain English, approved, and updated by our in-house legal editors.

Legal Articles
Get informed with thousands of free articles on everyday legal topics. Our articles are accurate, up to date, and reader friendly.

Find a Lawyer
Want to talk to a lawyer? Use Nolo to find a lawyer who can help you with your case.

NOLO
LAW for ALL

TENTH EDITION JANUARY 2021

Editor ANN O'CONNELL

Book Design SUSAN PUTNEY

Proofreader IRENE BARNARD

Index RICHARD GENOVA

Printer BANG PRINTING

Names: Portman, Janet, author. | O'Connell, Ann, author.
Title: Renters' rights / Attorney Janet Portman and Ann O'Connell.
Description: Tenth edition. | Berkeley, CA : Nolo, 2021. | Includes index.
Identifiers: LCCN 2020033199 (print) | LCCN 2020033200 (ebook) | ISBN 9781413328226 (paperback) | ISBN 9781413328233 (ebook)
Subjects: LCSH: Landlord and tenant--United States--Popular works.
Classification: LCC KF590.Z9 P673 2021 (print) | LCC KF590.Z9 (ebook) | DDC 346.7304/34--dc23
LC record available at https://lccn.loc.gov/2020033199
LC ebook record available at https://lccn.loc.gov/2020033200

This book covers only United States law, unless it specifically states otherwise.

Please note

We know that accurate, plain-English legal information can help you solve many of your own legal problems. But this text is not a substitute for personalized advice from a knowledgeable lawyer. If you want the help of a trained professional—and we'll always point out situations in which we think that's a good idea—consult an attorney licensed to practice in your state.

About the Authors

Janet Portman is an attorney, an editor, and Nolo's Executive Editor. She received undergraduate and graduate degrees from Stanford and a law degree from Santa Clara University. She is an expert on landlord-tenant law and the coauthor of *Every Landlord's Legal Guide, Every Landlord's Guide to Finding Great Tenants, Every Tenant's Legal Guide, Leases & Rental Agreements, Negotiate the Best Lease for Your Business,* and *First-Time Landlord.*

Ann O'Connell is an attorney and editor at Nolo. She received an undergraduate degree from Boston College and a law degree from U.C. Berkeley School of Law. She is also a licensed Colorado real estate broker, and is a coauthor of *Every Landlord's Legal Guide* and *Nolo's Essential Guide to Buying Your First Home*. Before joining Nolo, Ann focused on real estate and business matters as a practicing attorney, and represented both sellers and buyers as a real estate agent.

Table of Contents

Appendixes

Renters' Rights—Your Legal Companion

Dealing with your landlord can be a challenging experience: Maybe you have a well-intentioned landlord who doesn't know the law or is bad with business details; or maybe you have a mean, petty, and avaricious landlord. (If you have a perfect landlord, you're probably not reading this book.) You might know what you want to do in response, but the legal and efficient solution is likely quite different.

This book gives you the knowledge you need to thrive as a renter and push back against misinformed and malicious landlords. You'll learn about how your landlord must respect your privacy and provide you with a livable home; how your landlord can and cannot use your security deposit; and your right to being treated in a fair, nondiscriminatory manner by your landlord. It includes all kinds of important state-specific information, with many detailed charts on everything from state security deposit rules to state laws prohibiting landlord retaliation.

It's important to understand that, in many situations, tenants can't legally demand that landlords fulfill their legal responsibilities unless the tenants, too, have satisfied their own legal duties. For example, if you want to force your landlord to perform major repairs by using a rent withholding law, you must at least be current on the rent—and in many states, you must also give the landlord a certain type and amount of notice before you can withhold rent.

Consequently, throughout this book we alert you to your legal duties—not to be preachy, but to educate you and prevent legal difficulties should you need to take action. Once you understand the strength (or weakness) of your position, you'll know how far you can push—both informally through negotiation and formally by invoking your legal remedies, in court if necessary. In short, our goal is to make you a savvy, practical tenant who directs just the right amount of time and energy into solving (or better, preventing) a landlord-tenant dispute.

RESOURCE

Check out tenants' rights groups. Many communities, especially those with rent control, have active tenants' rights groups, such as the San Francisco Tenants Union (SFTU.org) and Tenants Together (California, TenantsTogether.org); and online resources, such as Tenant Net (New York City and state, Tenant.net). To find local tenant advocacy groups, check out the Resources section of the U.S. Department of Housing and Urban Development (HUD) website (HUD.gov). HUD provides a wide variety of local resources, including links to tenant unions and legal aid organizations for each state; even if you don't qualify for legal aid services, you will find useful information on tenant rights on many legal aid websites.

Rent Control Heads Up

If you live in a community with rent control, you're probably well aware of that fact (and thankful for it). It's important to understand that most rent control ordinances affect more than just the amount of rent a landlord may charge. Many of the legal principles explained in this book have a special twist when rent control enters the picture. Typically, rent control laws also regulate:

- when and why landlords can legally refuse to renew a lease or discontinue a monthly rental agreement
- the amount of notice, or warning, that a landlord must give a tenant before terminating a tenancy, and the language that must be used in a termination notice, and
- whether the landlord must pay interest on a deposit.

Throughout this book, you'll find rent control notes wherever it's likely that rent control will affect the main discussion. Chapter 12 is devoted entirely to rent control and explores the typical provisions in rent control ordinances in depth.

Other Helpful Nolo Resources for Tenants

Renters' Rights covers common problems encountered by most tenants. Each topic is discussed in more detail in Nolo's larger book, *Every Tenant's Legal Guide* (Nolo). The *Guide* also covers specific environmental hazards such as lead, asbestos, and mold; landlords' liability for tenant injuries and losses (including those caused by criminals); and permissible reasons for tenancy terminations. *Every Tenant's Legal Guide* includes an overview of the eviction procedure and dozens of forms such as a Rental Application, Receipt and Holding Deposit Agreement, Notice of Intent to Move Out, and more. To order, go to Nolo.com.

If you rent in California, be sure to see *California Tenants' Rights*, by Janet Portman and J. Scott Weaver. This Nolo book, written specifically for tenants in the Golden State, covers everything from California rent control rules to rules and procedures for rent withholding to the legal forms necessary to fight an eviction in court.

Also, be sure to check out the Tenants' section of Nolo.com for a wide variety of articles of interest to tenants, including detailed state-by-state charts on the topics covered in this book, as well as others, such as state rules on abandoned property.

Finally, if you need a lawyer, you might want to consider Nolo's Lawyer Directory (Nolo.com/lawyers). It includes comprehensive profiles of the lawyers who advertise there, including each one's education, background, area of expertise (such as landlord-tenant law), and more. You can also submit information about your legal issue to several local attorneys who handle real estate issues, and then pick the lawyer you'd like to work with.

Who shouldn't use this book? Don't use this book if you are renting commercial property or space in a mobile home park, hotel, or marina. If you are a tenant in government-subsidized or -owned housing (including the "Section 8" program), your lease will contain terms required by the government, which neither you nor your landlord can change. Tenants who lease residential space in condominiums are generally on the same legal footing as those who rent single-family houses, which means that this book will apply to them. However, condo tenants are also subject to the condominium association's operating rules and regulations (known as "CC&Rs"), which might impose obligations or restrictions on tenants and landlords in addition to those found in federal, state, and local law.

Rules to Rent By

You'll see "Rules to Rent By" at the conclusion of every chapter. It's our way of summing up the chapter's key points. Here are a few general rules to get you started:

The best way to win over a prospective landlord is to be prepared. Bring a completed rental application, written references from landlords, and a current copy of your credit report when you first check out a rental. If the rental accepts pets, bring a copy of your dog or cat resume and pet references (search The Humane Society of the United States' website, HumaneSociety.org, for "pet resume").

Carefully review all the important conditions of the tenancy before you sign on the dotted line. Make sure the lease or rental agreement doesn't contain a provision that you find unacceptable—for example, a no-pets clause.

To avoid disputes or misunderstandings with your landlord, get it in writing. Keep copies of any correspondence (sent return receipt requested) and follow up an oral agreement with a letter, setting out what was said (and decided). For example, if you ask your landlord to make repairs, put your request in writing and keep a copy for yourself. If the landlord responds orally, send a letter repeating and confirming the response. (See "Using Email for Notice or a Letter of Understanding," in Chapter 2, for information on how to use email to deliver written requests.)

Know and protect your privacy rights. Emotion-filled misunderstandings often arise over a landlord's right to enter a rental unit and a tenant's right to be left alone. If you understand your privacy rights—for example, the amount of notice your landlord must provide before entering—it will be easier to protect them.

Rules to Rent By (continued)

Know your rights to live in a habitable rental unit—and don't give them up. Landlords must offer tenants livable premises, including adequate weatherproofing; heat, water, and electricity; and clean, sanitary, and structurally safe premises. If your rental unit is not kept in good repair, you might have a number of options, from withholding a portion of the rent to pay for repairs to calling the building inspector (who can usually order the landlord to make repairs) to moving out without liability for future rent.

Communicate with your landlord. If there's a problem—for example, if the landlord is slow to make repairs—talk with the landlord to see if the issue can be resolved short of a nasty legal battle.

Make sure the security deposit refund procedures and allowable deductions are spelled out in your lease or rental agreement. This will help protect your deposit and avoid misunderstandings that can end up in court.

Get Updates and More at This Book's Companion Page on Nolo.com

If we become aware of important legal developments that affect the information in this book, we'll post updates on Nolo's website, on a page specifically dedicated to this book:

www.nolo.com/back-of-book/RENT.html

You'll find other useful information on this book's companion page, too, such as corrections to the text and links to related, helpful Nolo products.

CHAPTER

1

Play the Landlord's Game: How to Score a Great Apartment

Looking for a place? No problem—as long as you have plenty of money, great references, no pets, and not too many roommates. If your reaction to this line is, "Unfortunately, that doesn't describe me," read on. You don't have to be wealthy or squeaky clean to get the rental you want—just savvy.

The good news. Thanks to federal and state antidiscrimination laws, landlords are limited in what they can say and do when selecting tenants. Basically, landlords must have a legitimate business reason for turning you down, or they risk running afoul of these laws, which can create big legal trouble for them. Because antidiscrimination laws are so important, we devote a whole chapter to them: Chapter 5.

The sobering news. Aside from complying with antidiscrimination laws, landlords have a lot of leeway in choosing tenants. Landlords are legally free to choose whomever they think will be the best, most stable tenant—ideally, someone who pays the rent on time and won't cause any problems.

Tenant Traps

Read this chapter to find out why you should:

- **Never rent from a landlord who asks personal non–business-related questions or subjects you to intense grilling.** These are red flags that indicate that the landlord does not understand—or chooses not to follow—the law.
- **Never pay more for a credit check than a reasonable approximation of the landlord's actual costs.** A landlord who gouges you when you're applying to rent will continue to do so once you're renting.
- **Never let a prospective landlord see your credit report before you do.** If the report is inaccurate, you need to take immediate steps to fix it. If the report is correct but damaging, you should prepare your explanations and defenses in advance.
- **Never lie on the rental application.** It's the kiss of death.
- **Never rent a place that you have serious misgivings about—** whether it's the landlord, the neighbors, the neighborhood, or the unit itself. It might be harder than you think to get out.

Because landlords can choose tenants based on their assessment of how much maintenance the applicant might require, applicants with a shadow or two in their past (a bad reference, a few late rent payments) or a shaky present (low income relative to the monthly rent) need to know how to anticipate—and head off—the landlord's concerns before they solidify into a rejection. And, if you live in a tight rental market—like New York City or San Francisco—you'll need to act fast, be persistent, and be street-smart to score a reasonably priced rental.

This chapter alerts you to the main factors landlords consider when choosing tenants, such as credit reports and references, and gives advice on how to improve your chances of getting a place you like—and can afford.

Legal and Illegal Reasons for Turning You Down

Landlords can legally set whatever criteria they want for tenants, as long as they are reasonably related to their business needs and don't violate antidiscrimination laws. The Federal Fair Housing Acts (42 U.S.C. §§ 3601–3619) prohibit discrimination on the basis of race, color, religion, national origin, gender, age, familial status (having children), and physical or mental disability (including alcoholism and past drug addiction). In addition, many states and cities also prohibit discrimination based on other factors, such as marital status, sexual orientation, and gender identity. Chapter 5 discusses illegal discrimination and how to file a complaint with a fair housing agency.

A landlord may reject you for a variety of legal reasons, such as poor credit history, a debt-to-income ratio that a reasonable businessperson would deem too high to leave money for rent, negative references from a previous landlord or employer, a criminal conviction, or a prior eviction lawsuit (even one that you won). As long as they don't discriminate illegally, landlords can basically choose whomever they want. For example, a landlord can refuse to rent to smokers or disallow pets because smokers (and pet owners) as a group are not protected by antidiscrimination laws. (The exception would be animals used by a person with a legal disability.) If your lifestyle conflicts with a landlord's no-pets policy, no-smoking policy, or some other legitimate lease or rental agreement term, you're out of luck unless you can make some convincing arguments for your case. ("Negotiating With the Landlord," in Chapter 2, suggests ways to get around landlord restrictions.)

What about roommates? A landlord can limit the number of occupants for health and safety or legitimate business reasons. A landlord may not adopt a low occupancy standard if the result eliminates families with children—this is a violation of the fair housing laws, as discussed in "Discrimination Prohibited by Federal Laws," in Chapter 5.

CAUTION

You are your own worst enemy if you lie on your rental application. Your landlord can easily find out that you don't make $50,000 per year by talking with your employer. Misrepresentations on the rental application are always legitimate grounds for rejection. And even if you slip by, ask yourself whether you want to rent from a landlord who is so careless. Would you be concerned to learn that the "former schoolteacher" next door has twice been evicted for riotous parties? A landlord who didn't check up on you probably didn't check up on your neighbor, either.

Rental Application Questions—How Far Can They Go?

Most landlords will want you to fill out a rental application with information on your employment, income, credit and financial information, rental housing history, and any criminal convictions (but not mere arrests). It's legal (in most areas) to ask for all this information and use it to make rental decisions. Landlords may also legally ask you for your Social Security and driver's license numbers and (except in New York City and California) for proof of your legal residency in the United States. Landlords may even ask if you smoke or if you've ever been sued.

How far can landlords go? They can ask for any information that will:

- tell them whether you're likely to be a good tenant, and
- help them find you if you skip town owing them for rent or property damage.

Questions that don't relate to these two issues are probably not legal.

Keep in mind, however, that not all discrimination is illegal, so some questions that don't "sound right" might in fact be legal. (See "Are You Two, Like, Together?" below.)

Too Expensive? Says Who?

Money talks, especially in rental housing. If the landlord reasonably concludes that you can't afford to pay the rent in view of your income and existing debt level (which will be on your credit report), the landlord may legally refuse to rent to you. Many landlords use a rent-to-income ratio of one-to-three (rent can be no more than one-third of your gross income) as a rule of thumb.

As a broad generalization, you too probably don't want to spend more than 25% to 35% of your monthly income on rent, but this will obviously depend on your other expenses. And you won't want to live in a penthouse if it means you need to eat popcorn every night.

Question One, Question All

While landlords are entitled to ask business-related questions on a rental application or during an interview, there is an important hitch: They should subject all applicants to the identical set of basic questions. Because federal and state antidiscrimination laws make it illegal to single out members of certain groups (such as people of a certain race or ethnic background) for special treatment, interview or application questions that aren't directed at everyone constitute special treatment. For example, landlords who ask about immigration history (in states that allow this) should ask all tenants, not just those whom they suspect might be in the country illegally. Questioning only those from the Middle East would amount to illegal discrimination on the basis of national origin. Similarly, requiring credit reports only from African Americans would also be considered illegal discrimination.

Are You Two, Like, Together?

Most landlords don't care a bit about whom you share your bed with—they're much more interested in whether you pay your rent on time and are a decent housekeeper and a considerate neighbor. Unfortunately, a few landlords see themselves as enforcers of their chosen code of morality. For instance, some people do not want to rent to heterosexual, unmarried couples, and some refuse to rent to homosexual couples.

In many states, unmarried straight couples and gay and lesbian couples are not protected by antidiscrimination laws, meaning landlords can get away with these kinds of choices. (In Chapter 5, see "Discrimination Prohibited by State and Local Law.") In these states, it would not be illegal for a landlord to question you and your would-be roommate about the nature of your relationship.

If you and your friend are questioned concerning your relationship, what should you do? This is an issue for *all* roommates, even the ones who are just friends and heterosexual, whom the landlord would presumably welcome with no problem. Think about what this line of questioning bodes for future dealings with this landlord: Here is a businessperson who is inappropriately interested in his customers' private lives. Chances are he spends his time and energy checking up on his tenants' love lives, at the expense of running a pleasant and livable property. If at all possible, look elsewhere.

How to Check Out Potential Landlords

Conscientious prospective landlords will probably take the time to learn about your rental and employment history. There's no reason why you, too, can't ask a few questions to find out whether you want to rent from a prospective landlord. Ask current tenants and neighbors what it's like to live there; ask the tenant whose unit you're considering why she's moving out. If you learn that she's leaving in disgust over poor management or dreadful neighbors whom the landlord won't evict, you'll want to think twice about signing a lease or rental agreement. If possible, talk with other people and businesses in the neighborhood; they might know something about the reputation of the building, landlord, or manager. Keep in mind that a building with a large turnover rate, and especially one where evictions are common, is probably not run very well. As part of your research, check out ApartmentRatings.com. This comprehensive website is used by about 30% of apartment seekers nationwide. Along with ratings, it includes other useful information about rentals, such as estimated rents and pet policies.

Your Credit Report Can Make or Break Your Application

Many landlords consider credit reports to be a litmus test of how well you manage your money. Like it or not, your financial history is a powerful indicator of whether you will be a reliable tenant who pays rent on time and doesn't cause problems. A landlord can legitimately turn you down for a bad credit report.

Fortunately, the law imposes some restraints on collecting and reporting on an individual's credit history. The Fair Credit Reporting Act (15 U.S.C. §§ 1681 and following) covers all aspects of credit reports, including your access to your file, your right to dispute information in it, and steps you can take to correct inaccurate reporting. It also regulates investigative background reports, including your right to be told that such a report has been requested. Some states have their own laws that give consumers more protections.

What's in Your Credit Report

Credit reports show your credit history for the past seven years, including whether you have ever been:

- late paying rent or bills, including student or car loans
- the subject of a "charge off" (when a store declares an overdue account uncollectible)
- evicted from a rental unit, or
- involved in another type of lawsuit, such as a personal injury claim.

A credit report will also state whether you have filed for bankruptcy in the past ten years.

If you've never borrowed money or used a credit card, the report will have large blank spaces that would normally be filled with a consumer's history. Ironically, a landlord may refuse to rent to you because you don't have a good history of debt management, even if you have been a fastidious on-time, cash-only consumer! The landlord will be worried that the first time you encounter lean times might be when the rent is due—and the landlord has no way of knowing whether, if this happens, you'll be able to put your rental obligation at the top of your list. (See "How to Deal With Problems (Your Fault) in Your Credit Report," below, for advice on how to deal with this situation.)

Consumer Relief After the Coronavirus Pandemic

The coronavirus pandemic caused many consumers and businesspeople to lose their incomes, making it hard to pay their debts. In response, Congress passed the federal Coronavirus Aid, Relief, and Economic Security (CARES) Act. It prohibits creditors from adverse credit reporting during the COVID-19 crisis under certain circumstances.

Specifically, suppose your ability to pay rent was affected by the coronavirus, and you asked your landlord to defer your rent payment or even lower it. If your landlord agrees by deferring payments or modifying the rent, the landlord cannot report your account as delinquent to the credit reporting agencies, so long as you weren't already behind on your rent payments.

Verify Credit-Check Fees

Landlords can charge a fee for the cost of the credit report itself and their time and trouble to order it and read it—$30 or $40 is common. You can call the credit bureau to verify the actual cost of getting a report. Some states, such as California, regulate how much the landlord can charge (call your state's consumer protection agency to find out if your state has set a limit). Find your agency at USA.gov/state-consumer.

Your Right to a Refund of a Credit-Check Fee

Some unscrupulous landlords collect credit-check fees but never run a credit check, pocketing the money instead. If a prospective landlord has done this, you're entitled to a refund. If you suspect this illegal behavior, contact a credit reporting agency as soon as you've been rejected by a landlord to see whether the landlord actually requested your report. If not, ask for your money back; if you get no results, contact your state's consumer protection office.

If the landlord ordered a credit report and you decide not to take a rental unit or the landlord chooses someone else, you are not entitled to a refund.

Your Right to Know When Your Credit Report Does You In

A landlord who does not rent to you because of negative information in your credit report is legally required to give you the name, address, and telephone number of the credit agency that reported the negative information. The landlord must also tell you of your right to a free copy of your credit report from this agency, if you ask for it within 60 days. If a landlord won't rent to you based on what's in your credit report, it's a good idea to get a copy of the report and fix any incorrect items before applying to rent somewhere else.

Why and How to Check Your Credit Rating

Because your credit report is so important, you should always check it before you start your housing search. This will give you the opportunity to correct or clear up any mistakes, such as out-of-date or just plain wrong information. It's all too common for credit bureaus to confuse names, addresses, Social Security numbers, or employers. Especially if you have a common name (say, John Brown), chances are good you'll find information in your credit file on other John Browns—or even John Brownes or Jon Browns. Obviously, you don't want this incorrect information given to prospective landlords, especially if the person you're being confused with is in worse financial shape than you.

Spotting inaccurate information isn't the only reason to check your credit report. If your report contains accurate but damaging information, it's better that you know exactly what it says before a prospective landlord sees it. That way, you can anticipate any objections and formulate your explanation, which will better your chances of convincing the landlord that your financial troubles are all in the past.

Get a Copy of Your Credit Report

The three largest credit bureaus, with offices throughout the United States, are Experian, Equifax, and TransUnion. Virtually every credit report in the U.S. is generated by one of these three agencies. They compile credit information on individuals and provide reports to affiliate companies, landlords, and others upon request. You can obtain a copy of your own credit report from any or all of these agencies.

If you'd like to see a copy of your credit report, it's easy and cheap. You can get a free copy of your credit report once every 12 months. Go to AnnualCreditReport.com.

TIP

Copy your own credit report and save on credit check fees. If you're applying for more than one rental, you'll find that credit-check fees (at $30 or $40 a pop) mount up quickly when every landlord orders a report. Get your own credit report and make several copies to give landlords when you apply for a rental. While landlords might still want to order your credit report directly (some might fear that you've doctored your copy), it's worth a try.

How to Handle Errors (Not Your Fault) in Your Credit Report

If you see entries in your report that are wrong, take action. All three major credit reporting agencies—Experian, Equifax, and TransUnion—allow you to dispute inaccurate information by going online. To start the online dispute process, go to:

- Equifax: www.equifax.com/personal/disputes
- Experian: www.experian.com/disputes, and
- TransUnion: www.transunion.com/disputes.

You can also submit your dispute by calling the agency or sending a letter in the mail. If you send a letter, list each incorrect item and explain why it's wrong. Under federal law, the credit bureau must investigate within 30 days (under some states' laws, it's less). If the investigation confirms that you are right (or if the creditor who provided the information can no longer verify it), the bureau must delete the information from your file.

Unfortunately, a request for an investigation doesn't always right the situation to your complete satisfaction. If the credit reporting agency fails to remove inaccurate or outdated information, lists a debt you refused to pay because of a legitimate dispute with the creditor, or reports a lawsuit against you that was abandoned, you have the right to place a 100-word statement in your file, giving your version of the situation. Be sure to submit such a statement immediately if your situation fits one of the above descriptions. In addition, you can contact the Federal Trade Commission (FTC) and the Consumer Financial Protection Bureau (CFPB) to complain about the inaccuracies.

Keep in mind that if one credit bureau has inaccurate information on you, it's likely that others do, too. If you find errors in your report from one credit bureau, be sure to check your files at the other two agencies.

For more information on credit reports, including how to correct inaccuracies, visit the FTC's website (FTC.gov) and the CFPB's website (www.consumerfinance.gov).

How to Deal With Problems (Your Fault) in Your Credit Report

If your credit file shows negative but accurate information, or if you have no credit history, take these steps to give your rental application a boost:

- See if the prospective landlord will accept a cosigner—a creditworthy person who signs the lease or rental agreement and agrees to cover any rent or damage-repair costs you fail to pay. Keep in mind that the landlord will evaluate the cosigner with the same criteria used for you—so your willing but broke college buddy isn't likely to be accepted.
- Offer to pay a large security deposit (but within legal limits), or offer to prepay rent for several months. (Chapter 4 discusses security deposits and state limits.)
- Show proof of steps you've taken to improve bad credit—for example, enrolling in a debt counseling group, a recent history of making and paying for purchases on credit, and maintaining a checking or savings account.
- Get positive references from friends, colleagues, employers, and previous landlords.

RESOURCE

For a detailed description of how to obtain a credit report and challenge its contents, and for information on your state laws, see *Solve Your Money Troubles,* by Cara O'Neill and Amy Loftsgordon (Nolo). For suggestions on how to reestablish your good credit, see *Credit Repair,* by Amy Loftsgordon and Cara O'Neill (Nolo). For useful articles on consumer credit and credit reports, see the Debt Management and Personal Finance sections on Nolo.com.

References Are All-Important

Your past relationships with landlords, managers, and employers can make the difference between getting a rental unit and getting a rejection. Prospective landlords will usually want to talk with your current and previous landlords, your employer, and others who know you well.

When talking to other landlords and managers, a prospective landlord might ask if you:

- Paid rent on time?
- Were considerate of neighbors (no loud parties, out-of-control guests, or dangerous dogs)?
- Made unreasonable demands or complaints?
- Took care of the rental unit?

If your landlord says you were a pain in the neck, always paid rent late, and left the place a shambles, don't expect the next landlord to welcome you with open arms.

When speaking with your boss, a prospective landlord might ask:

- how long you have worked at this job, and how much money you make
- if you are a responsible person, and
- how well you get along with coworkers.

When talking to your friends (nonrelatives), a prospective landlord might ask if you:

- are a reliable, honest person
- have good housekeeping habits, and
- are considerate of others.

A landlord can't force you to give references. And you might not want to, particularly if your current landlord or boss is a complete jerk and will have nothing good to say about you. But if you cannot come up with a good substitute—another supervisor or maybe a resident manager—a prospective landlord will conclude that you're withholding the name because the person will give a negative—but accurate—report. If you really can't come up with references, at least have a reasonable explanation for your reticence.

Many employers and landlords refuse to act as rental references unless the prospective tenant has signed a release stating that it's okay to answer a prospective landlord's questions. Most of the time, this policy is based on a concern that talking about the prospective tenant without permission will result in their being sued for defamation or invasion of privacy. To head off this concern, you'll want to provide written permission that the references you list may discuss you and their relationship with you. This document should assure your previous landlord, current or past employers, credit sources, or personal references that you won't object if they respond truthfully to a landlord's relevant questions about your work and employment history.

Many prospective landlords will ask you to sign a form release, even if you provide your own. Even when you sign a release, though, you cannot force a prior employer or landlord to provide information.

Smart Moves: How to Find a Good Place

Knowing what questions landlords are legally allowed to ask and preparing your answers will give you confidence as you head into your rental search. But your success will also depend on some "street smarts," not just legal know-how. Here are some proven strategies that will make your efforts more efficient and successful:

Set your rental priorities before you start looking. Know how much rent you can pay, which neighborhoods you want to live in (and those you want to avoid), the number of bedrooms you require, and whether you want to keep a pet. You don't want to drive yourself crazy running around looking at places you could have easily eliminated from your search with a little planning.

Use your personal contacts. Let everyone in your social networks—online and off—know that you're looking for a rental. Don't be shy—tell friends, coworkers, even local businesspeople with whom you have a friendly relationship. You never know who might come through with a lead on the perfect apartment.

Check Craigslist and other websites. The advertising-free website craigslist.org is enormously popular in the hundreds of cities it serves, and is a great place to begin your housing search. Craigslist is free to both landlords and tenants.

Many major urban areas have online listing sites specific to the area. For example, Apartable (Apartable.com) lists rentals in New York City, allowing users to search by specific neighborhoods. And don't forget that many local newspapers post their classified ads online (if they don't, check the print editions).

Also look for the local listings posted on nationwide rental sites such as:

- ApartmentRatings.com
- Rent.com
- ApartmentGuide.com
- Zillow.com
- Zumper.com, and
- Lovely (livelovely.com).

Many of these sites provide more than apartment listings, offering information and links covering renters' insurance, moving tips, and more. Useful iPhone and Android apps are free for some of these sites, such as ApartmentRatings.com.

Work with a real estate broker or property management firm. If you're moving to a new city, these might be your best options. Be sure to check out fees. In New York City, where many property owners list their rentals exclusively with real estate brokers, you can expect to pay a fee that is tied to the rent (for example, 15% of the first year's rent) or a flat fee of $1,000 or more for a rental.

Check out university and corporate housing offices. Professors leaving on sabbatical and corporate employees who are temporarily transferred are often anxious to rent their homes for a year or more. University housing services and corporations sometimes maintain databases to help them in their leasing efforts.

Hit the streets. Walk, bike, or drive around the neighborhood you want to live in and look for "For Rent" signs in windows or notices on local bulletin boards. You might even come across some vacancies that aren't advertised elsewhere, reducing the competition. If you want to live in a particular apartment building or complex but you don't see a posted sign, stop and talk to the manager or doorman. Get on a waiting list.

Spread the word on your rental search. Consider posting your own "Apartment Wanted" flyer (and maybe even offer a finder's fee) in a local store, health club, yoga studio, laundromat, or other business; or put a classified ad in a local newspaper or newsletter.

Try not to compromise. Unless you're completely out of options, don't move into a place that's a complete disaster, next to a drug house, or run by a landlord who is well known by the housing inspectors and the local tenants' rights organization. Even if you consider it temporary, try not to settle for a questionable place. Keep looking.

Take your time. Unless you're positive that you've found your dream rental (and there are eager would-be tenants lined up behind you), don't commit yourself on the spot. Take some time, even a few hours, to think about it. Were there any little, nagging misgivings that need to be faced and resolved? For example, what about the manager's offhand remark about his tenants' private lives that, viewed in retrospect, might spell trouble ahead? Often a return visit, or candidly sharing your doubts with a wise friend, can bring important issues to the fore. You don't want to look back later and say, "I should have seen it coming."

How to Find a Roommate

If you want to find an apartment where current tenants need a roommate, or if you're looking for a roommate to share a rental, you have options. In addition to your own personal networks, Craigslist, and university housing offices, you can use many websites geared toward making roommate matches. Many services will screen and match compatible roommates, based on detailed questionnaires you complete. (See Chapter 6 for advice on renting with roommates.) Try Roomster.com, Roommates.com, SpareRoom.com, Roomi (www.roomiapp.com), and RoomieMatch.com, to name just a few.

How to Impress Prospective Landlords

To gain a competitive edge over other applicants, bring a completed rental application when you first meet prospective landlords. You can find a downloadable rental application form at Nolo.com. Or you can simply bring the following information:

- Written references from landlords, employers, friends, and colleagues. If that's not possible, be sure to bring a typed list of references' current phone numbers and addresses. It's always a good idea to alert references to expect a call from prospective landlords. And make sure they'll speak well of you.

- A signed release from you giving permission to these references to answer the landlord's relevant questions. Offer to furnish a digital version so the landlord need only email it to the reference.
- A current copy of your credit report. You can order one from any of the major credit bureaus.

Greasing the Wheels Now Can Backfire Later

If you're looking in a tight rental market, you might be tempted to improve your chances over other applicants by offering to pay more rent, prepay rent, pay more security deposit, or waive the protections of state or local laws (especially rent control). Applicants have been known to offer airline or sports tickets and attractive items. If you engage in creative bribery, be aware:

- **Waiving your rights might set the stage for having them trampled in the future.** If you offer a higher security deposit than the law allows, or agree to under-the-table rent in violation of a rent control ordinance, you've sent a signal that you are willing to overlook the law. If you later want to assert other rights (such as your right to basic repairs and maintenance), you might be out of luck—your landlord will surmise that if you were willing to waive legal protections once, you can be talked out of these, too.
- **Offering carrots now might make the landlord expect more.** You obviously don't want to have to bribe the landlord every time you make a reasonable request. But once you've established a precedent, the landlord might continue to expect "deal sweeteners." This could get expensive.
- **Choosing tenants based on the quality of their gifts is no way to run a business.** The best landlords are the ones who choose the best tenants—those who are responsible, considerate, and law-abiding. If you live in a multiunit building, these are the best neighbors for *you*, too. Chances are you'd rather live next door to someone who got the place because she came with great references and not because she could come up with six months' prepaid rent. Beware a landlord who hasn't learned this lesson.

Be on your best "good tenant" behavior. Show up on time, dress neatly, and present yourself as someone who is both conscientious and agreeable. Realize that landlords hate dealing with overly demanding or fussy tenants who constantly complain about trivial things, so don't start off asking for a long list of improvements and special favors.

To clinch the deal on a great place, you might need to sweeten the pot—for example, by offering to pay more rent or a higher security deposit. Be aware of the possible downsides of this strategy. (See "Greasing the Wheels Now Can Backfire Later," above.)

Rules to Rent By

- **Be prepared.** Get a copy of your credit report, and check it for accuracy (and press for corrections if necessary) before your prospective landlord lays eyes on it. Prepare explanations for damaging entries whenever possible. Get your references lined up before you start apartment hunting. Make sure that your roommates do the same.
- **Be creative.** Besides Craigslist, look for rental listings in newsletters, on bulletin boards, and anyplace else you can think of. Tap into all your contacts and social networks to find unadvertised rentals.
- **Be choosy.** Don't be in a rush. Check out the landlord, the rental unit, the neighbors, and the neighborhood by asking current tenants what it's like to live there.
- **Be realistic.** Don't take on a rent that will cripple your social life or make it impossible to make other necessary expenditures.
- **Be a negotiator.** Follow our tips throughout this book on how to negotiate more favorable terms at the start of your tenancy—for example, a lower security deposit.

CHAPTER

2

Leases and Rental Agreements

It's not smart for a tenant—or a landlord—to conclude rental negotiations with no more than a handshake and a promise to "See you on the first!" Especially if you've argued long and hard to get a landlord to lower the rent, bend the pet policy, promise to paint the kitchen, or add a parking spot, it's plain foolish not to ask that these understandings be written down and signed. Failing to get your rental terms on paper is the single most dangerous mistake you can make as a tenant.

On the other hand, your rental negotiations might end with the grand presentation of a lengthy lease document in seven-point type written in a language that purports to be English. It's easy for a landlord to reject you as a tenant if you won't sign on the dotted line. But signing a legal document that you don't understand is like playing chess without knowing the rules: You cannot understand whether the other side has played fair, and you cannot adjust your moves to be legal and advantageous. Signing a lease that you don't understand is the *second* most dangerous mistake a tenant can make.

This chapter discusses the key provisions typically included in leases and rental agreements and explains what to do if your landlord shies away from paper and pen. It highlights terms that are protenant and those that are clearly biased in favor of landlords. It also gives some tips on how to negotiate for better terms at the beginning of a tenancy.

How Written Leases and Rental Agreements Differ

Both leases and rental agreements are legally enforceable agreements that establish the terms of your tenancy. As with any contract, they can be written or oral—though you should always insist on a written agreement. (See "Oral Understandings—Legal but Unwise," below.) Leases and rental agreements both cover basic issues such as the amount of rent, security deposits, and who can live in the rental unit. The primary difference between the two types of agreements is the length of the tenancy.

Before you get into the nuts and bolts of leases and rental agreements, it's important that you understand the meaning of the word "term."

When you read a lease, rental agreement, or any other kind of contract, you'll come across the word "term" used in two ways:

- **As a synonym for "rule" or "condition."** For example, you might see a sentence in a rental clause that reads: "The terms of the lease include $2,200 monthly rent, no pets, and a duty upon the tenant to shovel the sidewalk when it snows." This means that you must pay this rent, not have a pet, and shovel that snow. If you don't do these things, you will have broken (lawyers say "breached") the agreement, and the landlord might be entitled to send you a termination notice.
- **As a way to describe the length (years or months) of the agreement.** For example, a clause might say: "The term of the lease is one year." This means that you must pay rent and abide by other rental rules and laws for one year (and you get to live there for that length of time).

Rental Agreements

A rental agreement establishes a tenancy for a short period of time, usually one month. A month-to-month rental agreement automatically renews each month unless you or your landlord gives the other the proper amount of notice (typically 30 days) to end the agreement. A landlord can change the terms of a rental agreement—for example, increase the rent (unless there's rent control)—with proper written notice. In most states, this amount of notice is also 30 days. (Chapter 9 explains the mechanics of how tenancies change.)

Leases

A lease obligates both you and the landlord for a set period of time, usually a year. Your landlord can't raise the rent or change other terms until the lease ends. And your landlord can't force you to move out unless you breach an important term of the lease such as failing to pay the rent, or violate nuisance or other property laws by repeatedly making too much noise or damaging the rental unit. Landlords who have rented their unit under a lease can't kick a tenant out simply because they feel like it.

At the end of the term, you or your landlord can decline to renew the lease, or can negotiate to sign a new lease with the same or different terms. (Landlords subject to rent control, however, often have less flexibility when it comes to deciding not to renew a lease. See Chapter 12.) Often, especially when the landlord and tenant are content with the arrangement, nobody does anything formal and the tenant stays and continues to pay rent. When this happens, in most states the tenancy will continue on a month-to-month basis, subject to the same terms and conditions, in effect converting the lease to a rental agreement. (Chapter 9 covers what happens when a lease runs out.)

Which Is Better—A Lease or a Rental Agreement?

Because a lease gives you more security than a month-to-month agreement, a long-term lease is usually the better option for tenants who plan to stay put for the foreseeable future. With a lease, you don't have to worry about being kicked out on short notice—unless of course you've done something bad enough to justify eviction, such as not paying rent. With a month-to-month rental agreement (except in most rent control situations), a landlord is free to sock you with a rent increase or terminate your tenancy even if you're a model tenant. (A landlord must, however, give you the proper notice, and cannot raise the rent or terminate the agreement for retaliatory or discriminatory reasons. Retaliation is explained in Chapter 11; discrimination is covered in Chapter 5.)

Also keep in mind that leases don't lock you in as much as you might think. In most states, if you move out midway through a lease, your landlord can't automatically charge you for the remainder of the lease term. Landlords must take reasonable steps to find a new tenant to take your place. As soon as the place is rerented, your obligation to pay the rent ends, and you'll have to pay only for the time between your leaving and when the new tenant moved in, plus the landlord's advertisement costs. (Chapter 9 covers your rights when it comes to breaking a lease.)

If you might want to move soon, you'll prefer the flexibility of a rental agreement. For instance, if you know that your job will relocate you in the near future, a rental agreement is probably your better option. Or, if you're in a real pinch and are forced to rent a place you're not happy with, a rental agreement will allow you to move out easily once you find a better place.

Will You Have a Choice?

It's ultimately the landlord's call whether to use a lease or a rental agreement, but you might have some bargaining power. If you live in an area choked with "For Rent" signs or where it is difficult to find tenants for a particular part of the year—for example, a college town where most students are gone during the summer—most landlords will probably insist on a lease. That way, the landlord has the security of knowing that the unit will be generating income for a significant and uninterrupted amount of time.

Oral Understandings—Legal but Unwise

While many landlords want tenants to sign some kind of written lease or rental agreement, written documents aren't legally required. Oral leases or rental agreements are perfectly enforceable for month-to-month tenancies and, in most states, for leases for one year or less.

While an oral agreement is legal and enforceable, it's usually unwise to rely on one. People's memories (even yours) can become unreliable, leading to arguments over who said what and when. You don't necessarily need a five-page legal document, especially if you know and trust your landlord, but you should at least get the basic terms in writing, including the rent, the length (or term) of the rental, when and where rent is due, and any other important aspect of the understanding, such as the landlord's willingness to let you have a pet. If your landlord shies away from written documents, you can put the basics on paper yourself. ("Get It in Writing: A Letter of Understanding" in this chapter explains how to prepare a letter of understanding.)

If you live in an area where vacancies are scarce and new tenants are easy to find, you might be offered a rental agreement. Many landlords prefer the flexibility of a rental agreement, because it allows them to raise the rent or get rid of a tenant on short notice. If a particular tenant turns out to be a good one and the landlord decides not to change the terms of the rental, the landlord will simply let the rental agreement renew month after month.

If you can convince the landlord that you'll be an excellent tenant (based on your credit history and references) and will be around for the long haul, you might be able to get a long-term lease. Wise landlords prefer to keep good long-term tenants and avoid the hassles and expenses of constant turnovers (cleaning, advertising, showing, and checking out applicants)—even if it means less flexibility in terms of increasing rent or ending the tenancy. If the landlord balks at your request for a lease, consider accepting the month-to-month arrangement for a few months and then ask again. Your track record at that point might tip the balance.

Who Should Sign a Lease or Rental Agreement

Landlords typically want all adults (18 years of age and older) who will live in the rental unit, including both members of a couple, to sign the lease or rental agreement. Doing this makes everyone who signs responsible for all terms, including the full amount of the rent.

The landlord isn't the only one who benefits when everyone signs on the dotted line. If you have roommates, you'll want them to understand that they are bound by the landlord's rules on guests, noise, pets, and so on. As explained in "Common Legal Gobbledygook," later in this chapter, it's important for everyone to realize that one roommate's serious transgression can result in the ouster of everyone.

Typical Provisions in Leases and Rental Agreements

Your lease or rental agreement can be as short as one page or longer than ten. It can be typed or handwritten, easy to understand, or full of legalese. Most landlords use preprinted forms they buy in stationery stores, order from a landlords' association, or find online.

Often, leases and rental agreements contain fancy legal language or complex, roundabout clauses. This section offers plain meanings for the most common terms you'll find in a lease or rental agreement.

Names and Addresses of Landlord and Tenants

You might see "lessee" used to refer to the tenant, and "lessor" used to refer to the landlord. Together, the tenant and landlord might be called the "parties" to the agreement. If the owner has authorized a property manager or company to receive notices and legal papers on the landlord's behalf, you should also see that name and address.

Chapter 6 provides complete details on the legal responsibilities of tenants and cotenants, and related issues such as adding a new roommate. "Discrimination Prohibited by Federal Laws," in Chapter 5, discusses occupancy limits that might restrict who lives in the rental unit.

Rental Property Address and Details

The property address is often called "the premises." Your lease or rental agreement might also include details on any furnishings, parking space, storage areas, or other extras that come with the rental property.

Organize Your Rental Records

This book is devoted to explaining your legal rights and how to secure them. If you're lucky, your landlord will also know the law. But there might be times when you'll have to press your point—in negotiation, mediation, or a courtroom, if necessary.

We want you to be prepared when entering a negotiation or mediation, or when bringing your case to court if you need to. And the first rule in preparing a winning case is to keep and organize essential documents. This material will be the evidence you need to clinch your argument. Establishing a simple record-keeping system will provide a valuable paper trail should disputes develop later—for example, regarding your landlord's failure to make necessary repairs. Without good records, the outcome of a dispute could come down to your word against your landlord's—always a precarious situation. To start organizing, set up a file for the following documents:

- a copy of your rental application, references, and credit report
- your copy of a signed lease or rental agreement
- any building rules and regulations from the landlord
- deposit information, including (if known) the location and interest rate terms of your deposit, and
- your photos and notes on condition of rental unit at move-in time.

After you move in, add these documents to your file:

- your landlord's written requests for entry
- rent increase notices
- records of your repair requests along with notes on how and when they were handled, and
- any other correspondence with your landlord, such as letters of understanding.

Be sure to include copies of emails, (although as we describe below, it's best to use mail or a delivery service for important notices and communications with your landlord).

Term of the Tenancy

The term is the length of the rental. The document should include the beginning date and whether it's a month-to-month (or other shorter-term) tenancy or a lease. If it's a lease, the ending date should also be specified. Leases often have a term of one year. The important differences between leases and rental agreements are discussed above. Chapter 9 explains how tenancies end.

Rent

Leases and rental agreements usually specify the amount of rent due, when and where it's due, acceptable forms of payment, and late fees. Chapter 3 covers rent rules in detail.

Deposits and Fees

Expect to see details about deposits, such as the dollar amount of a security deposit, cleaning deposit, or last month's rent. Chapters 4 and 10 explain state laws that govern the use and return of security deposits and why it's important to know your landlord's cleaning and maintenance requirements.

Utilities

The lease or rental agreement should state who pays for what utilities. Normally, land lords pay for garbage and sometimes for water, if there is a yard. Tenants usually pay for other services, such as phone, gas, cable, Internet, and electricity.

Condition of the Rental Unit

Most leases and rental agreements include a clause in which you agree that the premises are in habitable (livable) condition and you promise to alert the landlord to any defective or dangerous condition. Chapter 7 covers tenants' rights and responsibilities regarding repairs and maintenance.

Inspect Before You Sign

Always inspect the rental unit before you sign a lease or rental agreement. Think (and look) carefully before signing off on a clause that states that the rental is in fine shape. Look for damage, dirt, mildew, pest or rodent problems, and obvious wear and tear. Write down (be as specific as possible) serious problems, such as a broken heater or leaking roof, as well as minor flaws such as a stained kitchen counter, dirty drapes, or faded paint. Back up your written statement with photographs.

Try to get your landlord to fix problems before you move in. Write down any agreement in a letter of understanding as described in "Get It in Writing: A Letter of Understanding," below.

Keeping tabs on the condition of the rental at move-in is an excellent way to protect yourself when it comes time to move out and get your security deposit returned. Without reliable proof of the condition of the premises at the start of the tenancy, your landlord might keep all or part of your deposit, claiming you left the place filthy or damaged it—for example, stained the rug, cracked the bathroom mirror, or left behind a broken garbage disposal. Records of the initial inspection will establish that the problems existed at the start of the tenancy and are not your fault. Chapter 10 discusses how to avoid disputes over security deposits at move-out time.

Check your state statutes (listed in Appendix B): Some require landlords to give new tenants a written statement on the condition of the rental premises at move-in time, including a comprehensive list of existing damages.

Tenant's Repair and Maintenance Responsibilities

A carefully written lease or rental agreement will include a statement that makes you responsible for keeping the rental premises clean and in good condition and obligates you to reimburse the landlord for the cost of repairing damage caused by your abuse or neglect. Some agreements go further and spell out specific tenant responsibilities, such as fixing clogged drains or broken windows. Many leases and rental agreements also tell you what you can't do in the way of repairs—such as painting walls or adding built-in bookshelves without the landlord's permission. Chapter 7 covers important tenant rights and responsibilities regarding repairs and maintenance, and your options if your landlord fails to provide habitable housing.

When and How Landlords May Enter Your Rental Unit

Many state access laws specify when landlords may legally enter rented premises—for example, to deal with an emergency or make repairs—and the amount of notice required. Some landlords include this information in the lease or rental agreement. Others are ignorant of these laws and write entry provisions that are illegal. Chapter 8 covers the landlord's right to enter rental property and tenant privacy rights, and includes a good sample privacy clause.

Extended Absences

Some leases and rental agreements require you to notify the landlord in advance if you will be away from the premises for a certain number of consecutive days (often seven or more). Such clauses might give the landlord the right to enter the rental unit during your absence to maintain the property as necessary and to inspect for damage and needed repairs. You'll most often see this type of clause if you live in a cold-weather place where, in case of extremely cold temperatures, landlords want to drain the pipes to guard against breakage.

Limits on Your Behavior

Most form leases and rental agreements contain a clause forbidding you from using the premises or adjacent areas, such as the sidewalk in front of the building, in such a way as to violate any law or ordinance, including laws prohibiting the use, possession, or sale of illegal drugs. These clauses also prohibit you from intentionally damaging the property or creating a nuisance by annoying or disturbing other tenants or nearby residents—

for example, by continuously making loud noise. Leases and rental agreements can also prohibit smoking, in individual units as well as in common areas.

Restrictions on Number of Occupants

Most landlords will set a limit to the number of people who can live in each rental unit. Landlords are not free to set unreasonably low figures (for example, two people for a two-bedroom flat) in order to maintain a "quiet atmosphere" or to reduce wear and tear. Federal law requires landlords to allow two persons per bedroom unless the landlord can point to legitimate business reasons that justify a lower number (this is difficult to do). Chapter 5 explains occupancy standards in more detail and includes advice on what to do if your landlord sets a more restrictive occupancy policy than the federal or state standard.

Restrictions on Use of the Property

Landlords can throw in all kinds of language limiting your use of the rental property and who may stay there. For example, landlords can ban waterbeds, prohibit plants on wood floors, and require bikes to be left outside. These restrictions might be in the lease or rental agreement itself, or in a separate set of rules and regulations. Basically, landlords can set any kind of restriction they want—as long as it doesn't retaliate, discriminate, or otherwise violate the law. Chapter 5 covers discrimination in detail. Some common restrictions involving pets, home businesses, sublets, and guests are discussed below.

No Pets

Your landlord has the right to prohibit all pets, or to restrict the types allowed—for example, forbidding dogs or cats, but allowing birds. However, a landlord may not prohibit "service" (sometimes called "assistance") or "comfort" animals used by people with a physical or mental disability, as provided by the fair housing laws (discussed in Chapter 5). Many landlords spell out pet rules—for example, that the tenants will keep the yard free of all animal waste or that dogs will always be on leash.

No Home Businesses

Landlords may prohibit you from running a business from your home, by including a clause specifying that the premises are "for residential purposes only." The concern here is generally about increased traffic and liability exposure if one of your customers or business associates is hurt on the premises. Obviously, working at home on your computer is not likely to bother your landlord, and might not ever be noticed.

If you want to run a day care operation in your rented home, your landlord might not be able to flatly prohibit it. Some states, including California and New York, are anxious to encourage family-run day care. Landlords in these states may limit the number of children, however, and any business you run must comply with business licensing laws, state fire and health regulations regarding minimum size of the facility, and fire exits.

No Assignments or Sublets Without Landlord Permission

Most careful landlords will not let you do the following, without their written consent:

- turn over your rental to another tenant (called "assignment")
- let someone live in your rental for a limited time while you're away (called a "sublet")
- rent an extra bedroom to another occupant, with you as the "landlord" (also called a sublet), and/or
- host short-term (and paying) "guests" through services such as Airbnb (see Chapter 6 for details).

Limits on Guest Stays

It's common for landlords to limit overnight guests. For example, a lease might state that a guest can stay for no more than ten days in any six-month period, with written approval required for longer stays. Landlords do this to keep long-term guests (who haven't been screened or approved, and who haven't signed the lease or rental agreement) from gaining the status of full-fledged tenants.

Attorneys' Fees and Court Costs in a Lawsuit

Many leases and rental agreements specify who will pay the costs of a lawsuit if you go to court over the meaning or implementation of a part of your rental agreement or lease. These clauses do not apply to legal disputes that arise independently of the lease or rental agreement—for example, lawsuits over alleged discrimination.

CAUTION

Watch out for clauses that make only the losing tenant pay for the owner's lawyers' fees. In several states, including California and New York, these unfair arrangements will be interpreted to run both ways, even though the landlord didn't intend it that way (in other words, if *you* win, the landlord has to pay your costs). A common and evenhanded attorneys' fees clause will explicitly require the losing side in a landlord-tenant dispute concerning the lease or rental agreement—whether it's the landlord or the tenant—to pay attorneys' fees and court costs of the winning party (filing fees, service of process charges, deposition costs, and so on).

Grounds for Termination of Tenancy

You'll often see a general clause stating that any violation of the lease or rental agreement by tenants or their guests, is grounds for terminating the tenancy according to the procedures established by state or local laws. Chapter 9 provides an overview of how tenancies end.

Negotiating With the Landlord

Your lease or rental agreement is probably loaded with clauses written to maximize the landlord's rights and minimize yours. That's because rental documents are typically written by lawyers hired by landlords or their trade associations.

Don't assume, however, that every clause is written in stone. Armed with a little legal knowledge, you'll be able to figure out whether the terms and conditions of your lease or rental agreement—its clauses—are legal, illegal, or required by law. Here's how to evaluate your lease or rental agreement, and how to negotiate better terms when possible.

NEGOTIATE

Knowing *when* to negotiate is as important as knowing how. Don't start bargaining the minute you see a promising rental. Take some time to establish a rapport with the landlord, supplying reasons to choose you over other applicants. Even seemingly implacable rules, especially no-pets restrictions, might melt away if the landlord likes you and wants you as a tenant.

Four Types of Lease Clauses

Each rental clause falls into one of four categories, depending on the issue's connection to any federal, state, or local law on that subject. Determining how (or whether) to negotiate with your landlord over a rental clause depends on which category the issue fits into.

Category 1: A Restatement of Your Guaranteed Legal Rights

Many states have passed tenant-friendly laws covering key areas such as landlords' access to rental property, the amount and use of security deposits, and tenants' rights to a livable home. In addition, you might have important legal rights under federal law (particularly in the area of discrimination) and local law (especially if your community has rent control). *Your landlord cannot legally diminish these rights and cannot ask you to waive them.* This book explains which important tenant rights belong in this category.

Your landlord is obliged to comply with tenant rights but is not usually required to inform you of them in your lease or rental agreement. You don't have to bargain for legal rights that are guaranteed under local, state, or federal law. If your landlord spells out guaranteed tenant rights in your rental document, fine, but you've got them regardless.

Category 2: A Variation of a Negotiable State or Local Law

Not all tenant-protection laws are off-limits to landlord tinkering, as are the ones in Category 1, above. For example, in some states a landlord and tenant may agree to shorten the statutory notice periods for changing or ending a tenancy.

If you see a clause that restricts rights that are given you by a state or local statute, you'll obviously need to know whether this restriction is allowed in your state—in other words, whether the rule instead fits within Category 1, above.

If your state or local law allows landlords some wiggle room on a tenant-friendly procedure, they are allowed to take advantage of that liberty. You can't force the landlord back to the original law. Be prepared to offer reasons why the variation is either not necessary or not fair. You might be able to work out a compromise or offer a concession of your own in exchange for your full rights under the law. Ultimately, however, if a landlord won't budge and you feel very strongly about the issue, you'll have to look elsewhere.

Category 3: Illegal Clauses

Landlords cannot diminish certain tenant-protection laws, such as your rights to a habitable rental unit and to be free from illegal discrimination. These are the rights that fit within Category 1, above. Nonetheless, many landlords attempt to circumvent the law by rewriting it. The best example of this is when landlords try to limit their responsibility to provide habitable housing, despite the laws that exist in the vast majority of states to the contrary. Incredible though it might seem, you'll see lease clauses in which the landlord states that the premises are not warranted as fit, safe, secure, or in good repair. Most states will not uphold these clauses. This means that even if you sign a lease or rental agreement that contains a clause absolving the landlord of the duty to offer and maintain fit housing, you can still complain (or use a tenant remedy such as repair-and-deduct, explained in Chapter 7), and a court will not hold you to your "waiver."

A misstatement of a guaranteed tenant right isn't the only kind of illegal clause you may encounter. Some clauses are illegal because they violate an important public policy. For example, many landlords use a lease clause that states that the tenant will not hold the landlord responsible for any injuries the tenant suffers as a result of the landlord's negligence or carelessness. Most courts will not enforce these clauses because our society has decided that, for the most part, people should be held accountable for the consequences of their mistakes.

Remember that we are dealing here with tenant rights that can't be waived or diminished—in other words, they are nonnegotiable. If your landlord nevertheless attempts to avoid her responsibilities, it means that she is either unaware of your rights or deliberately violating the law. Your approach will depend on your reading of the landlord.

- **The landlord doesn't know the law.** If you think the landlord has made an honest mistake, and especially if you don't have a lot of other rental options, it might be worth pointing out to the landlord that the clause is invalid. Doing so lets her know that you're an informed renter and won't be a pushover, and hopefully she'll be more careful in the future. There is a risk, however: You might discover that she'll do everything possible to get rid of you, preferring to rent to people who don't know their rights.
- **The landlord is deliberately violating the law.** If every sign suggests that the landlord has deliberately circumvented the law, the wise course is clear: Move on. If you don't, you can count on problems ahead.

Category 4: A Policy or Rule Not Covered by State or Local Law

Finally, you'll see lots of lease clauses that are not regulated in the slightest by your local or state laws or court decisions. Examples include provisions for parking spaces, amount of rent (rent control excepted), rent due date, move-in date, rules regarding common area use, and procedures for registering complaints and repair requests. Some of these issues are written as clauses in the lease itself, but many are covered in "house rules," which landlords attach to leases.

But minor, day-to-day issues aren't the only ones that might not be tethered to a federal, state, or local law. In some states, extremely important issues, such as security deposit limits or rules governing landlords' access to rental property, are not governed by law. For example, New York (for nonregulated units) and Texas do not limit the amount of security a landlord may demand. Clearly, before sounding off with a haughty demand to reform an "illegal" clause, you'll need to know whether your state law does, in fact, regulate the issue.

Issues that aren't governed by law are the truly negotiable ones. Here you are both free to bargain, restrained only by the strength of your position. If it's a renters' market and the landlord's property is littered with "Vacancy" signs, you can expect more cooperation than if there are 17 applicants lined up waiting to take the unit with no demands. Rather than push now for a better deal, it sometimes makes sense to get the rental and then, after you have established yourself as a stable, desirable tenant, ask the landlord to revisit the issue and possibly change that lease clause. Changing rental agreements and leases is covered in Chapter 9.

Concluding Your Negotiations

Negotiation with your landlord should always end with a written version of what the two of you agreed to. For example, if the landlord agreed to omit an illegal clause, cross it out and make sure that both of you initial and date the cross-out. Similarly, add signatures and the date if you add a clause to a preprinted lease or rental agreement. If your landlord offers to fix the oven or install security bars on the windows, write this into the lease or rental agreement and set a deadline for work to be completed (ideally, before you move in). Or outline the terms of your agreement in a letter of understanding, explained below. Negotiation techniques are covered in more detail in Chapter 13.

Common Negotiation Issues

This section discusses some common issues you might be able to negotiate—pets, guests, home businesses, and roommates. Often, an offer to pay more rent or a higher security deposit will convince reluctant landlords to modify their policies.

Other chapters provide specific advice on negotiating:

- rent increases and late rent (Chapter 3)
- deposits (Chapter 4), and
- breaking a lease (Chapter 9).

Pets

Several humane societies across the country offer petowning tenants helpful materials on how to negotiate with a landlord who doesn't normally allow pets. For example:

- The Hawaiian Humane Society (www.hawaiianhumane.org) includes a special section (search for "Pets Are Family" on its home page) that offers lots of useful resources for tenants, including a pet addendum to a rental agreement; the site also includes information on state laws in Hawaii, such as recent legislation that allows landlords to charge an additional pet deposit to tenants.
- The Humane Society of the U.S. (www.humanesociety.org) includes useful tips for tenants, a sample pet resume, and tips for training your pets to be better tenants (begin by searching for "renting" on their home page).

Guests

As mentioned earlier, some leases limit guest stays. If you plan on having regular guests—for example, your college roommate stays with you two weekends a month when she's in town on business, or your boyfriend sleeps over a few nights a week—you'll need to think about how to handle this issue. If your landlord lives far away and doesn't have a resident manager, you might decide to take a chance that you'll never be found out. You might get away with it if you're always current with the rent and have no hassles with other tenants. (Be assured that when a disgruntled neighbor complains about you to the landlord, the first words out of the neighbor's mouth will be a description of your boyfriend's overnight stays, even if these visits have nothing to do with your problem with the neighbor.) But if the landlord lives downstairs, ask the landlord to revise this clause. Perhaps you can compromise by offering a little more rent. If you encounter unreasonable resistance, consider looking for another rental.

Home Businesses

If you are one of the millions of Americans who run a business from your house or apartment (or even simply work at home), make sure your lease or rental agreement doesn't specify that the premises are "for residential purposes only." If you're working alone or your job primarily consists of making phone calls or using your computer, you've probably got nothing to worry about (and landlords in California and New York may not prohibit tenants from operating a licensed child care facility). But if clients or deliveries will be coming on a regular basis, you'll want to discuss the issue with your landlord, who might be concerned that neighboring tenants will be inconvenienced. Where will your visitors park, for example? Will your piano students disturb the neighbors?

A landlord who does allow you to run a business from your rental unit might require that you maintain certain types of liability insurance. (In California, however, landlords cannot insist that tenants who operate licensed child care facilities obtain insurance.) That way, the landlord won't wind up paying if someone gets hurt on the rental property—for example, a business customer who trips and falls on the front steps. If you can obtain a quote for liability insurance before approaching the landlord, obviously your chances of an official okay go way up.

Also, be aware that if you use your residence as a commercial site, the property might need to meet the accessibility requirements of the federal Americans with Disabilities Act (ADA). For more information on the ADA, contact the Department of Justice, Office on the Americans with Disabilities Act, Civil Rights Division, in Washington, DC, at 800-514-0301 (or 800-514-0383, TTY). The ADA website (ADA.gov) is very helpful.

Finally, even if it's okay with your landlord, your home-based business might violate local zoning laws governing the type of businesses allowed (if any) in your residential neighborhood. The ordinances are often vague as to the type of business you can operate—for example, many allow "traditional home-based businesses," but don't provide a more specific definition. However, these laws are often quite detailed as to the following issues:

- restricting the amount of car and truck traffic the business can generate
- barring outside signs
- prohibiting employees or at least limiting their number, and
- setting a limit on the percentage of the floor space that can be devoted to the business.

Smoke Gets in Your Eyes (and Drapes)

Landlords often prohibit smoking in single-family homes and individual rental units, as well as common areas. The reason: Smoking damages carpets, drapes, and paint, thus increasing the landlord's maintenance costs. A blanket prohibition on smoking is not illegal. In fact, in several cities, smoking in common areas—and sometimes in tenants' private spaces as well—in multiunit buildings is against the law.

If you want to smoke in a declared smoke-free building, consider offering a higher security deposit, which will cover expected refurbishing costs. This might assuage your landlord's worries. However, this proposal isn't an option if your security deposit is already at a state law maximum. And keep in mind that the landlord might not be able to give in to your request without violating promises to other tenants: If a building has one ventilation system or windows that freely communicate air, allowing one tenant to smoke impinges on all, thereby destroying the smoke-free nature of the building that other tenants doubtless jealously guard.

Roommates

Landlords may set reasonable limits on the number of persons who will live in a rental. Landlords who limit your occupancy to the federal standard of two per bedroom (or the state limit, whichever is higher) are within their rights. Even if the rooms are big, you will have a hard time finding legal support for a higher number of occupants. But you might be able to convince a landlord to allow more tenants if you offer to compensate for the additional wear and tear that higher numbers of occupants cause. You could try offering a higher security deposit (assuming the deposit is not already at the state maximum) or even a higher rent.

Common Legal Gobbledygook

Here's the real meaning of some legal terms you might see in a lease or rental agreement.

Committing waste. This means seriously and intentionally damaging the property—something your lease or rental agreement will probably prohibit (even if it's not mentioned, you'll be liable if you do this and it's grounds for termination).

Hold harmless. Many form leases include a provision that attempts to absolve ("hold harmless") the landlord in advance from responsibility for all damages, injuries, or losses, including those caused by the landlord's carelessness. Such prolandlord language is usually illegal. If your landlord assaults you, or you're injured because of a dangerous or defective condition the landlord knew about but failed to fix in a reasonable time, no boilerplate lease provision will protect your landlord from civil and possibly even criminal charges.

Indemnify. This one usually accompanies the "hold harmless" clause. It means that if the landlord is sued or has to pay money for something you are responsible for, you agree to pay the landlord's costs. For example, if another tenant trips on the skateboard you've carelessly left in the stairwell and sues both you and the landlord, you agree to pay the landlord's legal fees along with any other monetary damages. It is not illegal to agree to indemnify your landlord.

Common Legal Gobbledygook (continued)

Joint and several liability. Many leases and rental agreements state that all cotenants are "jointly and severally" liable for paying rent and abiding by terms of the agreement. This bit of legalese means that each tenant is legally responsible for the whole rent, and that the misdeeds of one tenant—for example, keeping a pet in violation of a no-pets clause—will allow the landlord to evict all of you. Cotenants are jointly and severally liable even if the lease doesn't say so. (See "Renting a Place With Others," in Chapter 6, for a complete explanation.)

Liquidated damages or "termination fees." This item is often found in fixed-term leases. It means if you move out before the lease expires, you are supposed to pay the landlord a predetermined amount of money (damages) for the loss of rent caused by your early departure, irrespective of the amount of rent money that the landlord actually lost when you stopped paying rent. Usually landlords set the amount of liquidated damages (or the termination fee) at the entire security deposit or many hundreds, or even thousands, of dollars in addition to the deposit. In some states, liquidated damages clauses must be reasonable, to be enforced; in others, they are unenforceable—which doesn't mean that you can take off scot-free, just that you will be liable only for the landlord's provable, actual damages. In Florida, a lease can include a liquidated damages clause that provides for no more than two months' rent.

Quiet enjoyment. You have a right to live undisturbed, free from disturbance from your landlord or other tenants in the building whom the landlord has failed to control. Your landlord must not act (or fail to act) in a way that seriously interferes with your normal use of your home—for example, by allowing garbage to pile up or failing to correct a neighboring tenant whose constant loud music makes it impossible for you to sleep.

Validity of each part. Leases and rental agreements commonly include what lawyers call a "savings" clause, which means that, in the event that a judge decides that one of the other clauses in the lease or rental agreement is invalid, the remainder of the agreement will remain in force. Given the number of blatantly illegal clauses that lots of landlords stick in their agreements, it's not hard to see why they need this one.

Signing a Lease or Rental Agreement

At the end of the lease or rental agreement, there will be space to include your landlord's signature, street address, email, and phone number, or that of the person authorized to receive legal papers, such as a property manager. There's also space for your and other tenants' signatures and contact information, as well as any cosigner (someone who agrees to cover any rent or damage-repair costs you fail to pay).

If your landlord has altered a preprinted form by writing or typing in changes, be sure that you and the landlord initial and date the changes when you sign the document.

Make sure you sign the lease or rental agreement at the same time as the landlord and that you get a copy then and there. This assures both sides that no changes can be made before all parties have signed.

Get It in Writing: A Letter of Understanding

Some landlords don't want to bother with a written lease or rental agreement. Others provide a rental document that is unclear on key issues such as the circumstances under which the landlord may enter the rental unit. And some won't want to take the time to add clauses or promises that the two of you have negotiated. In any case, you don't have to settle for the hope that the two of you will remember precisely what agreement you made. There's a way to nail down an oral understanding that lawyers use all the time. It's called a "letter of understanding."

Here's a general overview of how it's done. We suggest specific ways to use a letter of understanding in later chapters. After you and the landlord have reached an agreement concerning basic terms—rent, deposits, repairs—write down that understanding in a letter to the landlord. At the end of the letter, ask for a response if the landlord feels you have misunderstood or misrepresented your agreement. (See "Using Email for Notice or a Letter of Understanding," below, for information

Sample Letter of Understanding

August 24, 20xx
Ms. Iona Lott
68 Seventh Avenue
Rockyport, Maine 12335

Dear Ms. Lott,

Thank you very much for agreeing to rent me apartment #4 at 68 Seventh Avenue. I understand that you will lease the apartment to me for $750, due on the first of every month, starting September 1, 20xx, and ending on August 31, 20xx. Thanks for including parking spot #5 and allowing me to bring my dog Ruff. When I move in on September 1, I'll have the $750 security deposit that you asked me to bring, along with the first month's rent.

If your understanding of our agreement differs from mine, please let me know as soon as you receive this letter. If I don't hear from you by August 30, I'll assume that I have noted these details correctly. I look forward to moving in on the first.

Yours truly,
Izzy Real, Tenant
1236 Williams Avenue
Rockyport, Maine 12335
207-555-4567
izzy@izzy.com

on how to use email to deliver written requests.) Hand-deliver or email your letter or, better still, mail it return receipt requested. Keep a copy of the letter and the post office receipt in a safe place. A sample letter of understanding is shown above.

What good does this do you? Let's say there's a dispute over an issue covered in your letter and the two of you end up in court. When you show the judge the letter and the receipt, in most states the judge will presume that your landlord received your letter and agreed with your version unless the landlord promptly wrote back and argued otherwise. A landlord who disputes your version for the first time in court will be facing an uphill battle convincing the judge otherwise.

Letters of understanding are useful in any situation where you rely on your landlord's (or anyone else's) oral promise. For example, suppose that you buy a clothes dryer after the landlord promises that he'll install an electrical outlet. If he reneges on his promise, you'll be stuck with a dryer you can't use. Without your letter of understanding safely tucked into your rental papers file, you'll have a hard time persuading a judge that the promise was made. Chapter 13 covers disputes and small claims court.

Using Email for Notice or a Letter of Understanding

You and your landlord are probably a lot more likely to send each other messages by email or text rather than by post. Will those communications serve you as well as a mailed letter, if you need evidence that the message was received at the other end?

Suppose, for example, that you want to give notice of your intention to end your month-to-month tenancy, and do so by sending an email that's 30 days in advance of your planned departure. Or, say you need to send your landlord a request for repairs (this is the first, necessary step before you can use a remedy like repair-and-deduct, if the landlord fails to take action). If you end up in a legal dispute and your landlord challenges you in court, saying that you never told him about your decision to leave or alerted him to the repair problem, you'll need confirmation that the emails or text messages were received.

Rules to Rent By

- **Get it in writing.** If the landlord won't offer a written lease or rental agreement, use the next best thing: a letter of understanding.
- **Cover the essentials.** Make sure you're clear on the key issues before you sign on the dotted line: rent (how much, when, where due, and how it's paid), deposits (the amount, use, and return policy), roommates, pets, and parking.
- **Understand what you sign.** Never sign a legal document without understanding what it means. Refer to this book, a tenants' rights organization, or an experienced friend or attorney if you aren't sure.
- **Know the difference between a lease and a rental agreement.** Bargain for the one that suits your situation.
- **Watch out for illegal lease provisions.** Understand your state laws so that you will know them when you see them.

Unfortunately, getting confirmation of delivery in the face of the landlord's claim that the email or text was never received can be next to impossible. While it might be theoretically possible to trace the journey of an email or text, it will be prohibitively expensive. For this reason alone, do not rely on emails or texts as the way to communicate important information to your landlord.

However, if you expect to rely on email as the method of communication (and your lease or rental agreement allows it), consider signing up for a service that promises secure and traceable emails (for example, RMail (RMail.com)).

CAUTION

Read the statute (or the lease) for notice instructions! Now and then, a statute will tell you exactly how to deliver notices and demands to the other party. As email and text communications become more and more common, lawmakers will begin to incorporate specifications for email and text communication in their laws. And lawyers will draft notice clauses that take email and text into account. For now, however, you'll mostly see the generic requirement that demands and notices be delivered "in writing," which doesn't help very much.

CAUTION

Text messages are hard to track, and evidence of receipt isn't available short of complex searches through users' accounts. Rarely would a landlord-tenant dispute support the expense of such a search. If you're worried about being able to prove the receipt of your text, you'd be best served to also print it and mail it return receipt requested ... the old-fashioned way. Consider doing the same for your emails (if you don't use a service such as RMail).

More Information on Leases and Rental Agreements

Questions about a lease term or clause

If you run across terms or whole clauses not discussed here, get more information before you sign the lease or rental agreement. Tenants' rights groups, which exist in many areas, will be able to answer your questions. Or, if you're signing a long-term lease for a valuable property, you might want to see a lawyer.

Questions about state law

The charts in Appendix B contain summaries of essential landlord-tenant laws. In addition, a few states require that specific information be included in leases and rental agreements, such as details on where security deposits will be held and interest payments or specific disclosures regarding the condition of the property. Check your state statute. (Appendix A provides a brief overview of legal research.)

Where to complain about illegal or questionable clauses

If you think a clause is illegal, check Appendix B to see whether your state has a statute that covers the issue. Contact your state's consumer protection or attorney general's office for landlord-tenant information (find yours at USA.gov).

Where to find model leases and rental agreements

Nolo has developed lease and rental agreement forms that are clearly written and fair to both landlords and tenants. When you use them in conjunction with the accompanying state-specific information, your document will be legal in every state. Forms are available in *Every Landlord's Legal Guide*, by Janet Portman, Marcia Stewart, and Ann O'Connell, and in *Leases & Rental Agreements*, by Janet Portman and Marcia Stewart. Nolo also publishes interactive online lease and rental agreement forms, including state-specific forms for many states. For more information on Nolo products, go to Nolo.com.

CHAPTER

3

Rent Rules

For most tenants, "What's the rent?" is the first question to ask when considering a rental. Little wonder, considering that rent is often the biggest chunk of your hard-earned income. Rent is one of the landlord's biggest concerns, too: The rent you pay each month probably covers the property's mortgage and operating costs, as well as some of the landlord's personal expenses. If you pay on time, your landlord will be happy. If you're late, you can count on trouble.

This chapter summarizes your rights and responsibilities when it comes to paying rent, and Appendix B provides information about your state's rules on when rent is due, the amount of notice required to change or end a tenancy, late rent fees, security deposits, and more. Tenants who live in a state or city with rent control (such as Oregon, California, New York City, and Newark, NJ) enjoy far more protections and rights than those in areas without rent control.

Get Your Rent Control Ordinance and Read It

If you live in an area covered by rent control, it is essential that you get the actual text of the law and become familiar with it. Typically, rent control laws cover more than just the amount of rent that a landlord can charge—they often regulate security deposits (such as requiring interest) and the allowable reasons for a tenancy termination. If you live in a city with a rent control ordinance, it should also have a rent control board that can provide you with a copy of the ordinance. (For more on rent control, see Chapter 12.)

Rent Gouging: Isn't There a Law Against It?

There's a short answer to this question: No, unless you've got the protections of rent control (or the gouging is in response to a disaster, such as a hurricane or a pandemic). The more popular the area and the fewer the rentals, the more you can expect to pay. You can always try to negotiate on rent, but if there's lots of competition, you probably don't stand much of a chance. In fact, it might be to your advantage to offer more than the advertised rent to clinch the deal.

It's perfectly legal for a landlord to set a higher rent in response to competition. It is not legal, however, to:

- Advertise a certain rent and then, after the tenant has signed up or paid a deposit, demand a higher one. This is a variation on the old "bait and switch" game and is illegal under federal and state law. If you encounter this tactic, contact the consumer protection division of your local prosecutor's office.
- Quote a higher rent based on your race, sex, or other group characteristic. (If you feel the landlord is discriminating against you by charging more than the advertised price, see Chapter 5 for advice.)

The Nitty-Gritty on Where and How to Pay Rent

Your lease or rental agreement should spell out the details on when rent is due and where and how to pay it. If these important items aren't covered in your tenancy agreement, be sure to clear them up with your landlord before you move in. (Write a letter of understanding, as explained in Chapter 2.) As with most rental issues, your landlord calls the shots on these things. It doesn't hurt to negotiate, however, if you really prefer a different rent due date or form of rent payment.

Rent Is Usually Due the First of the Month

Most leases and rental agreements call for rent to be paid monthly, in advance, on the first day of the month. However, landlords are normally legally free to establish a different monthly payment date—or even to require that rent be paid weekly or bimonthly. Some landlords make the rent payable each month on the date the tenant first moved in. Most find it easier, however, to prorate rent for a short first month and thereafter collect rent on the first of the month. (If you move in mid-month, expect to pay a prorated amount for that month, plus the next month.)

Expect to Mail Your Rent Check to Your Landlord

Your lease or rental agreement probably also states where you should pay the rent and how it should be paid. Mailing it to the landlord's business address is the most common method of rent payment, unless your landlord or manager has an on-site office. If you mail your rent check, make sure that it arrives on the due date. It is not sufficient to mail your check on the day it is due.

Tenants often feel that the form of payment—cash or check—should be up to them. Unfortunately, it's not your call. Just like restaurants and shops, landlords are legally free to insist on a particular form of payment. Most require rent be paid by check or money order, but some landlords allow payment by credit card or automatic debit (rent payments are debited automatically each month from your bank account and transferred into the landlord's account).

These days, many landlords won't accept rent in cash—they don't want the risk of keeping large amounts of cash on hand. Your safety, too, will be imperiled if the word gets out that you regularly make a trip to the manager's office carrying large amounts of cash. If you must pay in cash, be sure to get a written, dated receipt stating your name and the amount paid. It's your only proof that you did, indeed, pay the rent.

Isn't There a Grace Period?

Lots of tenants are absolutely convinced that if rent is due on the 1st, they actually have until the 5th (or sometimes the 7th or even the 10th) of the month to pay, because they are within what they believe to be a legal grace period. Sorry, but this is not true. Rent is legally due on the date specified in your agreement.

The only exception is when the rent due date falls on a weekend or legal holiday. Most lease and rental agreements state that when the rent due date falls on a weekend day or legal holiday, the tenant must pay rent by the next business day. This sensible practice is legally required in some states and is the general practice in most. If your landlord insists on receiving the rent check by the first of the month (or other due date), even if mail is not delivered on that day, take a look at the law in your state—you might find that your landlord is violating it. If not, you might have to bite the bullet and get your rent in early.

What will happen if you don't pay on time? Usually, your landlord will:

- send you a note or pay you a visit, demanding the rent
- begin assessing late fees if there is a late fee provision in your lease or rental agreement, and
- send you a termination notice stating that an eviction suit will be filed if you don't pay rent or move out by a certain date.

Laws in a few states restrict the amount of late fees and whether landlords must wait until tenants are a certain number of days late before imposing them. Likewise, some states make landlords wait a few days before sending a termination notice. But if you've been late with the rent before, some states allow your landlord to terminate immediately. ("Tenancy Terminations for Nonpayment of Rent," below, covers evictions for nonpayment of rent in more detail.)

What to Do—and Not to Do—If You Can't Pay Rent on Time

Rare is the tenant who's never had a problem paying rent on time or in full. If you are a conscientious and honest tenant who is temporarily short on funds, most landlords won't evict you for paying rent a little late one month. You're more likely to avoid problems by being up front about your situation and asking for an extension, rather than simply not paying rent (or sending a check that bounces). Expect to pay a late rent fee if your lease or rental agreement has this provision, and don't press your luck with repeated requests to pay late.

This section covers the dos and don'ts of paying late. The following sections discuss the consequences of being late—specifically, late rent fees and tenancy terminations.

Don't Ignore the Problem and Hope It Will Go Away

If you can't pay the rent on time, you might be tempted to hope the landlord won't notice—after all, your landlord has a lot of tenants to keep track of, and one late check will hardly be noticed, right? Wrong. Remember, it's likely that your landlord is counting on your timely check to cover the property's mortgage payment. Because the bank won't forgive tardiness, your landlord can't afford to ignore yours. And it's equally naive to think that you can ignore the landlord's phone calls or emails or think that the landlord will swallow ridiculously lame excuses.

Never Send a Check You Know Will Bounce

Nothing infuriates a landlord more than dealing with a sneaky tenant who consistently bounces rent checks. Stirring up your landlord's ire isn't the only consequence of a bad check: Keep in mind that sending a worthless check (or one that's not signed) is like sending no rent at all. If your landlord has a late fee policy, it will kick in regardless of your bounced check. And, a bounced check gives your landlord grounds to terminate your tenancy.

Like any other business, your landlord has the legal right to charge you for bounced checks. The charge must be reasonable—such as the amount the bank charges for a returned check, probably $15 to $30 per returned item, plus a few dollars for the landlord's trouble. In many states, the bounced check fee is set by statute.

Your landlord should tell you in advance—in the lease or rental agreement, orally, or by means of an obvious sign in the rental office where you bring your monthly check—that a bounced check fee will be imposed.

Negotiate a Partial or Delayed Rent Payment

A landlord who considers you a good tenant won't want to lose you—it's often difficult and expensive to evict someone, then find and move in good tenants. This means you can probably get the landlord to accept a portion of the rent now—maybe even a small portion—and the rest later. Here are some basic steps to take:

- Ask your landlord in writing (as far in advance as possible) for a few extra days.
- Explain your difficulties and emphasize (if you can) that they are only temporary.
- Offer (if at all possible) to pay at least some of the rent on time.
- Give your landlord written assurance of your plan to pay the full rent by a certain date, such as the 15th of the month—and make sure you keep your promise.
- Explain that the problem won't happen again and that you'll pay your rent on time in the future.
- Be prepared to pay a late fee if the landlord has a late fee policy. Or, if you think your landlord will be responsive and your late rent is a rare occurrence, see if you can get a late fee waiver.

Late Rent and the Coronavirus Pandemic

In response to the devastating pandemic in 2020, lawmakers on the federal, state, and local levels imposed moratoriums on terminations and evictions for rent nonpayment (when the tenant's inability to pay was caused by fallout from the pandemic). Most laws did not reduce or cancel the rent; they just required that landlords not demand it until a specified date (usually months after the state of emergency had been lifted).

How can a landlord know that a tenant's inability is traceable to the effects of the pandemic? Is proof of the loss or reduction of income alone sufficient? Can landlords expect tenants to dip into savings or retirement accounts? As of this writing, these and many other questions are simply unanswered. If you are unable to pay rent because of your own illness, that of a family member, the need to stay home to care for school-age children, or because your income has been reduced, you'll need to get up-to-date information about federal, city, county, and state eviction moratoriums.

The CDC's Temporary Halt of Residential Evictions

In early September 2020, the Centers for Disease Control and Prevention (CDC) issued an agency order titled "Temporary Halt in Residential Evictions to Prevent the Further Spread of COVID-19" (Order). The Order prohibited residential landlords nationwide from evicting certain tenants through December 31, 2020. The Order protected tenants who:

- used their best efforts to obtain government assistance for housing
- were unable to pay their full rent due to a substantial loss of income
- made their best efforts to make timely partial payments of rent, and
- would become homeless or have to move into a shared living setting if they were to be evicted.

In addition to the requirements above, tenants had to:

- expect to earn no more than $99,000 (individuals) or $198,000 (filing a joint tax return) in 2020
- not have been required to report any income on a tax return in 2019, or
- have received an Economic Impact Payment (stimulus check) under the CARES Act.

Tenants had to complete a declaration under penalty of perjury stating that they qualified under these criteria. Tenants who did not qualify for protection from eviction under the Order might still have been protected from eviction under state or local eviction bans.

At the time of this writing (September 2020), the Order is set to expire on December 31, 2020. Given the strong possibility that the economic strife caused by the pandemic will continue into 2021, the Order might well be extended in the same or a modified form into 2021. Any renter struggling to pay rent should research the current status of the Order, as well as state and local COVID-related eviction bans and tenant protections. We'll post updates about the Order on Nolo's website at www.nolo.com/back-of-book/RENT.html.

Late Rent Fees

Landlords often impose a late fee when rent is even a few days late. But the size of the late fee is subject to legal limits, and in some situations it's not legal to impose one at all.

Are Late Fees Legal?

If your lease or rental agreement says nothing about late fees, your landlord may not impose one, no matter how reasonable it is. For example, if you hand your rent check to the landlord two days late and he tells you he will accept it only if you pay an additional $20, you can refuse to pay it unless your lease or rental agreement includes a late fee clause, and the amount demanded is within it. Keep in mind, however, that being too hasty to assert your rights over a relatively modest sum of money might not be worth the bad feelings that could come back to haunt you in the future.

Limits on Late Fees

Most states do not put dollar limits on late fees. Does this mean your landlord can charge any amount? No. Under general legal principles, your landlord may not charge an unreasonably high late rent fee.

Here are some guidelines for judging what's unreasonable:

- The fee shouldn't begin immediately. Normally, a late fee should not apply until at least three days after the rent due date.
- The fee should be within a certain percentage of your rent. Any late charge that is 5% or more of the rent is unlikely to be enforceable—for example, a judge would likely consider a $60 late fee (5%) on a $1200-per-month rental to be excessive.

What to Do About Excessive or Questionable Late Fees

Obviously, the surest way to avoid a late fee is to pay your rent on time. But if you cannot do this, don't automatically assume that there's nothing you can do about the penalty.

When There's No Provision on Late Fees

Your landlord may not impose a late fee unless the lease or rental agreement has a late fee clause (or unless you've discussed the policy, if you have only an oral rental agreement). However, this rule of law won't stop some landlords.

If you refuse to pay the fee, be prepared to be asked to move at the first legal opportunity—with proper notice if you rent with a rental agreement, or by the landlord refusing to renew your lease when it expires. Remember, in most states a landlord can terminate a month-to-month tenant, or decide not to renew a lease, without having to give a reason. (If you live in a state that prohibits landlord retaliation, discussed in Chapter 11, you might have some protection, but you're still in for a legal fight.) To avoid the risk of losing your home, if the amount is something you can live with, it might make more sense to pay the fee and begin looking elsewhere for a better landlord.

When You've Agreed to an Outrageously High Fee

If you've signed a lease or rental agreement that contains an outlandish late fee policy, you can still refuse to pay it and challenge it in court when the landlord seeks to evict you for breaking a lease provision. Why? Most courts consider the imposition of enormous late fees, like outrageous high-interest loans, to raise an important public policy issue. They will listen to your defense (though not necessarily rule in your favor) in spite of the landlord's claim that you "waived" the right to protest when you signed the lease or agreement.

We suggest, however, that you not risk the threat of an eviction lawsuit (which involves expensive court costs and always includes the possibility that you'll lose). Instead, pay the fee if possible and file your own lawsuit in small claims court, asking that the judge order the landlord to return it. (Small claims court is covered in Chapter 13.) That way, the only thing at stake is your time and the small filing fee, not your home. But it goes without saying that once you've sued your landlord you can expect a termination notice at the first legal opportunity, and would do well to begin looking for a new rental.

Tenancy Terminations for Nonpayment of Rent

If you are late with the rent, landlords in most states can immediately send you a termination notice giving you a few days in which to pay up or move before the landlord can file for eviction. These are usually called pay rent or quit notices—you are given a few days to pay or move out ("quit"). If you do neither within the time limit, the landlord can then file an eviction lawsuit against you. The rules vary widely among states, including:

- **How soon landlords may serve a pay rent or quit notice.** While most states allow landlords to send the notice the first day the rent is late, a handful don't let the landlord send the notice until you're a certain number of days late.
- **How the notice must be served.** Some states require the landlord to serve the notice personally; most states allow mailing.
- **How quickly you must pay the rent before the landlord can terminate the tenancy.** In most states, landlords must give the tenant three to five days to pay up or face a termination. But some states don't give you any time at all. Instead, if you fail to pay rent on time—even just once—the landlord can simply demand that you leave, with what's called an unconditional quit notice.
- **What happens if you're late more than once.** In many states, if you're late with the rent a second or third time within a specified number of months, landlords don't have to give you the usual few days to pay—they can terminate the tenancy immediately, the moment the rent is late, with an unconditional quit notice.

Eviction itself—that is, physically throwing you and your possessions out of the property—can't be done until the landlord has gone to court and proved that you've done something wrong (like not paying the rent) that justifies eviction. For a discussion of the eviction procedure, including time periods, negotiation strategies, and an overview of an eviction lawsuit, see *Every Tenant's Legal Guide,* by Janet Portman, Marcia Stewart, and Ann O'Connell (Nolo).

Rent Increases

Rent increases are an inevitable part of any tenant's life. In most areas without rent control, there is no limit on the amount your landlord can increase the rent. But landlords cannot raise the rent at whim. The timing of a rent increase, and the way your landlord communicates it, are governed by statute in most states.

Also, in most states landlords cannot increase rent in retaliation after you exercise specified legal rights guaranteed to tenants, and cannot illegally discriminate in their system for raising rent.

When and How Your Landlord Can Raise the Rent

Except in cities and states with rent control, your landlord's legal right to raise the rent depends primarily on whether you have a lease or a month-to-month rental agreement.

If you have a lease, your landlord can't raise the rent until the end of the lease period, unless you agree to it or the lease itself provides for an increase (multi-year leases commonly include a schedule of increased rent for each year of the lease).

If you rent under a month-to-month rental agreement, the landlord can raise the rent (or change any other term of the rental arrangement) by giving you the proper amount of notice, which in most states is 30 days. Also, the rent increase notice must be in writing; some states require certified mail. Oral notices are ineffective in most states and, unless you specifically agree to the rent increase, you are not obligated to pay it.

Effect of Rent Increase on Security Deposit

Rent increases often trigger security deposit increases. Here's how it happens: Many states limit the amount a landlord can charge for a security deposit. Typically, deposits are capped as a multiple of the monthly rent—for example, the maximum deposit is twice the monthly rent. But this means that if the rent has gone up legally, the security deposit can also be legally increased. For example, if the highest allowable deposit is twice the monthly rent, and your $1,000 rent has gone up to $1,100, the deposit limit rises from $2,000 to $2,200. Your landlord may require you to add $200 to your deposit. (See Chapter 4 for more on security deposit increases.)

Responding to an Illegal Rent Increase

What should you do if your landlord doesn't give you proper written notice for a rent increase?

If you're a month-to-month tenant and it's not that big a deal, you're better off going along rather than insisting on your rights and facing a chill in your relationship. (Besides, because the landlord can "do it right" with typically 30 days' notice, your objections will only buy you one month's time.) It's usually a good idea to ask your landlord to put the increase in writing, so that the amount of the increase can't mysteriously grow. Ask the landlord to prepare a new lease or rental agreement confirming the new arrangement or write a letter yourself confirming the new terms. (See Chapter 2 on letters of understanding.) As with all correspondence, be sure to keep a copy in a safe place with your other rental papers.

It's a somewhat different situation, however, if you have a lease. Having thought that you were protected from rent increases (one of the main advantages of a lease), you won't take kindly to an increase midlease. But think carefully: It might be a mistake to point out to your landlord that the rent payment clause cannot be changed during the life of the lease. Especially if you have been habitually late paying rent or have broken some other significant provision for which you could be evicted (for example, your boyfriend has moved in, violating your lease's restrictions on occupants), you could end up winning the battle but losing the war. In short, if the landlord has a *legal* ground for eviction, it is probably far better to go along with the rent payment change than to stand on your rights and invite the end of your tenancy.

Rent Increases as Retaliation or Discrimination

Landlords may not raise the rent in a discriminatory manner—for example, only for members of a certain race or religion or for families with children. (Discrimination is explained in detail in Chapter 5.)

Also, in most states your landlord can't use a rent increase (or evict you or decrease services, either) in retaliation against you for exercising a specified legal right. For example, if you make a legitimate complaint to a housing inspector about defective conditions in your rental unit, your landlord may not raise your rent to punish you. (Chapter 7 discusses your rights to demand fit and habitable housing, and Chapter 11 explains what you can do about landlord retaliation.)

Talking the Landlord Out of a Rent Increase

Legally, there is nothing you can do about a legal rent hike that doesn't violate a rent control law and is not discriminatory or retaliatory. The landlord can charge as much as the market will bear. But, practically, you can appeal to your landlord's business sense.

Landlording is a business with the goal of making money, but smart landlords realize that high rents are not the only route to high profits. Solvent, long-term tenants are the best tenants because they are low-maintenance—they don't have to be evicted, sued, coddled, cleaned up after, scolded for breaking the rules, or interviewed and investigated as part of the time- and money-consuming new-tenant application process. If you are a good, long-term tenant and can convince your landlord that the rent hike will make you move, your landlord might think twice, or at least moderate the increase. (On the other hand, if you have been less than straight in your dealings with the landlord, don't expect any accommodations.)

NEGOTIATE

When faced with a rent hike, work together with other long-term tenants. Your leverage with the landlord will increase if you can show that many other stable, long-term tenants are also upset and considering moving. If the rent hike affects others in your building, work together to present your collective plea. Remember, even in a tight rental market, lots of long-term tenants are hard to find.

The Landlord's Right to Change Other Rent Terms

If you've bounced a check or two or lost your job, can your landlord suddenly refuse personal checks and accept only certified checks or money orders? Or, if you've been paying by mail, can your landlord now require you to bring your rent to the manager's office?

Legally, the answer to these questions is usually no—assuming your payment method has followed the instructions on this issue in your lease or rental agreement. If you have a year's lease, the payment arrangement is in force for a year; if you rent month to month, most states require your landlord to give at least 30 days' written notice before changing a rental agreement clause.

If your lease or rental agreement doesn't say where and how rent is to be paid, your landlord's past practice is likely to legally control how rent is paid. For example, a landlord who has always asked for your rent check on the first of the month has established a due date that both of you must honor until the landlord formally changes the system with proper notice (in most states, 30 days).

Rules to Rent By

- **Always pay rent on time.** Do whatever it takes, including hand-delivering your rent check. If you mail your rent check, make sure that it arrives on time—it is not sufficient to post your check on the rent due date.
- **If you can't pay on time, deal with it.** Contact the landlord, explain the situation, and offer a partial payment and a plan to pay the rest. If you reach an agreement, send a letter of understanding (see Chapter 2) that will protect you in case your landlord "forgets" and attempts to terminate for nonpayment of rent.
- **Think carefully before refusing to pay late fees.** Although they might be illegal, it might not be worth risking an eviction lawsuit to prove your point.

CHAPTER

4

Security Deposits

Most landlords will require a security deposit before you move in. If you damage the property or leave owing rent, your landlord can use your deposit to cover what you owe. Security deposits are usually several hundred, or even thousands of dollars. Because of the large amount at stake, landlords and tenants frequently clash over the amount charged, whether it's refundable, and how it's used.

Fortunately, many states impose fairly strict rules on how landlords can collect and use deposits and how they must return them when tenants move out. Some states and cities even require landlords to put deposits in a separate account and pay interest on them. Landlords who violate security deposit laws are often subject to substantial financial penalties. (Appendix B provides details on state security deposit rules, including limits, whether the landlord must keep your money in a separate account or pay you interest on it, and the deadline for returning the deposit after you leave.)

If you live in an area that regulates security deposits, count yourself lucky. If you don't, it's especially important that you follow our advice on clarifying the use and return of all deposits with your landlord *before* you move in. To protect yourself and avoid misunderstandings with your landlord, make sure your lease or rental agreement clearly states:

- what you must do to ensure the return of your deposit, and
- how soon after you vacate the unit your landlord will assess the condition of your rental and return all or part of the deposit.

If the game plan isn't contained in your rental documents, you can always ask the landlord about the requirements and procedures and then write a letter of understanding documenting the conversation. (Letters of understanding are explained in Chapter 2.)

Dollar Limits on Security Deposits

Half the states don't set any limits on deposits. As with rent, landlords are free to charge as much deposit as they want. But unless the rental market is especially tight, landlords won't find many takers if they charge a security deposit of more than a month or two of rent.

The other half of the states limit the deposit a landlord can collect to an amount equal to one or two months of rent. The deposit limit that applies to you might depend on factors such as:

- your age (some laws mandate lower deposit ceilings for senior citizens)
- whether the rental unit is furnished (sometimes larger deposits are allowed for furnished apartments)
- whether you have a pet (if so, you'll often pay a higher deposit), and
- the number of rental properties the landlord owns (landlords with only a few rentals might be exempt from security deposit limits).

(Check "State Security Deposit Rules" in Appendix B to see whether your state limits the amount your landlord can collect.)

NEGOTIATE

Negotiate the amount and payment of deposits. If you think you'll have a hard time coming up with the deposit, your landlord might be willing to reduce it or allow you to pay it in installments. Here are a few tips for approaching your landlord. Obviously, these strategies are more likely to work if you have a good credit history and references and live in an area with lots of rentals. And don't ask for a lower deposit or an installment plan until you know for sure the place is yours.

- Offer to pay half the deposit up front with the rest on an affordable installment plan. Some landlords will say yes only if you can come up with the whole deposit in 30 to 60 days, but others will let you increase the amount a little each month until it's topped off in six months or more.
- Offer to pay higher rent in exchange for a substantially lower deposit. For example, offer to pay $25 more per month for the first year in exchange for the landlord cutting the security deposit from $1,000 to $500. Even though the landlord would only get an extra $300 in one year while you get a break of $500, the landlord knows that the $300 doesn't have to be returned, unlike money paid as a refundable deposit.

When Landlords Can Increase Deposits

If you have a fixed-term lease, your landlord may not raise the security deposit during the term of your lease, unless the lease itself allows it (most don't). If you have a month-to-month tenancy, a security deposit can be increased the same way the rent can be, typically by giving you a written notice 30 days in advance of the change. (In Chapter 3, see "Rent Increases.") Of course, if your state regulates the maximum deposit that can be charged, your landlord can't exceed that amount.

What's the Money For?

By law in most states, your landlord must refund your deposit promptly after you move out, unless there is a valid reason not to return all or part of it. Most states give landlords a set amount of time (usually from 14 to 30 days) to either return the entire deposit or provide an itemized written statement of deductions and refund the rest.

Although state laws vary on the details, your landlord can almost always withhold all or part of the deposit to pay for:

- unpaid rent
- repairing damage to the premises that you or a guest caused (except for "ordinary wear and tear")
- cleaning necessary to restore the rental unit to its condition at the beginning of the tenancy (over and above "ordinary wear and tear"), and
- replacing rental unit property you've destroyed or taken.

Landlords don't need to wait until you move out to tap into your security deposit. Your landlord may use some of it during your tenancy—for example, because you broke or damaged something and didn't fix or pay for it. After using part of the deposit in this way, the landlord can require you to replenish it. (Chapter 10 explains how landlords may use the deposit when you move out.)

Last Month's Rent

A landlord might want you to pay a sum of money called "last month's rent" before you move in, as a form of insurance against your leaving without giving the proper amount of notice. If you pay in advance for the last month with a payment clearly labeled "last month's rent," you don't have to make a final payment on the last rent due date before you move out.

Many states consider a last month's rent payment as part of the security deposit when it comes to limits. In other words, if your state limits security deposits to twice the monthly rent, your landlord can collect for the last month and only one more monthly sum as "security." But the landlord can't collect twice the monthly rent as a deposit *plus* the last month's rent.

Using the Security Deposit as the Last Month's Rent

Many tenants whose deposit doesn't explicitly include "last month's rent" are tempted to skip paying their last month's rent, figuring that the landlord will just take it out of their deposit. This is a risky move.

- It forces the landlord to deplete your deposit to cover rent. This leaves your landlord with less money to use for repairing damage you've caused or replacing missing items in your unit. Even if you leave the place spotless, your landlord won't appreciate being manipulated this way. Don't expect a good reference when your next landlord calls the current one and asks about you.
- Even though you've announced that you're leaving, your landlord can still send you a termination notice and follow-up with an eviction lawsuit when you skip the final month's payment. Why bother, when you're moving out at the end of the month anyway? Because your landlord might not trust you to leave, and might not want to waste any time getting you out once your rent payments have stopped. Even if the eviction is dismissed, it could show up on your credit record, which will be a major problem for future rentals.
- Laws in a few states impose penalties on tenants who attempt to use the deposit as the last month's rent without their landlord's permission.

It's best to not use the deposit for the last month's rent, unless you've got the landlord's permission in writing.

Nonrefundable Deposits and Fees

Many landlords collect a fee that is not refundable—such as for pets or cleaning. Most states' security deposit statutes are silent on the subject of nonrefundable fees or allow them for specific purposes, such as cleaning. A few states (including California), specifically prohibit landlords from charging any fee or deposit that is not refundable.

If you're being charged a nonrefundable fee, check your state security deposit laws (citations are in Appendix B) to see whether your state regulates this practice. Even if the law allows nonrefundable fees, be sure you're clear on what the fee covers.

Are You Entitled to Interest on Your Deposit?

Unfair as it might seem, only a third of the states require landlords to pay interest on deposits. In other words, many landlords can simply put your deposit in a personal bank account, use it, and pocket the interest, as long as the original sum is available when you move out.

Some states that do impose interest requirements require landlords to give tenants information on the location of the account at the start of the tenancy, usually as part of the lease or rental agreement. These states typically establish detailed requirements, including:

- **The interest rate to be paid.** Usually, it's a little lower than the bank actually pays, because the landlord is allowed to keep a small portion for administrative expenses.
- **When interest payments must be made.** Most laws require payments to be made annually and/or when you leave.
- **Notifying the tenant.** Landlords must tell tenants where and how the security deposit is being held and the rate of interest it's earning.

Chicago, Los Angeles, San Francisco, and several other cities (typically those with rent control) require landlords to pay or credit tenants with interest on security deposits, even if the state law does not impose this duty. A few cities require that the funds be kept in interest-bearing accounts that are separate from the landlord's personal or other business accounts.

NEGOTIATE

Ask for interest. Excellent landlords are willing to pay interest on your deposit as an honest business practice, even if there is no law requiring it. If your landlord doesn't volunteer to do this, there's no harm in asking.

How Your Landlord's Bankruptcy or Property Sale Affects Your Deposit

If your building has been sold or the landlord has declared bankruptcy, your security deposit should still be available to you at the end of your tenancy (minus legitimate deductions for damage or unpaid rent). That's the theory, at any rate. You might still have to take steps to retrieve your deposit.

When the Landlord Declares Bankruptcy

When your landlord files for bankruptcy, the landlord's creditors cannot touch your security deposit. That's because, technically speaking, it's not your landlord's money—it's yours, and it must be returned to you unless you fail to pay the rent or damage the property. Of course, if the landlord has used up every bit of cash within reach, there simply might not be any funds immediately available to pay you.

Don't give up, however, if your landlord pleads poverty and shrugs. Remember, declaring bankruptcy doesn't mean that the landlord gets to walk away from debts and keep inessential frills. The court will appoint a bankruptcy trustee who will assemble the creditors and pay them with what's left of the landlord's assets. Sometimes the bankruptcy trustee orders nonliquid assets (cars, real property, or jewelry) to be sold to make funds available. Because you are not even a creditor, you should be at or near the top of the list. Contact the bankruptcy court (look online or in the government pages of your phone book under "United States Courts") and write to the trustee, explaining your situation and asking to be paid.

When the Building Is Sold

In most states, the law requires a landlord who sells the building to do one of two things: Return the deposit to the tenant or transfer it to the new owner. If the old owner simply walks off with the deposit, the new owner cannot require you to pay again. Rather, the new owner will have to come up with the money when it's time to return the deposit to you. If the new owner refuses, you'll have to sue, preferably in small claims court. (See Chapter 13.) In some states, you can also sue the former owner.

Rules to Rent By

The security deposit demanded by your landlord is likely to be a hefty chunk of change. Take steps to ensure that you get it back:

- **Know the law.** Check to see whether your state sets a maximum security deposit. If you're being asked to pay a nonrefundable fee, find out whether it's legal and, if so, if it counts toward your state's limit, if any.
- **Learn the landlord's rules.** Find out at the beginning what steps you must take to get the security deposit back. For example, does your landlord's definition of "clean" include shampooing the carpets, or simply vacuuming them?
- **Don't assume that the deposit will cover the last month's rent unless the landlord agrees.** In some states, this dodge will cost you plenty because it will allow the landlord to keep some of the remaining deposit that you otherwise would get back. And, in all states, you can count on a negative reference from this landlord when a prospective landlord calls for a read on you.

CHAPTER

5

Discrimination

Not so long ago, a landlord could refuse to rent to you or evict you for almost any reason—because of your skin color, or your religion, or because you had children or were elderly or disabled. Some landlords even discriminated against single women, believing that they would be incapable of paying the rent or would have too many overnight guests.

Recognizing that all Americans who can afford to pay the rent should have the right to live where they chose, Congress and state legislatures have passed—and continue to pass—laws prohibiting housing discrimination. Most notable of these are the federal Fair Housing Act of 1968 and the federal Fair Housing Amendments Act of 1988 (Fair Housing Acts), which outlaw discrimination based on race or color, national origin, religion, sex, familial status, or disability. These laws are administered by the Department of Housing and Urban Development (HUD). In addition, many states and cities have laws making it illegal to discriminate based on additional factors, such as marital status or sexual orientation.

Today, it is safe to say that unless a landlord has a legitimate business reason to reject a prospective tenant (for example, a poor credit history or terrible references from previous landlords), the landlord risks a potentially costly legal challenge.

In this chapter, we'll explain the federal antidiscrimination protections that apply to every tenant and alert you to some state protections as well. And we'll suggest what to do if you believe that you have been the victim of illegal discrimination.

Discrimination Prohibited by Federal Laws

Because federal law governs everyone, we'll start with it. A number of federal laws prohibit discrimination on the basis of the following criteria (called "protected categories"):

- race or color
- religion
- national origin
- familial status or age—includes families with children under the age of 18 and pregnant women

- disability or handicap, and
- sex.

The federal Fair Housing Acts apply to all aspects of the landlord-tenant relationship. Under these laws, landlords cannot:

- indicate a bias against or preference for any protected class in advertising
- falsely tell a member of a protected class that no rentals are available
- apply more restrictive screening criteria to applicants in protected categories
- refuse to rent to people in protected groups
- set different terms, conditions, or privileges for rental of a dwelling unit for members of a protected class at any point before or during the tenancy (for example, landlords cannot require larger deposits from certain tenants, or adopt different policies for responding to late payments depending on the tenant's inclusion in a protected class)
- provide different housing services or facilities to tenants based on their status as a member of (or not a member of) a protected class, or
- terminate a tenancy because a tenant is a member of a protected category.

Race or Religion

Landlords who treat tenants and applicants differently on the grounds of race or religion—for example, by advertising that they will accept only renters who belong to a certain religion—are clearly breaking the law. This form of discrimination is relatively rare, but subtle, less direct (and possibly even unintentional) discrimination is more common. For example, the landlord who turns away every black applicant is discriminating just as much as the one who announces that none need apply. And an apartment ad that says "safe Christian community" or "Sunday quiet times enforced" violates federal law, because applicants might reasonably conclude that Christians are preferred as tenants.

National Origin

Discrimination based on national origin is illegal, whether it's deliberate, unintentional, or indirect. For instance, an ad that offers special discounts to members of the Italian-American Club would be a likely candidate for a discrimination charge. And landlords cannot require proof of citizenship or immigration papers from applicants of one ethnicity but not from others, because doing so places a burden on one group that is not imposed on everyone else (in California and New York City, it's illegal to ask any applicant or tenant about immigration or citizenship status).

Federal Loopholes, State Plugs

Unfortunately, not every rental is covered by the federal fair housing laws. The following types of property are exempt:

- owner-occupied buildings with four or fewer rental units
- single-family housing rented without the use of advertising or without a real estate broker, as long as the landlord owns no more than three such homes at any one time
- certain types of housing operated by religious organizations and private clubs that limit occupancy to their own members, and
- with respect to age discrimination only, housing reserved exclusively for senior citizens. Two kinds of senior citizen housing are exempted: communities where every tenant is 62 years of age or older, and "55 and older" communities in which at least 80% of the occupied units must be occupied by at least one person 55 years or older.

Fortunately, some states step in with their own laws to protect tenants in properties or situations that are exempt under federal law. For example, tenants in owner-occupied buildings with four or fewer rental units in California are not protected by the Federal Acts, but are protected by California's fair housing laws.

Familial Status or Age

Landlords are not allowed to explicitly or indirectly turn you away based on your family status or your age.

Discrimination Against Families

While some landlords don't like renting to tenants with children, fearing the noise and wear and tear that kids might cause, the federal Fair Housing Acts prohibit discriminating on this basis. It is illegal for a landlord to reject an applicant or evict a tenant on the basis that the person has children or is pregnant. Even if the landlord has a worthy motive, such as believing that children won't be safe in the building or the neighborhood, it is illegal to deny the tenancy on that basis or to make other discriminatory moves such as steering families to certain parts of the property (usually the back).

Some landlords try to get around the laws prohibiting discrimination against families by setting unreasonably low occupancy limits, such as only two people for a two-bedroom unit. This too is illegal, as it has the effect of excluding families. Federal law (in this case, an opinion letter written by the Department of Housing and Urban Development) has established minimum occupancy standards that regulate how low an occupancy can go and still be legal. In general, landlords must allow at least two persons per bedroom. Landlords can be more restrictive only in rare instances, when they can show that legitimate business reasons justify a more restrictive standard. For example, a policy of only three persons in a two-bedroom unit might pass muster if the landlord can prove it is truly based on the limitations of the plumbing system or some other aspect of the building's infrastructure.

Some states are more generous to tenants (by law, states cannot reduce federal protections). For example, because California state law allows two occupants per bedroom plus one more occupant in the whole unit, California landlords renting a three-bedroom apartment must allow seven occupants, unless they can point to legitimate business reasons justifying a lower number. Finally, some local governments have also written occupancy laws (these local laws must be more generous to tenants than the Fair Housing Acts and any state law).

Age Discrimination

The federal Fair Housing Acts do not expressly ban discrimination based on age. Nevertheless, it is definitely forbidden under the broader prohibition against discrimination on the basis of familial status.

A landlord cannot refuse to rent to an older person or impose special terms and conditions on the tenancy unless these same standards are applied to all applicants and tenants. If you have excellent references and credit history, a landlord has no legal basis for refusing you, even if you are 85 and rely to some degree on the regular assistance of someone else. (Of course, a landlord could legally give the rental to someone else with equal or better references or financial stability.) However, if your current landlord reveals that you suffer from advanced senility to the point that you often wander into the wrong apartment, frequently forget to pay the rent, or are unable to undertake basic housekeeping chores, the prospective landlord can refuse to rent to you based on this age-neutral evidence that you are not likely to be a stable, reliable tenant.

Disability

Federal law prohibits discrimination against people who:

- have a physical or mental disability that substantially limits one or more major life activities—including, but not limited to, hearing, mobility and visual impairments; chronic alcoholism (but only if it is being addressed through a recovery program); mental illness; intellectual disability; being HIV-positive; and having AIDS or AIDS-Related Complex
- have a history or record of such a disability
- are regarded by others to have such a disability, or
- are associated with a person who has, had, or is regarded as having such a disability.

Mental or Emotional Impairments

Even if you had, have, or appear to have mental or emotional impairments, a landlord can evaluate your application only on the basis of your financial stability and history as a tenant. For example, the landlord can reject you if you cannot meet one or more of the good-tenant criteria that the landlord applies to all applicants (such as a minimum rent-to-income ratio). The landlord cannot reject you because of your mental health status.

Discriminatory Questions and Actions

Landlords are not allowed to ask you whether you have a disability or illness, or ask to see medical records. And no matter how well intentioned, landlords cannot make decisions about where and how you will live on the property that they would not make were you not someone with a disability. For example, if two units are for rent—one on the ground floor and one three stories up—the landlord must show both units to an applicant who uses a wheelchair, unless the applicant asks to see only one.

The Rights of Tenants with Disabilities to Live in an Accessible Place

Federal law protects tenants with disabilities after they have moved into a rental unit as well as during the application process. Landlords must reasonably accommodate the needs of tenants with disabilities, at the landlord's own expense. This means that a tenant with a disability can expect the landlord to adjust rules, procedures, or services to a reasonable degree in order to provide an equal opportunity to use and enjoy the dwelling unit or a common space. Examples include providing a parking space for a movement-impaired tenant and accepting a guide or service animal in an otherwise "no pets" building.

However, landlords need not undertake changes that would seriously impair their ability to run their business, such as installing an elevator to the third floor to accommodate a wheelchair-bound tenant's wish to live there.

Limited Protection for Alcoholics and Drug Users

Federal fair housing law extends limited protection to two carefully defined groups:

- recovering alcoholics—those who actively and regularly participate in a medically based treatment or AA program, and
- former drug addicts—including those who have prior convictions for illegal drug use (but not for drug dealing or manufacture).

It is important to remember that, despite these protections, other aspects of a recovering alcoholic's (or a former drug addict's) past might legally serve as the basis for a denial of housing. For example, if you are a recovering alcoholic who has bad credit, a spotty employment history, or negative references from your previous landlords, a landlord may reject you for these reasons just as readily as any other applicant with these flaws. What a landlord cannot do is reject prospective tenants solely on the basis of their status as a former addict or recovering alcoholic.

Fortunately, even when a tenant wants to bend the landlord's policies in a way that goes beyond what a landlord would reasonably be expected to provide, the tenant might still have options: Tenants with a disability have the right to modify their living space, at their own expense, to the extent necessary to make the space safe and comfortable. This rule has two caveats: First, the landlord is not required to allow the tenant to make major structural alterations. Second, if the modifications will make the unit unacceptable to the next tenant, the tenant with a disability must agree to undo the modification when moving out. The landlord has the right to insist that the tenant put money in an escrow account to cover the eventual cost of returning the unit to its original condition. Examples of modifications undertaken by a tenant with a disability include lowering of countertops, installing a ramp, or repositioning the light switches.

Landlords are entitled to ask for proof that the accommodation or modification you have requested will address your situation—without it, your landlord has no way of knowing whether your request is legitimate or a ruse to obtain special treatment. Ask your physician, therapist, counselor, or any other third-party health care professional who knows you and understands your situation for a letter attesting that what you are asking for will meet your needs. To protect your privacy, explain to the writer that there's no need to explain the disability. The writer need only certify that you are a person with a disability, as that term is defined by law; that the writer has personal knowledge of your disability; and that the changes you request are appropriate to your situation.

Sex and Sexual Harassment

You cannot be denied a place to live (or have special rules imposed on you) solely because you're female or male. Even well-intentioned policies are off-limits—for example, a landlord who is fearful that single women are more likely to be burglarized and assaulted than male tenants cannot require single females to live in upper-story apartments, even if, in fact, those units have been less prone to break-ins.

Sexual harassment is another form of unlawful sexual discrimination. For example, it's illegal to refuse to rent to a person who resists the landlord's sexual advances or to make life difficult for a tenant who has resisted such advances.

Discrimination Prohibited by State and Local Law

Most state and local laws prohibiting housing discrimination echo federal antidiscrimination law. But some laws forbid additional types of discrimination—such as discrimination based on marital status—that aren't covered by federal law. For example, in states that prohibit discrimination based on marital status, it is illegal to refuse to rent to divorced people, even though federal law does not prohibit this kind of discrimination.

Here we explain some of the common antidiscrimination laws that states and localities have adopted.

Marital Status

About 20 states ban discrimination on the basis of marital status. Most of these states' laws extend protection to married couples only (meaning that landlords cannot treat them differently from single tenants). What about the reverse—preferring married couples over single roommates or a single tenant? Courts in Maryland, Minnesota, New York, and Wisconsin have ruled that the term "marital status" only protects married people from being treated differently from single people, not vice versa.

What about unmarried couples? In most states, landlords may legally refuse to rent to you if you are an unmarried couple. This means that landlords in these states can ask if two applicants of the same or different sex are lovers or just friendly roommates. In Alaska, California, Massachusetts, Michigan, and New Jersey, however, courts have ruled that the term "marital status" extends to unmarried couples. In these states, landlords cannot refuse to rent to you simply because you and your roommate are not married.

Sexual Orientation and Gender Identity

Housing discrimination based on sexual orientation and gender identity is prohibited in the District of Columbia plus 22 states: California, Colorado, Connecticut, Delaware, Hawaii, Illinois, Iowa, Maine, Maryland, Massachusetts, Minnesota, Nevada, New Hampshire, New Jersey, New Mexico, New York, Oregon, Rhode Island, Utah, Vermont, Virginia, and Washington. Wisconsin prohibits housing discrimination based on sexual orientation. In addition, many cities prohibit discrimination on the basis of sexual orientation and gender identity, including Atlanta, Chicago, Detroit, Miami, New York, Pittsburgh, and Seattle. For more information on state or local law on sexual orientation, contact the National LGBTQ Task Force at 202-332-5177; or check out its website at www.thetaskforce.org.

If you or your roommate are gay, lesbian, or transgender and you live in a state or city that extends antidiscrimination protection to you, a landlord may not ask for details of your intimate lives.

Source of Income

In several states, including California, Connecticut, Delaware (limited protection for housing vouchers), the District of Columbia, Maine, Maryland, Massachusetts, Minnesota, New Jersey, New York, North Dakota, Oklahoma, Oregon, Utah, Vermont, Virginia, and Wisconsin, applicants who receive public assistance may not be turned away or otherwise discriminated against solely because of this fact. (Some cities also extend protection.) But a landlord may refuse to rent to you if your available income—regardless of its source—falls below a reasonable level, as long as the same standard is applied to every applicant. And landlords in most states are not required to participate in the federal housing subsidy program known as Section 8.

How to Fight Back

If you believe that a landlord has unlawfully discriminated against you, you can try to work things out with the landlord, or you can take advantage of the powerful antidiscrimination laws discussed earlier.

Your options (discussed below) include:

- trying to negotiate an acceptable settlement with the landlord, possibly with the help of a neutral mediator
- filing a complaint with a federal, state, or local government fair housing agency, or
- filing a lawsuit in federal or state court.

If successful, these strategies might force the landlord to do one or more of the following:

- Rent you a particular unit.
- Pay you "actual" or "compensatory" damages, which cover what you spent to find another rental, such as money spent on another apartment-finding service or taking several hours off from your job. These damages also cover any additional rent you had to pay elsewhere. In addition, you are entitled to be compensated for any humiliation or emotional distress (called "special damages") that you suffered due to the landlord's bad acts. If the landlord's conduct was truly awful, this amount can be substantial.

- Pay you punitive damages, which essentially punishes the landlord for especially outrageous, intentional discrimination.
- Pay your attorneys' fees and court costs, if any.
- Pay a penalty to the government.

What Do You Want to Accomplish?

Before you can make an intelligent decision about what strategy to pursue, you need to sit down and ask yourself what you're trying to achieve.

Quick results. If you simply want the offensive or unfair behavior to stop, and aren't interested in seeking compensation for your expenses, inconvenience, or humiliation, it doesn't make sense to file a complaint or lawsuit right away. A frank discussion with the landlord, perhaps in the company of a mediator or other neutral third party, might work better than a full-frontal legal assault. (Chapter 13 gives advice on how to negotiate with your landlord. If informal techniques don't work, you still can sue or complain to a government agency.)

Major changes. If negotiation hasn't worked, or if you want to seek compensation, a lawsuit might be necessary (see Chapter 13 for advice on finding an attorney). But be forewarned: Lawsuits and complaints to fair housing agencies are adversarial, miserable, drawn-out procedures. And keep in mind that even if you win, the fact that you filed a discrimination complaint might appear on your credit record for some years into the future. If a prospective landlord or employer asks the credit bureau to run an "investigative consumer report" (containing detailed information about your character, general reputation, personal characteristics, and mode of living), you can be sure that this episode will show up—and it might cause future potential landlords to be concerned that you are litigious. (Credit reports are covered in Chapter 1, in "Your Credit Report Can Make or Break Your Application.")

Before making a final decision as to which path to take, ask for the opinion of a trusted and reasonable friend. Discrimination can be a highly emotional subject, and it's always a good idea to seek the counsel of someone who is not involved.

How Strong is Your Case?

If you've decided you want to file a complaint with a fair housing agency or to sue the landlord, you need to evaluate the strength of your case. The following guidelines will help you judge how strong or weak a case you have.

- **The more serious the harm you suffered, the more likely you are to win.** Be realistic in your assessment: A muttered racial slur will not offend a judge as much as a landlord's flat-out statement that he will not rent to you because you're Jewish or Black.
- **Repeated acts of discrimination are more likely to earn the wrath of a judge than a single incident.** If you can point to a pattern of illegal discrimination rather than an isolated incident, you're way ahead. And don't forget that judges have long memories—your landlord might be well known in the local HUD office for prior behavior, which will add credibility to your case.
- **Although unintentional discrimination is as illegal as intentional acts, it is harder to prove.** For example, although a landlord's policy of "one person per bedroom" has the effect of discriminating against families, it's easier for the landlord to dispute—and for the judge to give the landlord the benefit of the doubt—than if the landlord had a stated policy of "no children."
- **If you have only your word against the landlord's, you have a weak case.** As with any lawsuit, you need independent, physical evidence of your claims—like witnesses who will testify, newspaper ads, or house rules that establish the discriminatory policy—to corroborate your word.

RESOURCE

Mediate, Don't Litigate: Strategies for Successful Mediation, by Peter Lovenheim and Lisa Guerin (Nolo), contains important information on choosing and working with a mediator. This eBook is available at Nolo.com.

CAUTION

Don't proceed alone. If the landlord's insurance company or lawyer realizes you have complained to a fair housing agency (or are about to do so) or are poised to file a lawsuit, they might offer to settle. Be wary of dealing with insurance or legal professionals without the presence of a third party such as your own lawyer or a mediator. (In Chapter 13, "Using a Mediator" explains the mediation process and gives you information on locating and working with a mediator.)

Complaining to a Fair Housing Agency

You can file a discrimination complaint with the federal department of Housing and Urban Development (HUD) if you believe a federal law has been violated. Similarly, you can file with a state antidiscrimination agency if you believe your state's antidiscrimination law has been violated. Some areas also have local fair housing agencies that handle complaints.

A complaint to HUD must be filed within one year of the alleged violation. HUD will investigate the allegation and, if it concludes that there is a basis for your claim, will attempt a conciliation (compromise) between you and the landlord. If a compromise isn't reached, HUD will bring the case before an administrative law judge who, without a jury, will decide the matter. Administrative law judges can order the landlord to take certain actions to remedy the situation, pay you money, or pay a fine. State and local laws might have different procedures, including shorter filing deadlines, than those used by HUD.

Filing a Lawsuit in Federal or State Court

If you have experienced clear and outrageous discrimination, going directly to court might be quicker and more rewarding than going to a government agency. You'll need the help of an experienced lawyer if you choose this route. If you file in federal court, you must do so within two years of the alleged violation.

Right away, your lawyer might seek a temporary restraining order or a preliminary injunction ordering the landlord to do (or not to do) something (such as offer you the rental or cease treating you in a negative way) pending a full trial. Often, cases settle after an order like this is made.

You'll need to understand how lawyers typically charge for these types of cases. Some lawyers ask clients to pay an up-front amount called a retainer. Others might take the case "on contingency," which means that the lawyer will take a certain percent (usually 20% to 40%) if you win.

Rules to Rent By

- **Remember that landlords are allowed to discriminate for legitimate business reasons** such as whether you smoke, have pets (except in the case of animals used by people with a disability), or have a poor credit history. But landlords are not allowed to discriminate on grounds that are prohibited by federal, state, or local law.
- **Federal law prohibits discrimination on the basis of race or color, religion, national origin, familial status, age, disability, or sex.** State and local laws sometimes offer additional protections, such as prohibiting discrimination on the basis of marital status, sexual orientation, or gender identity.
- **Discrimination takes several forms.** It can be explicit ("No children allowed") or subtle ("A quiet, adult community"). Either way, if it results in discrimination against a protected group, it is illegal.
- **If you feel that you've been discriminated against,** before marching into the nearest lawyer's office, sit down with a friend who can give you straight advice. Ask yourself: What do I want to accomplish? Do I have a realistic appraisal of the harm I've suffered, and do I have solid evidence to back it up? Am I willing to become entangled in a lawsuit? Formulate your strategy accordingly.

More Information on Discrimination

The law. The federal antidiscrimination laws (the Fair Housing Act of 1968 and the Fair Housing Amendments Act of 1988), are in a set of code books called the United States Code and can be found at 42 United States Code Sections 3601–3619 and 3631. You can read the law by going to the Law and Legal Research section of Nolo's website (www.nolo.com/legal-research).

Where to complain. Start by calling HUD's Housing Discrimination Hotline at 800-669-9777, and checking out the HUD website: HUD.gov.

For information on state and local housing discrimination laws, contact your state fair housing agency (find yours on the HUD website at HUD.gov —under the "Resources" tab in the top menu, click on "State Information").

CHAPTER

6

Roommates

If you're like most tenants, you've got at least one roommate. And chances are that the names on your mailbox will change at least once before you, too, move on. Unfortunately, many landlords aren't as flexible as you would like when it comes to adding new roommates or letting others out of a lease.

This chapter discusses key aspects of sharing your home, including:

- your legal obligations and responsibilities with respect to your roommates
- what to do if your roommate takes off, leaving you with the rent to pay and maybe damages to cover
- moving in a roommate and what to do if your landlord objects
- what to do if your roommate becomes incompatible or won't pay the rent
- whether you can rent space to a roomer, and
- your rights to bring in paying "guests" through Airbnb and similar services.

Legal Jargon You Need to Know

Try as we might, we couldn't completely eliminate the legal buzzwords in this chapter. You need to understand them, because your rights and responsibilities vary depending on the term that fits your situation. For example, tenants can make some demands on their landlords that subtenants cannot, as explained below. Here's a rundown of some essential landlord-tenant terminology.

Original tenant. The initial tenant (or tenants) who entered into the lease or rental agreement (oral or written). This is our own shortcut term with no precise legal meaning.

Tenant. Someone who has signed a lease or a rental agreement, or was part of an oral rental agreement, or whose residency has otherwise been accepted by the landlord (by accepting rent, for example). Because a tenant has a direct relationship with the landlord, a tenant can hold the landlord to all the landlord's promises.

Legal Jargon You Need to Know (continued)

Cotenants. Two or more tenants who rent the same property under the same lease or rental agreement. Each is 100% responsible for carrying out the agreement (see "Joint and Several Liability," below), including paying the rent in full. Someone who is added to another's lease or rental agreement becomes the original tenant's (or tenants') cotenant.

Subtenant. Someone who rents from a tenant. The tenant becomes the subtenant's landlord. The subtenant might take over the rental for a portion of the lease term (for the summer, for example, with the tenant returning in September), or might live there at the same time as the tenant. Subtenants don't have a direct contractual relationship with the main landlord, and therefore aren't entitled to enforce many of the lease or rental agreement terms. Throughout this book, when we speak of "tenants," we do not mean subtenants unless specifically noted.

Roommates. Two or more people living under the same roof and sharing rent and expenses. Roommates are usually cotenants (they've signed the same lease or rental agreement), but a roommate might instead be a subtenant of the original tenant. Unless the landlord has accepted the presence of the roommate (by making the person a cotenant or explicitly or tacitly allowing the subtenancy), a roommate has the legal status of a long-term guest, with few if any legal protections.

Joint and several liability. This refers to the sharing of legal obligations by two or more people. Cotenants are "jointly and severally liable" for rent and other obligations of the lease, which means that each one can be held responsible for the misdeeds of the others and the landlord can look to any one of them to pay the entire rent. This rule applies even if your lease or rental agreement does not include this clause. It applies to oral leases, too.

Roomer. A person who rents space in your home from you while you live there. If you are a tenant, the roomer (sometimes called "lodger") is your subtenant, and you are that person's landlord. In most situations, landlords can legally prohibit roomers.

Renting a Place With Others

When two or more people sign the same rental agreement or lease—or enter into the same oral rental agreement—they are cotenants and share the same legal rights and responsibilities. But there's a special twist, which you might have noticed when reading "Legal Jargon You Need to Know," above. The legal principle known as "joint and several liability" has enormous implications for cotenants.

Keep in mind that here we are talking about housemates who are *cotenants*, not tenant and subtenant. This is an important distinction. Tenants and subtenants do not share the same rights and responsibilities with respect to each other or to the landlord. If you are a tenant who has rented out part of your place to someone else, or who has allowed someone to take your place in the rental for a portion of time, you are dealing with a subtenancy. Skip ahead to "Taking in a Roomer," below, in which we explain the legal landscape of tenants and subtenants.

Joint and Several Liability: You're in This Together

Joint and several liability is the legal version of the Three Musketeers' slogan, "One for all and all for one":

- **One for all.** The landlord can demand the entire rent from just one cotenant. The rent-sharing understanding you have with your roommates is immaterial to the landlord. In other words, even if you pay $400 for your tiny room and your roommate pays $800 for a master suite, your landlord can come to you for the entire $1,200 rent if your roommate doesn't pay.
- **All for one.** Even innocent cotenants will suffer the consequences of one cotenant's misdeeds. Unfair as it seems, the raucous party that your roommate threw when you were out of town can result in a termination notice directed to all of you.

It's that simple. So how can you avoid being burned by your roommate's screw-ups? The best answer, of course, is to choose your housemates carefully. Even when your roommate is a close friend, your relationship will benefit from considering and discussing possible areas of friction and planning ways to avoid problems.

CAUTION

Only landlords can evict tenants. This means that cotenants cannot force each other out. If your roommate becomes insufferable, you'll have to deal with it, unless the roommate's behavior is also a violation of law or of a lease or rental agreement clause (for example, illegal drug use). Be aware though: A violation of this nature would justify the termination of both your tenancies (joint and several liability!). You might get lucky if your landlord pities you and lets you stay, but you'll need to produce adequate proof that you can handle the entire rent on your own (or come up with an acceptable new cotenant quickly).

Talk It Out and Write It Down

Roommates make lots of informal agreements about splitting rent, sharing chores, and choosing bedrooms. It's important to understand that such agreements do not change the fact that all cotenants have joint and several liability to the landlord. And just as your landlord isn't bound by any agreements between roommates, your landlord cannot enforce them, either. If one roommate breaks an agreement made with the rest of the cotenants to pay one-third of the rent, don't bother asking your landlord to force the roommate to pay up.

Because the arrangements between you and your roommates will have a huge effect on your day-to-day life, you should take them seriously. Before you move in, sit down with your roommates and discuss the major issues that are likely to come up, including:

- **Rent.** What is everyone's share? Also, many landlords won't accept multiple checks or payments for the same unit, so you'll need to decide who is responsible for collecting everyone's share and making a timely payment to the landlord.

- **Space.** Who will occupy which bedrooms and use which bathrooms?
- **Household chores.** Who's responsible for cleaning, and on what schedule?
- **Food sharing.** Will you be sharing food? How about shopping and cooking responsibilities? How will you split the costs and work?
- **Noise.** When should music be turned off or down low? How late can guests stay?
- **Overnight guests.** Is it okay for friends to stay over? How often?
- **Moving out.** If one of you decides to move, how much notice must be given to the rest of you? Must the departing tenant find an acceptable substitute?
- **Spats.** How will you handle disagreements among yourselves about your living arrangement? (Don't kid yourself—they will come up.) If you want a roommate to leave, how can it be done fairly?

It's best to put your understandings in writing and ask every roommate to sign it. Oral agreements are too easily forgotten or misinterpreted after the fact. (See the Sample Roommate Agreement, below.)

TIP

A written and signed description of how you'll share the rent can help you collect if your roommate misses a payment. Remember, if one roommate hasn't paid, it's your problem—not the landlord's. You'll need to make up the deficit in order to avoid a termination. If your deadbeat roomie refuses to reimburse you, you can sue in small claims court. A written and signed roommate understanding is important evidence in your favor.

Sample Roommate Agreement

Catherine Davis, Kelli Halister, and Stacy Fremont are cotenants at 3901 Bay, #123, Collegetown, CA, under a $2,400/month, yearlong lease that begins on July 1, 20xx, and expires on July 1, 20xx. They have all signed the lease with the landlord, Will Stevens; and have each paid $800 toward the security deposit of $2,400. Catherine, Kelli, and Stacy agree as follows:

1. Rent. Because Will has agreed to accept three separate checks; each will pay $800 on or before the first day of each month.

2. Food. Each roommate is responsible for her own food.

3. Cleaning. Each will clean her own room. Cleaning the bathroom and kitchen (appliances, counters, vacuuming, and mopping) and the living room (vacuuming and dusting) will be done once a week on a rotating basis.

4. Utilities. Everyone will pay an equal share of the electricity, gas, Internet, and cable bills. Catherine will arrange for these services, receive each monthly bill, and show it to the others within two days of receiving it. Kelli and Stacy will give Catherine their checks, made out to Catherine, within one day. Catherine will make the payments.

5. Guests. Each roommate agrees to have no more than one overnight guest at a time, except in extraordinary situations; and no more than four overnight stays in one month.

6. Parties. Each roommate agrees that there will be no social gatherings of more than three guests at which alcohol is served on school nights. Parties on Saturday or Sunday evenings will be reasonably managed by the hostess, who will clean up afterwards.

7. Exam Periods. During exams, no roommate will have overnight guests or parties.

8. Violations of This Agreement. The roommates agree that repeated and serious violations of this agreement will be grounds for any two roommates to ask the other to leave. If a roommate is asked to leave, she will do so within one month and will forfeit any prepaid rent.

Sample Roommate Agreement (continued)

9. Leaving Before the Lease Ends. If a roommate wants to leave before the lease ends, she will give as much notice as possible (and not less than one month) and diligently try to find a replacement tenant who is acceptable to the remaining roommates and the landlord. The departing roommate will remain responsible for her share of the rent until a replacement has been found and accepted by the landlord. The departing roommate's obligation for rent will cease as of the date the replacement begins paying rent.

10. Security Deposits. The roommate who leaves early (voluntarily or involuntarily) will get her share of the security deposit returned, minus rent, costs of repairs, replacement, and cleaning attributable to the departing roommate, when and if an acceptable new roommate signs the lease and contributes his/her share to the security deposit. If an acceptable replacement cannot be found, the departing roommate will not receive any portion of her share of the deposit.

11. Dispute Resolution. If a dispute arises concerning this Agreement or any aspect of the shared living situation, the roommates will ask the University Housing Office Mediation Service for assistance before they terminate the cotenancy or begin a lawsuit. This will involve all three roommates sitting down with the mediator in good faith to try to resolve the problems.

Catherine Davis   *June 15, 20xx*
Catherine Davis   Date

Kelli Halister   *June 15, 20xx*
Kelli Halister   Date

Stacy Fremont   *June 15, 20xx*
Stacy Fremont   Date

Getting Rid of a Roommate

Sometimes, for various reasons, you might want a roommate to leave. However, you can't legally force out a roommate who is also a cotenant unless the roommate has broken one of the landlord's rules or engaged in illegal activity (and even then, it's the landlord, not you, who has the power to terminate the lease and file for eviction if needed). So how can you convince the person to move on? As is usually the case, the answer lies in preparation and negotiation.

Think ahead. At the start of your tenancy, before any tensions develop, design a fair way to address the situation where a cotenant (or cotenants) wants the other to leave. Paragraph 8 in our Sample Roommate Agreement, above, shows how three roommates decided they will deal with one who needs to go. If there are only two of you, you might agree that you'll go through mediation and abide by the mediator's suggestions (mediators usually don't impose decisions, but you can agree that you'll ask for one). The important point is to have a plan already in place that all have agreed to; that way, the problem roommate will be hard-pressed to opt out of the process.

Be creative. If you haven't planned ahead and are faced with an insufferable and stubborn roommate, you might need to use a little bribery. Paying someone to go is often very effective. And although most landlords won't get involved in their tenants' internal squabbles, you can try enlisting your landlord's help, anyway—the problem roomie might not know that the landlord cannot terminate the cotenancy except for violations of the lease or of law, and a stern "Take off!" from the landlord might just do the trick.

When a Roommate Walks Out

All too frequently, living arrangements that look promising when you're just friends turn into disasters when you become housemates. Maybe it's the gym bag dumped on the kitchen table every evening, the inconsiderate parties on work nights, or the "occasional" visitor who turns out to be a regular, unpleasant presence. Getting a roommate to leave can be difficult. But what happens to those left behind when the table is turned and a roommate leaves suddenly or against the wishes of the others?

When cotenants split, there can be serious consequences beyond hurt feelings. The remaining roommates must scramble to cover the departed tenant's rent share, and might feel forced to file a small claims court case demanding the departing tenant to pay up. (Chapter 9 explains in detail the likely consequences to the departing tenant. Here we discuss the predicament of the remaining cotenants.)

First, some rules. In a month-to-month tenancy, a cotenant who wants to leave must give the landlord the required legal notice—30 days in most states. Forget trying to leave on short notice—most landlords won't prorate a month's rent. This means that the remaining tenants will have the same amount of time to hustle up a replacement. Of course, there is nothing wrong with cotenants deciding among themselves that they will give *each other* a longer notice period. If a cotenant violates this internal agreement, the remaining tenants can go after the departed roommate in small claims court for the time (expressed as rent money) they were shorted. But the remaining tenants will still have to pay the full rent to the landlord as long as the departing tenant gave the landlord the statutorily required notice.

If there's a lease, the cotenant should either get permission from the landlord to leave early or, if this is impossible, find a new tenant acceptable to the landlord to take over. Again, if the cotenants all have an understanding that no one will leave without giving a longer notice period to the others, it's up to the cotenants to deal with the problem if one of them splits early.

Unfortunately, cotenants often leave with not so much as a "good-bye," let alone a substitute. Here are the options for the ones left behind.

CAUTION

Domestic violence victims might have special rights. Many states allow domestic violence victims to break a lease and leave without responsibility for future rent. (See "Domestic Violence Situations," in Chapter 9.)

What to Do If You Want to Stay

Let's start with the worst-case scenario for tenants who have a lease (see the section just above for month-to-month situations): Your cotenant leaves without the okay of the landlord. In this situation, the landlord has the option of evicting the rest of you, even if you can pay the full rent. How so? It goes back to joint and several liability: Moving out without the landlord's permission is a violation of a lease clause, and one cotenant's lease-breaking is a transgression for which all tenants are liable.

In practice, however, most landlords will probably let you stay if you're decent tenants and you can pay the rent. But if you're a trouble-some group, your landlord might see this as a golden opportunity to be rid of all of you.

NEGOTIATE

Hustle to cover the rent until you can replace your roommate. A landlord who fears that the remaining cotenants cannot cover the rent after one cotenant leaves might think it's necessary to terminate the lease (to bring in new, paying tenants as soon as possible). If you can assure the landlord that you can promptly bring in a good new cotenant, you might be able to salvage your tenancy. If you must, ask permission to pay the rent late or in installments. (See Chapter 3.)

CAUTION

Never bring in a new roommate without the landlord's consent. Moving in a new roommate without first getting approval gives your landlord a watertight reason to evict you, because your lease or rental agreement undoubtedly has a clause prohibiting unauthorized occupants.

What to Do If You Want to Move Out, Too

If your cotenant skips out, leaving you in the lurch, you might decide that you don't want to stay, either. To protect your security deposit and your good name at the credit bureaus, follow these steps:

- If you are a month-to-month tenant, give the required amount of written notice (usually 30 days) immediately. Don't wait until you can't pay the next month's rent and receive a termination notice. (Chapter 9 shows how to give proper notice.)
- If you have a lease, let the landlord know in writing that you plan to move because you cannot afford the rent without your cotenant. Before you move, be extra accommodating when it comes to showing the unit to prospective renters. Facilitating a quick rerental is not just a courtesy to your landlord, but benefits you as well, because the sooner a new tenant takes over, the sooner your liability for the balance of the rent due under the lease ends. In addition, do your best to find an acceptable replacement tenant yourself. (See Chapter 9 for an explanation of the landlord's responsibility to look for a new tenant, and "Adding a New Roommate," below, for advice on finding and presenting a replacement.)

Adding a New Roommate

If you want to add a roommate, most landlords will insist that the new roommate become a cotenant rather than a subtenant. Why? Unlike subtenants, cotenants are subject to joint and several liability, which allows the landlord to demand the entire rent from the cotenant as well as you. On the other hand, in some circumstances, you might want to ask the landlord to allow the newcomer to be a subtenant who rents from you and has no direct relationship with the landlord. For example, if you want to have the power to evict your new roommate, you'll need to set up a subtenancy, discussed in detail below in "Taking in a Roomer." Keep in mind no matter whether your roommate is a subtenant or a cotenant, you'll need the consent of the landlord.

Getting the Landlord's Approval

Obviously, you won't choose to live with someone who is financially unstable or inconsiderate. But even if you're satisfied with a prospective roommate's resume, your landlord might not be. There are many reasons a landlord might object to your chosen roommate, even if you've chosen someone who seems responsible and trustworthy. To increase your chances of an official okay, consider the following issues:

- **Will adding a roommate exceed the occupancy limit?** Landlords are entitled to set reasonable limits on the number of occupants per rental unit. (In Chapter 5, see "Discrimination Prohibited by Federal Laws.")
- **Will the new roommate meet your landlord's good-tenant criteria?** If your landlord subjected you to a thorough screening process, checking credit, employment, rental history, and references, put yourself in your landlord's shoes and do the same for your prospective roommate. If the results are dismal, don't waste your time further. If there's a small issue in your proposed roommate's situation that you think might raise your landlord's eyebrows, do your best to prepare a plausible explanation (along with the reasons why it won't pose a problem for the landlord).

Adding a Roommate to the Lease or Rental Agreement

If your intended roommate passes your landlord's credit and background checks, the landlord will probably ask both of you to sign a new lease or written month-to-month agreement. From your landlord's point of view, this is far more than a formality, because it makes the new arrival a cotenant who is 100% liable to pay rent and make good on any damage. It's also desirable from your perspective, because it makes it completely clear that your new roommate shares the same legal responsibilities that you do.

More Roommates, More Rent

If you add a roommate and sign a new rental agreement, technically speaking you're beginning a new tenancy, not changing an existing one. Consequently, if the landlord wants to increase the rent, the normal notice requirements for month-to-month tenancies (typically 30 days) don't apply and the rent can be increased as soon as you sign the new lease or rental agreement. The landlord might give you no notice other than presenting you with the new agreement containing the new rent provision. In this situation, landlords can set the rent at whatever level they choose (rent control areas excepted).

If you're adding a roommate to a lease, the same holds: Your landlord can increase the rent on the spot, because you're now beginning a new tenancy.

More Roommates, More Security Deposit

If you sign a new rental document, *all* bets are off, including the amount of the security deposit. If your state regulates the deposit in multiples of monthly rent, this is the only check on your landlord's ability to increase the deposit. Incidentally, the landlord can also change other lease clauses, such as those dealing with pets or late fees.

Taking in a Roomer

What if you're reluctant to share your entire home with a cotenant whom you have no power to evict, but want someone to share costs? The answer might be to take in a roomer as a subtenant.

When you take in a subtenant, you become that person's landlord. The main advantage of a subtenancy over a cotenancy is that it gives you the legal right to terminate the roomer's tenancy if things don't work out as planned. By contrast, you can't end the tenancy of a roommate who is a full-fledged cotenant—only your landlord can do this.

We suggest that you sign a month-to-month rental agreement with any subtenant, specifying rent and any restrictions on the use of your home. And, although your roomer doesn't sign the rental document you have with *your* landlord, the roomer must comply with its rules as well as yours. Think of the arrangement as a set of nesting dolls: You live within your landlord's rules and regulations, and your subtenant lives within yours *and* the landlord's. So if your landlord prohibits using the pool after 10 p.m., you can't promise your roomer the joy of midnight swims. And, most important, if your roomer breaks your landlord's rules, the landlord can evict *you* to get rid of the roomer.

Don't get too enthusiastic about bringing someone in as a roomer until you get your landlord's approval. And be forewarned that many "landlords" in your position have problems getting a roomer to leave. You'll probably have to follow the same legal procedures all landlords use to terminate a tenancy.

Tenant Rights to Use Airbnb and Similar Vacation Rental Services

If you're a renter, you might be tempted to earn some extra cash by renting out your apartment on a short-term basis though websites such as Airbnb, HomeAway, or FlipKey. But for most tenants, this can result in your landlord filing—and winning—an eviction lawsuit against you. Here are some things you should do before engaging in short-term hosting.

Read Your Lease or Rental Agreement

As discussed in Chapter 2, your lease likely prohibits sublets without your landlord's prior written consent (and many even explicitly forbid your use of services such as Airbnb). If you violate a no-sublets provision, or a lease clause limiting guest stays, your landlord can evict you.

Work Something Out With Your Landlord

Most renters who do short-term hosting on sites such as Airbnb never tell their landlords about it (especially when their landlord lives out of town and rarely stops by the rental). But if the neighbors complain or the landlord otherwise discovers what you're doing, you could be in trouble. Instead of taking this chance, consider asking your landlord's permission before you list your apartment on Airbnb or another short-term hosting site. Offering to split with your landlord part of the money you earn, or pay more rent, might seal the deal.

There are other things you can do as well to make your landlord more amenable to your short-term hosting, such as:

- promise to have paying guests only occasionally, rather than all the time
- promise that you'll follow any local regulations (see below)
- screen your Airbnb, HomeAway, FlipKey, and similar guests as well as you can, and
- rent out only a portion of your apartment, rather than the entire unit, so you'll be present to deal with the guests (and limit problems with neighbors).

If you do get your landlord's permission to short-term host, be sure to summarize your agreement in writing. If you don't have it already, you should also obtain renters' insurance with plenty of liability coverage. (That said, having renters' insurance might not, in the end, cover you if a paying "guest" causes damage. The insurance company might claim that its coverage extends only to damage caused by you and your true guests, not damage caused by a paying occupant.)

TIP

Check out any insurance provided by the short-term rental host. If you end up renting your place through one of the many online rental services out there, find out what sort of insurance it offers to hosts. For example, Airbnb provides hosts (free of charge) with $1 million in protection for property damage, and $1 million in liability insurance as part of its services. Having this coverage as backup might help convince your landlord to approve your request to become a short-term rental host.

If your landlord won't agree to permit you to short-term host, don't do it unless you're prepared to lose your tenancy. The extra money you might earn likely won't make up for getting evicted.

Research Your Local Zoning or Land Use Laws

Some cities prohibit short-term rental hosting. If that's the case where you live, forget about it—even if it's okay with your landlord. Others impose complicated restrictions, including limits on the number of days per year that the property is rented to short-term guests, registration requirements, and other conditions. Be sure to learn the rules, but keep in mind: A landlord with a clear "no sublets" clause in the lease can stop you cold, no matter what regulations your city has devised.

Rules to Rent By

- **Choose your roommates carefully.** Cotenants are jointly and severally liable to the landlord, which means that each individual cotenant is legally responsible for complying with the lease terms, including payment of rent in full. To be blunt: When it comes to paying rent and making good on damage, you are your cotenant's guarantor—if your cotenant flakes, you pay.
- **What's between roommates is beyond the landlord.** Any agreements you make with your roommates aren't binding upon the landlord. Arrangements for splitting rent, paying utilities, or cleaning house don't affect each cotenant's joint and several liability to the landlord.
- **No covert move-in operations.** Any roommate changes should be approved by the landlord, especially the addition of new roommates. Landlord approval is necessary whether a new tenant becomes a cotenant or a subtenant.

CHAPTER

7

Repairs and Maintenance

In almost every state, you're entitled to a safe and livable home, regardless of how much rent you pay or whether your landlord tries to get you to accept a hovel. We're talking about basic, important items such as a leak-proof roof, hot water, heat, and floors and walls that aren't in danger of imminent collapse. This list of necessary features includes the absence of significant danger from lead, asbestos, vermin, and mold, plus reasonable protection from criminal intrusion. If the landlord refuses to provide or repair these aspects of your home, you might, depending on where you live, be able to:

- withhold rent
- pay for repairs yourself and deduct the cost from your rent
- sue the landlord, or
- move out without notice and without liability for future rent.

It's another ball game, however, when it comes to minor repairs such as clogged kitchen sinks, broken ovens, or leaky faucets. Unlike the big-ticket items mentioned above, minor repairs usually aren't directly addressed by state law. There are other legal ways, however, that you can get some action out of your landlord, as we'll explain in "Laying the Minor Repair Job on the Landlord," below.

If you've come to this chapter because you're bedeviled by a repair problem, help is at hand. Here's the drill:

- First, you must figure out whether your problem is, legally speaking, a "major" repair or a "minor" one.
- Second, having correctly classified your problem, you need to choose the appropriate course of action, from friendly persuasion to invoking legal remedies designed to empower tenants. *Many of the legal steps you can take to force a landlord to deal with a major repair will not work for a minor repair and can result in eviction if used improperly.*
- Finally, you need to carry out the chosen strategy correctly. Usually, a necessary part of any plan will be to make sure that *you* have fulfilled the tenant's responsibilities to use your rental with reasonable care.

Tenant Traps

Read this chapter to find out why you should:

- **Never agree to move into or later accept a rental that lacks basic health and safety features** such as heat, plumbing, hot water, and weatherproofing. In most states, it is illegal for a landlord to offer a substandard rental or refuse to maintain a fit one.
- **Never push for repairs before figuring out whether it's a habitability problem or a minor repair.** Your bargaining power is vastly different depending on the seriousness of the problem.
- **Never delay in reporting major repair problems.**
- **Never use a "big stick" (such as rent withholding, discussed below) without first telling your landlord of the problem.** Your landlord is entitled to a reasonable amount of time to fix the problem.
- **Never use a big stick if you are behind in the rent, have an unauthorized roommate, or are violating some other important tenant obligation.**
- **Never make a big deal over a minor repair unless you are prepared for an uphill fight with your landlord.**

Your Right to a Livable Place

Your right to livable housing has a lofty-sounding legal name: You're entitled to the benefit of the landlord's "implied warranty of habitability." This means that by simply renting out a property, landlords promise tenants that the rental is—and will continue to be—livable, even when the landlord isn't aware of this promise. This basic right originated in court decisions in the early 1970s. By now, all but one state (Arkansas) have embraced this notion, either by decisions from their highest courts or by statute.

TIP

Some tenants in Arkansas do have rights to livable rentals. Although the Arkansas legislature has failed to adopt the implied warranty on a statewide level, some local governments (cities and counties) have enacted ordinances that come close to establishing at least minimal habitability standards. The situation in Arkansas is subject to change, as every few years or so an implied warranty bill is introduced. Check your local housing laws (found in most public libraries or online) for details. (Appendix A shows you how to find statutes online.)

So what does it mean to say that your landlord is expected to fulfill an implied warranty of habitability? It means that the owner must:

- keep basic structural elements of the building, including floors, stairs, walls, and roofs, safe and intact
- maintain all common areas, such as hallways and stairways, in a safe and clean condition
- keep electrical, plumbing, sanitary, heating, ventilating, air-conditioning systems, and elevators operating safely
- supply cold and hot water and heat in reasonable amounts at reasonable times
- provide trash receptacles and arrange for trash pickup
- manage known environmental toxins such as lead paint dust and asbestos so that they don't pose a significant danger
- in most states, provide rental property that is reasonably safe from the threat of foreseeable criminal intrusions, and
- exterminate infestations of rodents and other vermin.

In virtually every state, these rights are yours, no matter what the landlord has asked you to sign or agree to. (However, in Maine, tenants can agree to accept conditions that might violate the warranty in exchange for a reduction in rent (more restrictions apply to the provision of heat); and in Texas, tenants can undertake responsibility for repairs in narrow, specified situations.) In other words, the landlord cannot shrug off these responsibilities in a "disclaimer" when the tenancy begins. And landlords can't effectively ask you to waive your right to them. (Any so-called waiver will not be upheld by a court.)

CAUTION

Don't wait until you move in to discover major repair problems. Always inspect the rental unit—and have the landlord do necessary repairs—before you move in, as recommended in Chapter 2.

Environmental Hazards

Federal, state, and local laws have identified several environmental hazards that can pose serious health risks. The presence of airborne asbestos, deteriorating lead paint or dust, certain molds, and bedbugs could, in certain circumstances, constitute a violation of the landlord's duty to maintain fit housing. In turn, the tenant might be justified in using a remedy such as rent withholding, repair-and-deduct, or moving out, as explained later in this chapter. Here is a brief rundown of these problems. (For a more in-depth description, see *Every Tenant's Legal Guide*, by Janet Portman and Marcia Stewart (Nolo).)

Asbestos

Asbestos fibers that have begun to break down (from the passage of time or by being disturbed through repair work) will enter the air and pose health risks to those who breathe them. Under regulations imposed by the U.S. Occupational Safety and Health Administration (OSHA), owners of buildings constructed before 1981 must install warning labels, train staff, and notify people who work in areas that might contain asbestos. (29 Code of Federal Regulations (C.F.R.) §§ 1910.1001 and following.) Although these rules are designed to protect workers, they are also a boon to tenants, because once landlords learn about the presence of airborne asbestos fibers, they're on notice of a dangerous situation. If they fail to take action (by not encapsulating the asbestos, for example), they risk a costly lawsuit if one of their tenants is injured. The landlord generally does not have to take action if the asbestos is intact and is not entering the airstream. For further information on asbestos rules, inspections, and control, contact

OSHA's nearest office (see the section "Find an OSHA Office" under the "OSHA" tab at the top of the home page, OSHA.gov) or call the national office at 800-321-OSHA (6742). You can also learn more by visiting the OSHA website at OSHA.gov. (For additional information on asbestos, including negative health effects, see the EPA website, at www.epa.gov/asbestos.)

Lead

A federal law known as Title X ("Ten") of the United States Code requires landlords of pre-1978 buildings to tell every new tenant about the presence of lead-based paint if the landlord knows it's on the property. (42 U.S.C. § 4852d.) Your landlord should have given you a disclosure form and the government booklet "Protect Your Family From Lead in Your Home" when you signed the lease or rental agreement. Federal law does not, at this time, require the landlord to test for lead paint dust. In addition to the federal rules, many state laws impose maintenance and remediation duties, which might involve covering the lead-based paint or carefully removing it. For more information on Title X, contact the National Lead Information Center at 800-424-LEAD (5323), or check the EPA website at www.epa.gov/lead. To learn whether your state has laws in this field, contact your state's consumer protection agency.

Mold

Mold is a relative newcomer to the list of environmental hazards. In some sense, it's the most difficult to deal with, because not all mold is hazardous—unsightly, yes, but not necessarily bad for your health. If you discover mold in your rental, follow these steps.

First, determine whether something as simple as not opening the window when you shower has created the problem. The solution—to ventilate the room—is your responsibility. On the other hand, perhaps it's clear that the mold in the cabinet under the sink is due to a leaky pipe fitting. The landlord needs to address that.

Landlords Cannot Just Give Up

Some habitability problems can be addressed with decisiveness: A malfunctioning heater can normally be fixed with new parts and/or service, or a lead-based paint problem can be tackled with an appropriate abatement plan. But what about persistent problems that just won't go away despite the landlord's efforts—for example, roaches in an older urban building that are firmly entrenched and resistant to repeated exterminations? The answer is that the landlord must keep trying. In the meantime, assuming the problem has made the rental legally unlivable, you have the right to move out, as explained below in "Using Heavy Artillery for Major Repairs."

Second, if you believe that the presence of mold is the result of structural failure and/or your landlord's poor maintenance, and the landlord refuses to take care of it, use caution before invoking one of the self-help remedies described below. Unless the condition is significant and you have evidence that it has seriously affected your health, it might be just a minor repair, no matter how annoying it is. Using a self-help remedy for a minor problem will imperil your tenancy if the landlord chooses to fight back.

Bed Bugs

Bed bugs might win the "yuck" contest, though the damage they do to your health is quite minor compared to asbestos fiber inhalation or lead-based paint poisoning. Still, they make life miserable for their unhappy hosts, and landlords have learned the hard way that leaving a bed bug infestation untreated can quickly result in an unrentable building.

The tricky thing with bed bugs is that it's practically impossible to prove where they came from. They're expert hitchhikers, and could have entered your rental in your luggage, second-hand furniture, or through the electrical outlets from the unit next door. For this reason, arguments between landlords and tenants as to who is responsible for the critters—and who should pay to deal with them—often get nowhere. But because no one seriously argues that they are not a habitability problem, tenants who move out (or use other big-ticket remedies) can usually do so without legal repercussions (that is, without continued responsibility for the rent). All but the most dense landlord will act quickly to rid the building of the pests.

Major Habitability Problems Versus Minor Problems

As you look over the above list of repairs and maintenance that make up the landlord's duty to provide fit housing, you can see why these are called major, not minor, issues. When they pop up, reasonable occupants would be concerned for their health or safety. Put another way, a reasonable person wouldn't freely choose to live in a place with any of these problems. On the other hand, a minor repair is annoying, limiting, or distasteful—and it might be close to driving you nuts—but it wouldn't seriously endanger the health or safety of a reasonable tenant. The chart below gives more examples of major versus minor repair problems.

CAUTION

A defect is "minor" not because of its cost, but because it doesn't make your rental uninhabitable. For example, if the only thing between you and a heated apartment is a $50 furnace part, the repair is "major," because an unheated home is unlivable. If the landlord refuses to fix it, you can use the "big stick" remedies explained in "Using Heavy Artillery for Major Repairs," below. On the other hand, replacing an ugly but otherwise safe carpet might cost thousands, but it is a "minor" repair, because floor coverings that are merely shabby do not make your home unfit.

What *Exactly* Does "Fit and Habitable" Mean?

Chances are you aren't yet satisfied with our description of the implied warranty of habitability. If your repair problem is clearly a big deal (no heat in South Dakota in December), no one's going to argue with you. But often the line between major and minor isn't so clear. To better place your problem in the right category, you'll have to go to the source of your state's implied warranty—a state code or statute or, in some states, a court decision. Your local government (city or county) might also have ordinances that establish habitability standards. If so, you might find specific requirements (such as a minimum hot water temperature) that can help you label your problem.

This section discusses what these laws typically require of a landlord. Then, in the section just below, we'll show you what you can do to encourage your landlord to comply. And if you have to get heavy (by withholding the rent or repairing the problem and deducting the cost from your rent), we'll show you how in "Using Heavy Artillery for Major Repairs," below.

Local Ordinances

City or county building or housing codes regulate structural aspects of buildings and usually set specific space standards, such as the minimum size of sleeping rooms. They also establish minimum requirements for light and ventilation, sanitation and sewage disposal, heating, water supply (such as how hot the water must be), fire protection, wiring (such as the number of electrical outlets per room), and security devices such as locks.

Most local housing codes also prohibit "nuisances." A nuisance is something that is dangerous to human life or detrimental to health or morals—for example, overcrowding a room with occupants or providing insufficient ventilation, illumination, or sewage capacity. Drug dealing on the premises is also a legal nuisance, because it invariably involves the comings and goings of a criminal element with a potential for violence.

Classifying Your Repair Problem

It is essential that you correctly classify your repair problem—major or minor—before approaching your landlord or taking stronger measures. Following are some concrete examples of the two types of problems. The test for every repair problem is: Does this make my rental unfit to live in? If so, it's major; if not, it's minor.

Major Repair	Minor Repair
A roof leak that results in a wall of mildew in the bedroom	A roof leak that has caused a slight stain in the ceiling plaster in the hallway
A totally broken hot water heater	A hot water heater that heats to five degrees less than the temperature required by state statute
A furnace that won't turn on	A furnace that clanks and creaks when the fan runs
A front door that will not lock	A screen door (in front of a door that locks) with a broken latch
A toilet that won't flush in a one-bathroom rental	A toilet that flushes poorly in a two-bath unit
A lobby that is filled with tenants' garbage because the landlord has failed to provide trash bins and has not arranged for pickup	A lobby that's in need of a good vacuuming and paint job
A broken heater during the winter	A broken heater in the summer during a warm spell
An apartment rented to a family with young children where there is deteriorating lead paint	An apartment with faded and dirty latex paint

Contact your local building, housing, health, and/or fire departments for information on the exact requirements your landlord must meet.

State Housing Codes

Many states have general laws requiring landlords to keep rental units fit. These laws are usually less detailed than local codes, but in some states they're rather specific—some have statewide door and window lock laws, for example. To find out whether your state has any laws in this area:

- Go online and check your landlord-tenant statutes. We've listed the statute numbers by state in Appendix B; in Appendix A, we explain how to find them online.
- Look in the index of your state codes for subentries under Landlord-Tenant, such as "Duty to Maintain" or "Repairs."
- Contact your state's consumer protection agency and ask for any informational booklets. Find yours at www.usa.gov/state-consumer.

Who's Responsible for Crime?

Landlords are increasingly held accountable for criminal incidents that they should have foreseen and taken reasonable steps to avoid. Buildings that are crime-ridden or open invitations to criminals might qualify as uninhabitable, though the willingness of state courts to reach this conclusion varies widely. If your state considers a vulnerable building to be a violation of the implied warranty of habitability, you might be able to pressure your landlord to address the problems by using one of the tenant remedies discussed below.

If your building or neighborhood has had recent break-ins, your landlord's duty to take reasonable precautions (such as installing lighting and locks) goes up. However, courts will usually not hold landlords responsible for an isolated incident; nor will they expect landlords to erect virtual moats around their property. And remember: You, too, bear some responsibility for your own safety. A tenant who foolishly courts danger in a high-crime neighborhood might find little sympathy with the jury.

The statute that sets out the specific requirements for a habitable building usually won't tell you what to do if yours doesn't measure up. Your legal recourse (called your legal "remedy") is usually found in other landlord-tenant statutes, and sometimes in the code sections that deal with unlawful detainer (eviction) procedures.

Your Repair and Maintenance Responsibilities

Your landlord isn't the only one with responsibilities to keep the rental unit reasonably maintained. State and local laws require you, the tenant, to keep house a certain way, as the list below demonstrates.

Being familiar with your upkeep responsibilities is important: If a major habitability problem is the result of *your* not keeping up your end of the maintenance bargain, you cannot expect the landlord to pay for the repair, and you cannot use any of the tenant remedies, such as rent withholding, to accomplish the job. For example, if your only toilet is clogged because your babysitter tried to flush a diaper, it's a habitability problem, true, but the cost of repairing it will fall squarely on you.

You are obligated to:

- Keep your rental unit as clean and safe as the condition of the premises permits.
- Dispose of garbage, rubbish, and other waste in a clean and safe manner.
- Keep plumbing fixtures as clean as their condition permits.
- Use electrical, plumbing, sanitary, heating, ventilating, air-conditioning, and other facilities and other systems, including elevators, properly.
- Fix things you break or damage.
- In many states, notify the landlord promptly of defective or dangerous conditions on the property.

Your landlord can't, however, charge you for problems caused by normal wear and tear—for example, a carpet that has worn out from years of use. (Chapter 9 discusses the difference between normal wear and tear and damage.)

Knowing about—and fulfilling—your own responsibilities as a tenant makes you more than just a virtuous renter. The dividends of living up to your duties include the confidence that:

- You can expect a positive reference from this landlord when you move on to the next rental.
- You are well positioned should you need to ask an occasional favor, such as paying the rent late or letting your sister stay with you for a month while she looks for her own place.
- Your actions have entitled you to safely withhold rent or use a repair-and-deduct statute (if your state allows these remedies)—remedies that you probably could not use if you were in violation of a lease clause or other important tenant responsibility.

Persuading Your Landlord to Do Major Repairs

Suppose now that you're comfortable that you have correctly classified the problem you're living with as a major one. But it's one thing to have the law on your side—it's often quite another to get your landlord to follow it. Here are some tips for getting results, short of hauling out the big guns like rent withholding or repair-and-deduct. If this approach doesn't get results, head for the discussion below.

- **Put your repair request in writing.** Be as specific as possible: Describe the problem, its effect on you, what you want done, and when. This will get your landlord's attention better than a casual chat on the stairs. It will also be important proof that you gave your landlord "notice" of the problem, a step you must take in case you have to resort to a self-help remedy such as repair-and-deduct. Of course, if it's an emergency, call first and then follow up in writing. (See "Using Email for Notice or a Letter of Understanding," in Chapter 2 for information on how to use email to deliver written requests.)

Sample Request for Repairs

May 3, 20xx

Ms. Lisa Bilding
23 Oakmont Street
City Center, MD 55555

Dear Ms. Bilding,

As you know, I am your tenant at 57 Washington Street, City Center. I spoke to you last night about a serious problem with the hot water in my flat. Yesterday I discovered that the hot water temperature fluctuates randomly—one moment it's cold, and the next it is scalding. I think the mixing valve is deficient.

I am concerned that I and my children could be burned by the very hot water. I would very much appreciate it if you could attend to this problem as quickly as possible. Please email or call me (contact information below) so that I can arrange to be there when you (or a repairperson) come to work on the water heater.

Yours truly,
R.U. Lisning, Tenant
57 Washington Street
Home: 301-555-4546
Work: 301-555-5432
rulisning@lisning.com

- **Put the landlord's promises in writing, too.** If the landlord agrees on a requested repair, follow up with a letter confirming that promise. (This is called a letter of understanding, which we explain in Chapter 2.) If you don't receive a response, the landlord is legally committed to your version of the promise. This could come in handy if the landlord later reneges on the plan and you need to take self-help steps.
- **Emphasize the dire consequences.** If the repair problem poses a safety threat, it won't hurt to point that out to the landlord in your written request for repairs. For example, a broken lock will make it easy for a burglar to enter, and a loose carpet edge is an accident waiting to happen. Even lazy landlords will take care of business when they sense that a lawsuit could be on the horizon. The Sample Request for Repairs, above, provides an example of how to word your request.
- **Strength in numbers.** If you're not the only one living with a major problem—such as poor building-wide security or lack of heat—gather forces and present your request as a group. The specter of multiple tenants complaining to the building inspector or withholding rent often gets results.

Using Heavy Artillery for Major Repairs

If, despite your businesslike requests, the landlord hasn't fixed or addressed a serious problem that truly makes your rental unit uninhabitable—rats in the kitchen, for example—you will want to take stronger measures. Your options include one or more of what we call the "big sticks" in a tenant's arsenal. Big stick remedies include:

- calling state or local building or health inspectors
- withholding the rent (if allowed by your state law)
- repairing the problem, or having it repaired by a professional, and deducting the cost from your rent, called "repair-and-deduct," (if allowed by your state law)
- moving out, or
- paying the rent and then suing the landlord for the difference between the rent you paid and the value of the defective premises.

It's important to understand that you shouldn't use a big stick remedy rashly. Before you withhold rent, move out, or adopt another extreme remedy, make sure every one of these conditions is met:

- The problem is serious, not just annoying, and imperils your health or safety. Not every building code violation or annoying defect in your rental home justifies use of a "big stick" against the landlord.
- You (or a guest) did not cause the problem, either deliberately or through carelessness or neglect. If so, you can't pursue big stick options.
- You told the landlord about the problem and gave a reasonable opportunity—or the minimum amount of notice required by state law—to get it fixed. You can't use big stick options without taking these first steps. You'll need to check your state's law for the exact notification requirements for the specific option you are pursuing.
- As a tenant, you are squeaky clean. Under most rent withholding laws you cannot withhold rent if you are behind in the rent or in violation of an important lease clause.
- You are willing to risk termination of your tenancy by an annoyed landlord. Exercising any of the rights discussed here will not endear you to your landlord. Many states forbid your landlord from retaliating against you by raising the rent or terminating your tenancy, but, unfortunately, some states don't. If your lease is about to run out (or you're a month-to-month tenant) and your state does not protect you from retaliatory rent increases or evictions, a complaint to health inspectors or the use of a big stick could end up causing you to lose your rental. (See the Chapter 11 discussion on retaliation and "State Laws Prohibiting Landlord Retaliation" in Appendix B.)
- You are willing to risk eviction if a judge decides that you shouldn't have used the big stick, and your credit report can bear this negative mark. Even if you're sure that you were justified, a judge could decide otherwise. For example, if you withhold rent, the landlord might sue to evict you based on nonpayment of rent.

In most states and in most situations, you'll have a second chance to pay the balance before being evicted, but not always. For some tenants, additional negative marks on their credit records will cause extremely serious problems not only for future rentals but for loans and employment as well.

- You can find a comparable or better unit if you move out, either voluntarily or because the building is closed due to code violations you have reported. In some states, landlords whose buildings are closed due to code violations must help their tenants with relocation expenses.

TIP

Before doing repairs yourself, withholding rent, or using another "big stick," make sure you have proof of how bad the situation was. Take pictures of the problem or ask a reputable and impartial contractor or repairperson to examine the defect and give you a written, signed, and dated description of the problem and an estimate for repair.

Reporting Code Violations to Housing Inspectors

If the problem you're facing is a violation of a state or local housing law, you can contact the agency in charge of enforcing the law. This might be a housing or building department, or a health or fire department. The inspector will investigate and give the landlord a notice of violation and a deadline, typically 30 to 60 days, to correct the problem. The deadline can be shortened for extremely serious violations.

A landlord's failure to abide by the correction order can result in fines, losing control of the building to a "receiver," and even imprisonment. Keep in mind that there is wild variation in the actual effectiveness of inspectors, depending on their workloads and budgets. In some large cities, landlords have learned to evade and postpone. But take heart: You have more arrows in your quiver.

CAUTION

Health, fire, or building inspectors could order the building closed. If the problem you report is extremely serious, the inspectors could close your building and order all tenants to leave, sometimes on very short notice. Typically, you won't even have a chance to voice your objections. Think carefully and plan ahead if there's a chance that your phone call could result in actually worsening your living situation.

Withholding the Rent

If your landlord has not met the responsibility of keeping your unit livable, you might be able to stop paying any rent to the landlord until the repairs are made. This is called rent withholding. Many states allow rent withholding under certain circumstances, either by statute or court decision. (See "State Laws on Rent Withholding and Repair-and-Deduct Remedies" in Appendix B.) Rent withholding can be done only in states that specifically allow it by law. If yours isn't one of them, you'll have to use another approach.

The term "withholding" is actually a bit misleading, since in some states and cities you can't simply keep the rent money until your landlord fixes the problem. Instead, you often have to deposit the withheld rent with a court, a neutral third party, or into an escrow account set up by a local court or housing department until the repairs are accomplished. (And even if your statute doesn't require it, it's a good idea to escrow the rent yourself, as explained below.)

In states that have not established an escrow scheme, your right to withhold the rent is somewhat indirect: When you don't pay the rent and the landlord tries to evict you (which surely will happen), the statute allows you to argue in your defense that you didn't owe any rent because the unit was unfit. If the judge or jury believes you, you will win the eviction lawsuit and will be allowed to stay.

CAUTION

Never reduce the rent unless your state law authorizes rent withholding, either directly (by escrowing) or as a defense to an eviction. If you do, you can expect a speedily delivered termination notice, followed by an eviction lawsuit, for nonpayment of rent. Your theory—that the landlord was entitled to less rent because the premises weren't livable—is not likely to be well received in a state that hasn't taken the issue seriously enough to establish orderly procedures (rent withholding) that will pressure landlords into providing habitable housing. If you lose, you'll lose your rented home. Instead, use one of the other remedies mentioned here, including repair-and-deduct (if available), moving out, or filing a lawsuit in small claims court asking for a retroactive rent reduction for substandard conditions.

Before you can properly withhold the rent, remember that all of these requirements must be met:

- The lack of maintenance or repair has made your dwelling unlivable. ("Your Right to a Livable Place," above, discusses habitability requirements.)
- The problems were not caused by you or your guest, either deliberately or through neglect.
- You told the landlord about the problem and gave the landlord a reasonable time to fix it, or the minimum amount required by state law.
- You are not behind on the rent or in violation of a lease or rental agreement clause.

How to Withhold Rent

Needless to say, your landlord won't be pleased to get a short rent check. The landlord might respond by terminating your tenancy for nonpayment of rent and file for eviction if you don't pay up (or move). You'll survive the eviction action if you've used the withholding remedy correctly *and* you have good proof to back you up. And, let's face it—you'll need a bit of luck, because even a solid case can't overcome an ignorant or biased judge.

Here are the steps to follow if you decide to withhold the rent.

Step 1: Research the law. If rent withholding is allowed in your state, the statute (law) will be listed in Appendix B. Also, check if any local laws apply. In a few localities subject to rent control, the procedure might be part of your local ordinance. Read the law to find out:

- what circumstances justify rent withholding
- whether you must give the landlord a certain amount of notice (ten to 30 days are typical) to fix the defect, or whether the response time must simply be "reasonable" under the circumstances, and
- whether you must place the unpaid rent in a separate bank account or deposit it with a court or local housing department.

Step 2: Notify your landlord. Give your landlord written notice of the problem and your intent to withhold rent. Refer to your state's law or statute that allows withholding and include a copy of it. Give your landlord a reasonable deadline for repairs. (Or the legally required one, if your statute specifies one). Send the letter certified and ask for a "return receipt." (See "Using Email for Notice or a Letter of Understanding," in Chapter 2, for information on how to use email to deliver written requests.)

Step 3: Collect evidence. Start preparing your defense for a possible eviction suit from day one: Keep copies of all correspondence with the landlord, plus photographs of the problem.

Step 4: Repeat your request for repairs. If the landlord hasn't responded satisfactorily to your first letter, give the landlord one last deadline—say, 48 hours or whatever period you feel is reasonable (or legally required) under the circumstances.

Step 5: File any court papers. Under some state laws, you must ask a local court for permission to withhold rent, provide compelling reasons why your rental is not livable, and follow specific procedures. You can get the necessary information and forms from the court or housing department that is named in your rent withholding statute.

Step 6: Deposit your rent in escrow. In some states, you might have to deposit your rent with the specified local court or housing department or in a separate bank account. Even if your statute does not require this, we recommend that you deposit the withheld rent into an escrow account held by a neutral third party. This will dispel any suggestion that you are withholding rent simply in order to avoid paying it.

If a court or housing department is not set up to handle withheld rent, try asking a mediation service if it will establish an account for this purpose. You can also set up a separate bank account of your own and use it only for withheld rent.

What Happens to the Withheld Rent

If the rent money is being held by a court or housing department, landlords can sometimes ask for release of some of the withheld rent to pay for repairs. While repairs are being made, you might continue to pay the entire rent to the court or housing authority, or you might be directed to pay some rent to the landlord and the balance to the court or housing department. When the dwelling is certified as fit by the local housing authorities or the court, any money in the account is returned to the landlord, minus court costs and inspection fees.

If your withholding law does not require you to escrow the rent and a court has not been involved, you and the landlord are free to make your own arrangements as to the distribution of the money. Once your landlord has made the repairs, you will probably have to make full payment of the withheld rent. If you don't pay up, you can expect your landlord to file an eviction lawsuit for nonpayment of rent.

Understandably, you probably don't feel like paying full rent, in retrospect, for the months you spent living in a substandard home while politely trying to convince the landlord to take care of business. In short, you might want a retroactive reduction in rent, starting from the time that the premises became uninhabitable. (Some states will limit you to a reduction starting from the time you notified the landlord of the habitability problem.) Reducing the rent after the fact is known in legalese as rent "abatement." You can get a retroactive rent abatement through a court process or through negotiation with your landlord.

NEGOTIATE

Don't pay full fare for a substandard unit. Ask your landlord or the court to fix the rent at what a unit with these defects would have rented for on the open market; compare this sum to your stated rent, and argue that you deserve the difference. Or, if the defect rendered a portion of the rental unusable (a leak in the living room, for example), estimate what percentage of the rental was affected and calculate the reduced rent accordingly.

Making Repairs and Deducting the Cost: "Repair-and-Deduct"

Depending on where you live, you might be eligible to use another powerful legal remedy called "repair-and-deduct." Over half the states and some large cities allow it. (See "State Laws on Rent Withholding and Repair-and-Deduct Remedies" in Appendix B.) If your state doesn't allow repair-and-deduct, check your local housing ordinances to determine whether your city has independently adopted it. *If your state or city does not have a repair-and-deduct statute, this procedure is not available to you.*

It works like this: If you have tried and failed to get the landlord to fix a serious defect, you can hire a repairperson to fix it or fix it yourself and subtract the cost from the following month's rent. The statute will usually specify:

- the circumstances justifying your use of the remedy (usually only habitability problems can be addressed with repair-and-deduct)
- the amount of rent you can use for repairs (such as one month's rent), and
- the frequency with which you can use the remedy (once in an 18-month period, for example).

The repair-and-deduct remedy is a poor choice when it comes to big-ticket projects such as a major roof repair. Obviously, if you're limited to a twice-a-year expenditure of half your monthly rent, you are not going to be able to pay for a $20,000 roof job. However, a number of tenants might pool their dollar limits to accomplish a costly repair.

Moving Out

If your dwelling isn't habitable and hasn't been made so despite your complaints and repair requests, you also have the right to move out—either temporarily or permanently. You can also move out if the landlord has tried but failed to remedy the problem. For example, you are entitled to leave even if your landlord has made several unsuccessful attempts to rid a building of vermin.

These drastic measures are justified only when there are truly serious problems, such as the lack of essential services, the total or partial destruction of the premises, or the presence of environmental health hazards such as asbestos or lead paint dust.

If you have time remaining on a lease and use this remedy improperly, you risk losing your security deposit or even being sued for the remainder of the rent due under the lease. Therefore, check your state law for details, which might include:

- whether you must first call the building inspectors
- how much time you must give your landlord to fix the problem, and
- the amount of notice, if any, you must provide before moving out.

NEGOTIATE

Consider a temporary move. If your landlord learns that you are serious about abandoning ship, you might suggest that the landlord pay for temporary lodging while the problem is fixed. After all, this is cheaper in the long run than losing a rent-paying tenant and trying to rerent a substandard place. In some states, landlords *must* pay for temporary housing while court-ordered repairs are made, typically when lead paint problems are being remedied.

Suing the Landlord

A consumer who purchases a product—be it a car, a hair dryer, or a steak dinner—is justified in expecting a minimum level of quality and is entitled to compensation if the product is seriously flawed. The same goes for tenants. In nearly every location, if your rental is not habitable you can sue the landlord—whether or not you move out. You can probably use small claims court, which allows claims of up to several thousand dollars. You won't need to hire a lawyer. (In Chapter 13, "Small Claims Court" discusses procedures. Chapter 13 also discusses how to find an attorney, should you need one.)

Suing the landlord makes sense only if you can safely continue to live in your rental. For example, if the roof leaks only into the second bedroom and you can move the kids into the living room for a while, you might want to stay and sue in order to avoid the hassle of moving, arranging for the repair yourself (repair-and-deduct), or figuring out the complications of rent withholding. But you wouldn't want to stay and sue if you are without heat in the winter or in danger of electrocution every time you turn on the lights.

What are the pros and cons of suing your landlord instead of using repair-and-deduct or rent withholding? On the positive side, if you lose your lawsuit you'll have lost some time and money, but you won't be evicted, as can happen with the unsuccessful use of repair-and-deduct or rent withholding. But suing isn't entirely risk-free, especially if you're a month-to-month tenant or nearing the end of a lease you would like to renew. Your annoyed landlord might simply decide to terminate or not renew. Tenants who are protected by state antiretaliation laws will have some protection, but to assert your rights you'll have to bring a lawsuit, a dreary prospect. (Landlord retaliation is covered in Chapter 11.)

In your lawsuit, you ask the judge to rule that your unrepaired rental was not worth what you've paid for it. You want to be paid the difference between the monthly rent and the real value of the unit, times the number of months that you've lived with the substandard conditions. In short, you'll ask for a retroactive rent decrease—rent "abatement" in legalese. In addition, you can sue your landlord for lost or damaged property (for example, furniture ruined by water leaking through the roof).

In some states, you can also ask the court for an order directing the landlord to repair the defects, with rent reduced until they are fixed. In others, small claims courts can only order the landlord to pay you for your losses, but usually the money judgment gets the landlord's attention and the repairs get done.

Laying the Minor Repair Job on the Landlord

Until now, this chapter has focused on major repairs: how to know what they are and how to get them fixed. But it's not just major repairs that are a nuisance. In fact, ask a group of tenants which rental problems are most annoying and chances are you'll hear a recitation of day-to-day but nonetheless important problems that everyone encounters now and then: leaky faucets, malfunctioning appliances, worn carpets, noisy heaters, and dozens of other frustrating breakdowns.

Unfortunately, if your landlord refuses to attend to minor repairs, you can't use most of the "big stick" legal weapons discussed above. Even so, there are several proven strategies for getting results.

Ways to Put the Problem on the Landlord

There are several legal justifications for why your landlord should shoulder the responsibility for minor repairs.

Building Codes

State and local building codes mainly concern structural requirements such as roofs and flooring and essential services like hot water. If your repair problem is also a significant violation of the building code, you might be dealing with a habitability problem that can be addressed using one of the remedies explained above. But some codes also regulate less vital matters, such as the number of electrical outlets that must be present in rentals. Check your state's building code and any local ordinances to see whether your problem fits within them. If it does, you might get some results from the governmental department that administers the codes, as explained below.

Landlord-Tenant Laws

A number of states place the responsibility for some minor repairs directly on the landlord. Check your state's statutes, which you'll find listed in "State Landlord-Tenant Statutes" in Appendix B. Note that in many states, renters of single-family homes can agree to take on responsibilities that would belong to the landlord in a multiunit setting, usually in exchange for a reduction in rent or other tangible benefit relating to the rental.

Promises in the Lease

Your own lease or rental agreement might require the landlord to fix the problem. Even if the requirement isn't explicit, a simple list of the amenities that come with the rental—such as a dishwasher, sauna, or washing machine—constitutes an implied promise that the landlord will provide them in a *workable* condition for the duration of the tenancy.

Promises in Ads

If an advertisement for your unit described or listed a feature, such as a swimming pool, that significantly affected your decision to move into the particular rental unit, you have the right to hold the landlord to providing what was promised—as long as a breakdown is not your fault. (See "Tenant Responsibilities for Minor Repairs," below.) The promise doesn't have to be in words—a glossy photo showing a pool suggests that the landlord will provide one (and keep it up), and that's enough to obligate the landlord. Such a promise can also be oral, made during rental negotiations. ("You'll love our four-court tennis area!") The landlord who turns the tennis court into a parking lot will do so at some expense if the tenants are savvy—read on.

Implied Promises

Finally, you might be faced with a minor repair problem that doesn't fit within any of the above ways to nail the landlord: no code or law violation, no promise to fix it in the lease, no promise in an ad or during an enthusiastic prerental tour. Still, something was working or in good repair when you moved in and has since deteriorated.

Your theory for holding the landlord accountable here is rather simple: You are entitled to get what you pay for. Many courts will hold a landlord legally responsible for maintaining all significant aspects of your rental unit. If you rent a unit that already has certain features—light fixtures that work, doors that open and close smoothly, faucets that don't leak, tile that doesn't fall off the wall—many judges reason that the landlord has made an implied contract to keep them in workable order throughout your tenancy.

The flip side of this principle is that if you pay for a hamburger, the waiter doesn't have to deliver a steak. In other words, if your rental was shabby when you moved in and the landlord never gave you reason to believe that it would be spruced up, you have no legal right to demand improvements—unless, of course, you can show health hazards or code violations. As when you buy secondhand goods "as is" for a low price, legally you are stuck with your deal. (But see below for some strategies that might convince a reluctant landlord to take better care of the property.)

Your landlord's past conduct might also demonstrate an implied promise to attend to this repair. If your landlord has consistently fixed or maintained a particular feature of your rental, this behavior has created an implied promise to continue doing so. For example, if your landlord has regularly fixed the finicky timer on the hot tub but suddenly gives up on it, you can argue that the past efforts established a promise to continue to fix the tub.

Tenant Responsibilities for Minor Repairs

All tenants are responsible for keeping their units in a clean, safe condition and reimbursing the landlord for damage they might cause. Many leases also prohibit tenants from making alterations or improvements without the landlord's consent.

These rules often work in tandem. If you damage the garbage disposal by dropping a piece of silverware into it, you'll have to pay for replacing the disposal, but you'll need your landlord's okay before you hire the plumber. Minor repairs that are necessitated by normal wear and tear, however, are the landlord's responsibility.

Getting the Landlord to Make Minor Repairs

By now you should have a good idea as to whether your landlord is legally responsible for fixing the minor problem that is bedeviling you. Your next job is to get the landlord to do it. First, try for some cooperation. If the landlord won't budge, it might be time to take a confrontational approach.

Appealing to the Landlord

If simply voicing your concerns has been met with delays or refusals, it's time to write a request. Keep in mind your landlord's guiding lights: making money, avoiding tenant hassles, and staying out of legal hot water. An appeal designed to further *these* concerns is likely to succeed.

If possible, write your letter using one or more of the following approaches:

- It's a small problem now, but likely to get bigger (the landlord reads: less expensive to deal with it now).
- There is potential for injury (the landlord reads: a personal injury lawsuit in the making).
- It's a security problem that imperils your safety (another lawsuit).
- The problem affects many tenants (oh no! many lawsuits!).
- You'd be more than happy to fix it yourself, but it's clear you don't know the difference between a chisel and a screwdriver (a botched job that could be ruinous).

Often, even the most stingy and dense landlord will spring to action when it appears that the results of not taking care of business could be worse than dealing with your request now.

Reporting Code Violations

If the problem you want fixed constitutes a code violation, such as low water pressure, you might find an ally in the building or housing department in charge of enforcing the code. Whether you'll get any action out of the agency will depend on the seriousness of the violation, the department's workload, and its ability to enforce its compliance orders. Because by definition your problem is minor, don't expect lots of help if code enforcement officials are already overworked.

Think Before You Leap

If you have a month-to-month tenancy, in most states your landlord can terminate your tenancy with just 30 days' notice, without having to give a reason. And if your lease is about to expire and you'd like a renewal, the landlord can likewise simply decline to renew it. (Rent control ordinances might restrict the landlord; see Chapter 12.)

The ease with which your landlord can get rid of you means you should think twice before trying one of the adversarial strategies discussed here—reporting your landlord for building code violations or suing in small claims court—over minor problems with your rental.

An antiretaliation law, if one is in force where you live, might protect you from a termination or nonrenewal. (Retaliation is discussed in Chapter 11.) But if you have to go to court to argue about it as part of your defense to an eviction lawsuit, spending precious time away from work and your free time, you might end up wishing you'd never complained about that cracked mirror.

Suing in Small Claims Court

If you can reasonably argue that you aren't getting what you paid for, you might decide to sue in small claims court. But before you do, write a demand letter stating what you want and that you intend to sue if necessary. Write a second letter if you don't get results.

If the second letter doesn't do the trick, it's time to head for the small claims court website or clerk's office. We know of one tenant who successfully sued her landlord for failing to repair a dishwasher that was functioning when she moved in. In her lawsuit, she calculated how much time she spent hand-washing the dishes each day, multiplied that figure times the number of days she had been without the dishwasher, and multiplied that figure by her state's minimum wage. She won.

CAUTION

Don't withhold rent for a minor repair problem. If you do, you invite an eviction lawsuit. (The only time to withhold rent is when you have followed a statutory withholding process, described above.) Instead, ask for a retroactive rent abatement (or reduction) in your lawsuit, which, if granted, will accomplish the same thing without the risk of an eviction lawsuit.

Rules to Rent By

- **Never agree to rent a substandard unit.** Your landlord is breaking the law, and you can expect nothing but trouble.
- **Remember your own duties as a tenant**—keeping your unit clean and safe and paying for any damage you or your guest may cause.
- **Put all repair requests in writing and keep a copy for your files** along with all correspondence with the landlord—you may need evidence later to prove that you told the landlord about the problem.
- **Use a letter of understanding to document your landlord's promise to do a repair.** It will commit him to the promise unless he writes back and disputes your version.
- **Be certain** that you are paid up in rent and not in violation of any major lease clause before using the "big stick" remedies of rent withholding or repair-and-deduct.
- **Think twice before launching a campaign for a minor repair.** If you are not protected by antiretaliation laws, you might win the battle but lose the war (your tenancy).

CHAPTER

8

Tenants' Rights to Privacy

You might have already encountered a landlord who cannot stop fussing over the property or who frequently tries to wangle an invitation into your home to look around. Even worse are landlords and managers who use a passkey to enter without notice when there is no emergency.

This chapter covers your basic rights to privacy and what to do about a landlord or manager who violates these rights. You can sue your landlord for entering unlawfully—but it's rarely worth the time or trouble, unless the entries are extreme (involving serious sexual harassment, for example). You can also use the landlord's unreasonable intrusions as a grounds to break the lease, citing a violation of your right to quiet enjoyment. But if you want to keep your rental and just want the landlord to stop annoying but not outrageous actions, you might find that you'll either have to grimace and bear the actions of an intrusive landlord or move on.

TIP

Get the lowdown on the landlord before you sign up. Talk to neighbors or the tenant whose unit you're considering: Is this a nosy landlord? If so, look elsewhere.

Tenant Traps

Read this chapter to find out why you should:

- **Never sign a lease or rental agreement waiving your rights to privacy.** Many courts will refuse to uphold such a waiver, but you'll have to spend miserable hours arguing with your landlord in court before the lesson will sink in. Besides, any landlord who wants to do business this way is likely to be a sleaze in other respects, too.
- **Never complain to your landlord about privacy violations without putting the complaint in writing (in a follow-up letter after a conversation, if necessary).** If the landlord doesn't back off and you need to go to court, you might need this letter as proof that you've complained of the behavior. And if the landlord agrees to a reasonable plan covering times and reasons for entry, reduce that understanding to a letter, too.
- **Never go away for extended periods of time without notifying the landlord.** Some states give landlords the right to enter if they discover you're not around. To avoid the possibility that the landlord will enter to check up, alert the landlord of your plans and comply with reasonable requests such as turning off the heat in winter, draining the pipes, or securing the windows. If you take care of these matters, management will have less need (or excuse) to come in.
- **Never withhold rent in response to your landlord's unauthorized entry.** Unfortunately, rent withholding is not the proper legal response to even the most obnoxious entry.
- **Never change the locks without the landlord's consent.** If your landlord is violating your privacy rights, your answer lies in the law (filing in small claims court for violations of your privacy, or breaking a lease and moving out), not locksmiths.

Entry by the Landlord

Your rental unit is your home and ought to be respected as such. About half the states have statutes (laws written by state legislators) specifying when and how landlords can legally enter rented property. (See "State Laws on Landlord's Access to Rental Property" in Appendix B for details.) In some states, your right to privacy might instead be the product of judge-made law and will be contained in court opinions issued by your state's appellate courts. And, in some states, you'll find that neither the legislators nor the judges have made law that protects the privacy rights of tenants. (In this event, your only hope is that your state constitution includes a broad right to privacy, which you can cite if you need to press the point with your landlord.)

If you find, after checking Appendix B, that your state lacks a privacy statute, chances are that there's a "rule of thumb" practice in your state that judges tend to follow (this doesn't mean it's necessarily fair, unfortunately). To learn the practice in your state, research the case law or get help from a lawyer or tenants' rights group to find out how much privacy protection you can expect.

Sample Privacy Clause

Clause ________. Entry by the Landlord. Landlord or Landlord's agent will not enter Tenant's home except to deal with an emergency; to make necessary or agreed repairs; to supply necessary or agreed services; or to show the unit to potential purchasers, tenants, or repair persons. Unless there is an emergency, Landlord will give Tenant at least 24 hours' written notice of the date, time, and purpose of the intended entry and will schedule entries during normal business hours, Monday–Friday.

NEGOTIATE

You can bargain for privacy protection if your state has no statute. During lease negotiations, simply ask the landlord to include a reasonable clause covering reasons for entry, amount of notice, and time of entry. A sample is provided above. Most landlords will be hard-pressed to say no to such a reasonable clause. If the landlord balks, it's a sure sign that this person won't be reasonable in other respects, too. Continue your housing search!

Allowable Reasons to Enter

Landlords can always enter your rental unit under certain situations:

- **When you give permission.** There's nothing wrong with agreeing to a landlord's request to inspect for needed repairs. Many landlords ask for once- or twice-yearly walk-throughs to check for necessary maintenance. (You might see a provision establishing this practice in your lease or rental agreement.) Actually, most tenants are delighted when the landlord is so conscientious! But more frequent visits are generally unnecessary (unless there is a need to address a persistent problem, such as an insect infestation). Don't let yourself be coerced into "agreeing" to excessive visits that become harassing. These are illegal.
- **Any time there is a genuine emergency.** Common sense is the name of the game here: a broken dishwasher hardly qualifies, yet windows left wide open in the face of a driving rainstorm would.
- **To make needed repairs or improvements.** Most states allow the landlord to enter to perform required maintenance duties. This includes entry with contractors or designers as well as repair people. Your landlord must still give proper notice and enter at reasonable hours, as explained below.

- **To show property to prospective tenants or purchasers.** If you've given notice or your lease is about to expire, you must accommodate your landlord's reasonable efforts to rerent. The same is true when the owner attempts to sell the building or refinance. However, you are not obligated to hold endless open houses or accommodate showings with insufficient notice. Losing the use of your home every Saturday morning for an open house or being expected to clear out while potential buyers tramp through two or three times a week would be unreasonable in most people's estimation.

NEGOTIATE

Ask for a reduction in rent in exchange for short notice or frequent showings to prospective tenants or buyers. After all, you are hardly getting what you've paid for (a quiet, undisturbed home) with strangers constantly waltzing through. A smart landlord will realize that your gracious cooperation is well worth a few dollars less each month.

CAUTION

Never put up with a lock box. These are metal boxes affixed to the front door that hold a key to your home and can be opened by anyone knowing the code—typically, local real estate agents. It enables them to enter without notice and at any time, completely circumventing any state law on tenant privacy. Say "No," and if the owner or agent objects, write a letter to the real estate agent's main office with a copy to your state's real estate licensing board.

- **When the landlord believes you have abandoned the property.** When landlords can reasonably conclude that you've skipped out without giving any notice or returning the key, they can legally enter. For example, if a neighbor reports seeing a moving van drive away and the utilities have been shut off, it's reasonable to conclude that you've left for good. Some states allow landlords to enter when you have left for an extended period of time, in order to perform needed or preventive maintenance.

Your Right to "Quiet Enjoyment"

Every landlord is bound by a legal principle known as the "covenant of quiet enjoyment." This archaic-sounding bit of legalese actually packs quite a punch: It's your right to be left in peace, free of your landlord's illegal intrusions. Especially in states that do not have specific access statutes, this age-old principle can come in handy if your landlord persists in unlawful entries that significantly interfere with your right to kick back, relax, and not worry about who's coming in the door unannounced. You might need to rely on it if you want to sue in small claims court or break your lease and leave early.

You're Entitled to Fair Warning

Most state access laws require landlords to give you 24 hours' to two days' notice before entering your rental unit in nonemergency situations. A few states simply require landlords to provide "reasonable" notice. (See "State Laws on Landlord's Access to Rental Property" in Appendix B.)

If your state requires your landlord to give you only "reasonable" notice, you'll want to know how this translates into hours and days. Twenty-four hours is about right. In some circumstances, less notice (say, ten or 15 hours) might be fine—for example, think twice about objecting if your landlord finds out Thursday evening that an electrician is available Friday morning to install the extra outlets that you requested. Except for an emergency, less than four hours' notice is not ordinarily considered reasonable.

What Time of Day or Night?

Most state access laws either do not specify what hours a landlord can enter your rental unit or simply allow entry at "reasonable times." Weekdays between 9 a.m. and 6 p.m. would seem to be reasonable times, and perhaps Saturdays between 10 a.m. and 1 p.m. Some states specify "normal business hours," which leaves it open as to whether Saturday would be a reasonable time.

Standing on Your High Horse Is Risky

Common sense suggests that if your landlord does not have a history of invading your privacy, you're better off accommodating requests for entry, especially if the purpose is to make repairs that will benefit you. Objecting to legal entries without solid reasons may result in:

- **An eviction.** As long as your landlord complies with your state law as to reasons for entry and notice periods, your refusal to allow access can result in an eviction lawsuit.
- **A termination at the end of the month or a nonrenewal at the end of the lease.** Your landlord can simply give you a 30-day notice or not renew the lease rather than deal with your objections.
- **A difficult working relationship.** Don't expect much help or understanding when you make repair requests or float an occasional plea to pay the rent late. Landlords have long memories.

This is not to say that you should surrender your rights to privacy out of craven fear. By no means should you. But don't be hard-nosed just for the principle involved.

Entry by Others

Your landlord is not the only one who can enter your rental unit. This section describes situations when other people such as municipal inspectors might want to enter your home.

Health, Safety, or Building Inspections

While your state might give you significant protections against entry by your landlord, the rules are different when it comes to entry by state or local health, safety, or building inspectors. Generally, inspectors can enter when they have reliable information, such as a complaint from a credible source, that there's a health or safety problem inside. For example, neighbors, repairpersons, or delivery persons might report evidence of dangerous hoarding, the presence of many animals, or extreme uncleanliness. If you refuse entry, usually they'll return with a warrant and sometimes a police officer, who will make sure that you don't prevent access.

Many cities run random multidwelling inspections, to catch building and health code violations before tenants complain. You are entitled to reasonable notice (many ordinances specify notice periods). Your refusal to allow the inspectors to enter will simply delay the inevitable.

Law Enforcement

If the police have a valid search or arrest warrant, you have to let them in. The "notice" period is rather short—about as long as it takes them to knock and announce their presence! In addition, they can enter with no notice at all (forcibly if necessary) in order to interrupt a serious crime, apprehend a fleeing suspect, prevent the imminent destruction of evidence, or prevent a catastrophe such as a fire. More expansive rules might apply if law enforcement suspects terrorist activity by a tenant.

CAUTION

Don't expect your landlord to let your friends in. Aside from the situations explained above, your landlord has no authority to allow anyone into your home without your consent. If your landlord lets in someone who purports to be your long-lost auntie but turns out to be a creative burglar, the landlord will be liable. Landlords who understand the risk they are taking are naturally unwilling to open tenants' doors for others.

Limits on Your Guests

Some landlords limit guests' visits—for example, no more than ten days in any six-month period—to avoid having a guest turn into an unauthorized new tenant. (See Chapter 1 for an explanation of the landlord's right to screen and approve occupants.) A few overly concerned landlords go overboard by keeping tabs on legitimate guests who stay overnight or for a few days.

More Landlord Muzzles

Your landlord should refrain from:

- **Giving information about you to strangers who have no legitimate need to know.** This means that your landlord can give information about your creditworthiness or stability to prospective landlords, employers, banks, or creditors, but only if the question is directly related to a legitimate business need, such as your request for credit or a loan. Cautious landlords will ask you for a signed release before they answer even legitimate questions, but legally they are not required to have a release as long as the questions are legit.
- **Bothering you at work.** While you want your landlord to have your work phone number in case of an emergency, you don't want calls unless it's absolutely necessary. If you get persistent and embarrassing calls, write a tough letter demanding that they stop. If you lose your job or a promotion as the result of the landlord's conduct, see a lawyer—you might have the makings of a worthwhile lawsuit.
- **Spying on you.** Nosy interrogations and surveillance give you reason to sue a landlord for invasion of privacy.
- **Turning off the power or changing the locks.** In most states, no matter how far behind you are in the rent, your landlord may not lock you out or turn off any utilities. Known as "self-help" evictions, these moves expose the landlord to significant liabilities. The only legal way to evict you is through an actual eviction lawsuit.
- **Sexual harassment.** Harassment of a sexual nature is a form of discrimination that is illegal everywhere. If your landlord engages in persistent, serious, unwanted advances, see an attorney. If you fear for your safety, contact your local police department.

Some leases, rental agreements, or rules and regulations will require you to register any overnight guest. As you probably would suspect, it's overkill to require you to inform your landlord of a guest who will stay only a day or two. Extreme behavior in this area—whether by an owner or a management employee—can be considered an invasion of privacy for which you could sue in small claims court if gentle persuasion fails.

Limits on Guests in a Pandemic Era

In response to the 2020 coronavirus pandemic, some tenants have of necessity invited additional residents to share their homes, due to the newcomers' loss of their own housing, the need to have someone care for homebound children, and other virus-related causes. And landlords in multifamily settings have attempted to limit social visitors (visitors who are not overnight guests), arguing that such gatherings increase the risk that residents will become infected. Let's look at each position.

Adding Residents

In spite of a "no unauthorized resident" clause, some tenants have added permanent or semipermanent residents, citing COVID-related reasons. Can a landlord successfully object and terminate if the newcomers have not been screened or create overcrowding?

At this writing, there's very little established support for a tenant who has violated an unauthorized occupant clause, in spite of the best of reasons. Some states have addressed the situation by directing landlords to relax their occupancy rules if doing so is needed to address a COVID-related need. If you find yourself in this position, the best approach will be to try to work things out with your landlord, by offering additional rent, for example. Check with local legal aid offices and tenant organizations for any legal developments in your area.

Limiting Social Gatherings

Tenants who object to a landlord's attempt to limit or stop guest visits cite their rights to privacy and the lack of any such clause in their leases and rental agreements. A persistent landlord could theoretically terminate and evict on the grounds that the tenants were creating a dangerous situation.

Whether a landlord's rule would hold up in court is not clear. The landlord's position would be strengthened if a shelter order or law were in place, because the landlord would be able to truthfully claim that the tenants are engaging in illegal activity at the rental.

Expect to see new variations of lease "guest" clauses addressing unauthorized residents during times of emergencies. A concerned landlord will write one that clearly gives the landlord the right to warn and then terminate if the tenant hosts social gatherings in the face of a government order that prohibits them.

How to Get Your Landlord to Back Off

As you no doubt know too well, it's one thing to *have* a right, while it's sometimes quite another to enjoy that right. Alas, getting your nosy landlord to cool it might not be an easy task, especially if the intrusiveness is annoying but just this side of illegal. Still, proven methods might, with persistence, get results.

Have a Chat

The first step is to simply have a conversation, as friendly as possible, and ask that the behavior stop. If there is anything redeeming in your landlord's actions—unannounced entries are for the purpose of fixing something that really needs to be done, for example—be sure to acknowledge that you appreciate the good intentions. Then explain that it would *really* be great if you could get reasonable notice and so on. Follow up with a letter of understanding. (See Chapter 2.) A sample is shown below.

Friendly Letter Asking Landlord to Respect Tenant's Privacy

August 5, 20xx

Frank Lee Nosee
123 Main St.
Portland, Oregon 33221

Dear Mr. Nosee:

Thanks for sending your plumber over yesterday to fix my bathtub leak. I really appreciate your prompt response. As I mentioned when we spoke in the hall, I would have preferred to be notified when the plumber was scheduled to come because my dog can sometimes be temperamental around strangers. Thanks for your promise to give me at least 24 hours' notice in the future so I can arrange to be home.

Sincerely,
Heywood U. Bachoff
Green Gables Apartment #4B
526 Grover Road
Portland, Oregon 33221
503-555-4567

Get Tough

If your friendly chat and confirming letter don't get results, it's time to get heavy. Write another letter, this time directing your landlord's attention to the legal consequences of the refusal to respect your rights. Be sure you've done your homework first, by checking to see whether your state has a statute that covers tenant privacy or, failing that, whether court decisions uphold your rights.

These letters are not just exercises in futility—if you decide to press on and sue or utilize another significant remedy, you'll need evidence that you *first* brought the problem to the landlord's attention and did all that a reasonable person could do to persuade the landlord to shape up. Be sure to keep a copy of your letter (and all landlord communications) in a safe place, and send the letter return receipt requested. Another sample is shown below. (See "Using Email for Notice or a Letter of Understanding," in Chapter 2, for information on how to use email to deliver written requests.)

CAUTION

Never change the locks without permission. Many state statutes expressly forbid tenants from doing so. Violating the law might result in the termination of your tenancy. And if your lease or rental agreement forbids you from altering the premises without the landlord's okay, the installation of a new lock will trigger this clause—again with the risk that your tenancy will be terminated.

Get-Tough Letter Asking Landlord to Respect Tenant's Privacy

September 19, 20xx

I. Sellum Real Estate Co.
11 Peach Street
Cleveland, Ohio 77665

Dear Mr. Sellum:

Several times in the last two months your resident manager, Pete Tuttle, has entered my apartment when I was not at home and without notifying me in advance. Following the second such visit, I wrote to you on August 20, 20xx, demanding that these unannounced entries stop at once.

In spite of my letter, Pete continued to enter when I was not home and without notice. One time when I was home sick from work, he simply walked in without knocking.

None of these entries involved an emergency—in fact, there was no real purpose for these visits. These intrusions have caused me considerable anxiety and stress, to the point that my peaceful enjoyment of my tenancy has been seriously disrupted.

This letter is to formally notify you that I highly value my privacy. I insist that my legal rights to that privacy, as guaranteed to me under Ohio Rev. Code Ann. Sec. 5321.04 & 5321.05, be respected. Specifically, in nonemergency situations, I am entitled to 24 hours' notice of your (or your employee's) intent to enter my home, plus a clearly stated and legal purpose of the entry.

I assume this letter will be sufficient to correct this matter. If you want to talk about this, please call me at home (555-7890) at night before 10 p.m.

Yours truly,
Ivanna Favor
789 Porter Street, #3
Cleveland, Ohio 77665
216-555-7890

Sue Your Landlord

If your words and letters get nowhere, it's time to see a lawyer or head for small claims court. Depending on the circumstances, you might be able to sue your landlord for:

- trespass: entering your rental space without consent or proper authority
- invasion of privacy: interfering with your right to be left alone
- breach of implied covenant of quiet enjoyment: interfering with your right to the undisturbed use of your home (see "Your Right to 'Quiet Enjoyment,'" above), and
- intentional infliction of emotional distress: a pattern of illegal acts by someone (in this case, the landlord or manager) who intended to and did cause serious emotional consequences to you.

Be forewarned that it might be hard to prove much in the way of money damages if the intrusions are annoying but not extreme. Most likely, a judge will figure that you have not been harmed much if, on one occasion, your landlord merely walked on your rug and opened and closed your door, and you won't be awarded much money for compensation.

However, if you can show a repeated pattern of illegal entry and the fact that you asked the landlord to stop, or even one clear example of outrageous conduct, you might be able to get a substantial recovery. You'll probably want an attorney for this kind of case, especially if you bring your case in a court other than small claims court.

Move Out

Repeated abuses of your right to privacy might justify your breaking the lease and moving out, without liability for future rent. Some state statutes even include this as an available remedy.

If your statute doesn't explicitly give you the option of leaving when the landlord violates the privacy laws, or if you don't even have the protection of a privacy statute, don't despair. There's still a way to leave legally. Your legal theory is that the landlord's actions violated the "implied covenant of quiet enjoyment." Because that covenant, or promise, is automatically present in every rental situation, your landlord has broken the lease. That breach leaves you free to leave.

It's a good idea to try mediation before packing up and moving out or heading for court. In fact, in many small claims courts you'll be sent to mediation before your case will be heard by a judge, so you might as well do it yourself early on. (Mediation is explained in more detail in Chapter 13.)

Rules to Rent By

You can go a long way toward ensuring your rights to privacy by following these tips:

- **Learn your state's law on tenant privacy,** particularly the permissible reasons for landlord entry and the amount of notice required.
- **Bargain for an access clause in your lease or rental agreement** if you aren't protected by a state statute or court decision.
- **Contact the owner if it's the manager or supe who's giving you a bad time.** Often, the owners don't know what their employees are doing.
- **Speak with other tenants to learn whether they, too, are the unhappy recipients of nosy intrusions.** If many complain, more attention is paid.
- **Suggest mediation before filing suit or moving out.** Community-based landlord-tenant mediation services might help.

CHAPTER

9

How Tenancies Change and End

Sooner or later, you'll move on. Although not as complicated as the application and move-in process, moving out does involve more than dropping the keys on the manager's desk and waving good-bye as your U-Haul pulls away. You need to think about:

- how much advance notice you must give to end a month-to-month tenancy
- what happens if you *don't* give the required notice
- what can happen if you give notice and then don't leave
- what your options are if you want to get out of a lease
- what to do to make sure you get your deposit back, and
- how to deal with your landlord's bankruptcy or foreclosure.

Tenant Traps

Read this chapter to find out why you should:

- **Never leave without giving legal notice.** You'll be liable for at least a month's rent (if you have a rental agreement) and perhaps several months' rent (if you have a lot of time remaining on a lease). At the very least, you can kiss your deposit good-bye.
- **Never stay on after your lease has expired without signing a new rental document.** You might think that your lease self-renews, but in most states it doesn't, it simply changes to a month-to-month tenancy. Unless you're protected by just cause eviction protection, renting on a monthly basis puts you in a precarious position if you want to stay for a while.
- **Never prepare to move without understanding your landlord's rules for cleaning up and getting them in writing.** Not only will you not know what's required, but your landlord will have a golden opportunity to change the standards after you've done all the work.
- **Never expect the landlord to use the security deposit for the last month's rent unless you've reached an agreement.** Some states impose significant penalties for this ploy.

Changing Your Tenancy Without Ending It

Once you sign a lease or rental agreement, it's a legal contract between you and your landlord. Every understanding in it is binding for the life of the agreement: one month for month-to-month rental agreements and the term of the lease for leases.

So how can you or your landlord make changes in the lease or rental agreement? The rules are different for leases and rental agreements. And if the proposed change is something you both agree to, there are even more rules, as we'll explain below.

Changes in Month-to-Month Rental Agreements

If you rent month to month, chances are you'll see at least one change during your time at this address: a rent hike. Your landlord might also make other changes, such as the amount of the security deposit or whether to allow pets. You, too, might be able to negotiate your way toward more favorable terms—like the parking spot you've wanted for months. How you or your landlord can accomplish these changes depends on whether you both agree to the change. Here's how it works.

Changes That You Both Agree To

Because your rental agreement is a binding contract for its one-month life, neither you nor the landlord may unilaterally decide that there will be immediate changes, such as a rent hike or the removal of a guaranteed parking spot. A landlord who wants to impose these new rules despite your objection will have to follow the notice rules, as explained below. And if you feel that you cannot continue living there unless the landlord makes changes in your favor, you too will need to follow the notice rules in order to avoid legal trouble.

However, there is nothing to stop you and the landlord from mutually agreeing at any time to make a change. To make immediate changes in a rental agreement, simply write the changes into the original document, note the date the change will take effect, and make sure both of you sign and enter the date of your signatures in the margin. Or, if the rental agreement is saved in electronic format, the landlord can simply enter the changes into the electronic document and print out a new agreement, ready for signatures.

Changes Proposed by the Landlord

Often, landlords announce one-sided changes such as an increase in rent, a decrease in services, or a variation on a common area rule. Your landlord doesn't need your consent when announcing a change in your rental agreement—but it can't be imposed immediately, either. All that's required is that the landlord give you the legal notice period: 30 days in most states.

Assuming you stay, you don't have to redo the entire rental agreement. The landlord can cross out the old language, write in the new (including when it takes effect), and initial and date the changes (you should initial it, too). Or, the landlord can use an addendum page. If the change is significant and the landlord has the agreement on a computer, it's easy to print out a new agreement, incorporating the change.

What can you do if you don't like the landlord's proposed change? If negotiating is unsuccessful, you can move out. Remember, though, you'll still need to give legal notice to end your tenancy, which is usually the same length of time as the notice period to change its terms (typically 30 days). If you give notice of your intention to leave on the same day you get notice about the landlord's change, you'll be legally free to leave before the change takes effect. However, if you wait a period of time before giving notice, the changes will take effect before your obligations as a tenant end. (See "How Month-to-Month Tenancies End," below, on ending a tenancy.)

Changes Proposed by the Tenant

Tenants, too, can propose changes in a rental agreement, such as asking for permission to bring in an additional roommate. If the landlord agrees, great—follow the advice in "Changes That You Both Agree To," above. In most situations, however, you have very little bargaining power if the landlord balks. Your best ally when pressing for better terms is your track record as a stable, good tenant (a sluggish rental market will be helpful, too). Smart landlords will take steps to retain you as a tenant by keeping you happy. If you don't prevail and it's an all- important issue, your only alternative is to give your own termination notice, as explained below.

Changes in Leases

One of the advantages of having a lease is knowing that its terms are set until it runs out. But there are ways to modify leases, as explained below.

Changes That You Both Agree To

The two of you are free to change the terms of your lease at any time if you both want to. Follow the instructions for making changes in rental agreements, above.

Changes Proposed by the Landlord

Knowing that leases can't be changed except by mutual consent makes some landlords nervous. Predictably, they want to be able to raise the rent midlease, or they anticipate that they might want to make other changes (such as decreasing services) that they aren't intent on imposing at the start of the tenancy.

Landlords give themselves some flexibility by *writing the change into the lease itself.* You can think of it as a kind of option—to the landlord's benefit! For example, you might see a clause that specifies that the landlord "reserves the right to increase the rent by $50 at the end of six months." As long as the proposed change is certain as to time and amount (or other specific factors), by signing the lease you become bound by it if the landlord decides to impose it.

Watch out, however, for open-ended change rights, such as a clause giving the landlord the right to "raise the rent at any time." A court would not enforce a lease clause that is so vague. If you encounter a landlord who presents you with such a slippery clause, think carefully about doing business with this owner.

CAUTION

Some landlords use a lease clause giving them the right to make insubstantial changes during your lease. Some states have statutes giving landlords the right to make small changes midlease. Naturally, there is often great debate over the meaning of an "insignificant" change. There will be little argument about truly minor changes (keeping the pool open an hour less on weekdays, for example) or obviously major ones (an increase in rent), but the situations that fall into the middle will invariably cause trouble. As a rule of thumb, if an issue is important enough to be included in a written lease in the first place (such as the provision of a parking spot), it's hard to imagine how it could also be classed as "insubstantial."

Changes Proposed by the Tenant

Just as the landlord can't tinker with the lease terms while the lease is still in effect, neither can you. The landlord is entitled to hold you to your bargain, and vice versa. This doesn't mean, however, that you can't try some creative negotiating, as suggested below.

NEGOTIATE

To convince your landlord to change the terms of a rental agreement or a lease midterm, point out that the change is one or more of the following:

- Not a burden—it's a small matter to the landlord but an important one to you, such as allowing you to bring in a roommate. Of course, your pal must have the same good-tenant qualifications that you did, and your place must be big enough to accommodate an additional resident. (See Chapter 6 for more on bringing in a roommate.)
- Actually a benefit—such as your request to set up a home business. After you point out the security advantages of having someone who's consistently at home during the weekdays and able to spot suspicious or dangerous conditions, your landlord might like the idea.
- Necessary to enable you to stay—for example, if you've just inherited your aunt's pooch, you'll have to move to a place that allows pets unless your landlord bends the no-pets policy. This will only work if you're someone the landlord wants to keep.

- Something the landlord ought to do anyway—for instance, give you a nearby parking spot for the two months you'll be on crutches with a broken leg. While you could probably prevail by complaining to a fair housing agency or a judge (the rights of the disabled are explained in Chapter 5), you would certainly rather do it informally. For best results, don't threaten, just explain the strength of your position and the wisdom of doing things your way.

How Month-to-Month Tenancies End

A month-to-month tenancy renews (sometimes termed "rolls over") every 30 days. This means that if no one says anything about leaving, you can theoretically stay forever. But if your landlord wants you out, do you get any advance warning? And what are your obligations if *you* decide to pack up?

When Your Landlord Wants You Out

It's easy for landlords to end a month-to-month tenancy. In most situations, they needn't give a reason (though acting on discriminatory or retaliatory motives is illegal; see Chapters 5 and 11). Except in New Hampshire, New Jersey, and most rent-controlled states and cities, where a legally recognized reason ("just cause") is required for terminations, landlords can give you the boot just because they feel like it.

Landlords must, however, give you fair warning. Thirty days is typical. Unless the rental agreement specifies otherwise, notice needn't be delivered on the day rent is due. If notice is given midmonth, then your tenancy will run out in the middle of the next month.

All states, and even some cities (typically those with rent control) have their own very detailed rules and procedures for how landlords must prepare and serve termination notices. For example, some states specify that the notice be printed in a certain size or style of typeface. If your landlord doesn't follow these procedures, the notice terminating your tenancy might be invalid. But once you point out the mistake, either informally or as a legal defense to an eviction lawsuit, your landlord will probably just correct the mistake and do it right the next time. If you want information on your state's exact requirements, consult your state statutes. (See "State Landlord-Tenant Statutes" in Appendix B.) Your state consumer protection agency or local tenants' rights organization might also have useful advice.

CAUTION

Notice to terminate by mail. Most states allow landlords to mail termination notices when they are unable to deliver them to the tenant personally. If you receive a notice in the mail, don't assume that you can add a few days to make up for the time in transit. For example, a notice to terminate in 30 days that was mailed on the first but delivered by the mail carrier on the fifth might still be effective on the first of the next month, in spite of the fact that you have really received only 25, not 30, days' notice. Check your state statutes to find out for sure.

If your landlord attempts to terminate your tenancy without giving proper notice, you can decide to stay, wait for the eviction lawsuit to be filed against you, and fight it with the defense that the notice was defective. If the notice is truly defective, you'll probably survive the eviction, but the landlord will simply do it right the next time. Your gain: a few additional weeks at your old place. Your loss: time and effort spent in court, plus an eviction mark on your credit report, even though you won. You do the math.

NEGOTIATE

Landlords hate courtrooms. If you need a few extra days, or even a week or two before moving, ask the landlord to extend your tenancy. In exchange, promise to go quietly at the appointed time. From the landlord's point of view, unless you're a troublemaker or the unit is needed immediately, it's far more efficient to strike a deal than go through the expense and hassle of going to court. Put your offer in writing, which will assure the landlord of your good intentions—but note, it will be devastating evidence against you in court should you renege on your promise, requiring the landlord to file an eviction to get you out.

CAUTION

When landlords claim you've violated the lease—such as by failing to pay the rent—they can move quickly to terminate and evict. Notice periods for these situations are often much shorter, usually three to five days to pay up or move. Sometimes, tenants don't have the option of paying the rent or correcting the violation and thereby saving their tenancies—they must move or face an eviction lawsuit. Defending yourself against an eviction for an alleged lease violation isn't covered in this book.

When You Want to Leave

When it's you who wants to end the month-to-month tenancy, simply give the required amount of notice to your landlord. If you mail the notice, be sure to take into account the amount of time your notice will spend in transit. To be safe, assume that the time begins running when you mailed the notice, not when the landlord receives it. That way, if the landlord rerents the unit upon getting your notice, it will be available to the next residents a few days after you have left. To be safe, contact the landlord and make sure you both agree as to which day will be your last (take a look at your state statutes first).

Usually you can send in your termination midterm, as can your landlord. But check your rental agreement—some landlords, anxious to avoid the hassles of being left with partial months, insist that notice be given on the day rent is due so that tenants move out at the end of a full rental period. This means that if rent is due on the first but you decide on the second that you want to move, you'll have to wait until the start of the next month before giving notice. In other words, if your rental agreement requires you to give notice on the first day of the month, and you give notice on any other day, in the eyes of the law it hasn't been given until the first day of the *next* month and won't expire until one month after that.

CAUTION

Watch out for rental agreements that lengthen your notice period and shorten your landlord's. Some rental agreements establish a notice period for tenants that is longer than the one specified by state law for terminating a tenancy. Or, landlords sometimes attempt to shorten their own notice period. Both moves are designed to give the landlord more flexibility and you less. In some states, these agreements are valid. Check your state statute and, if the issue isn't addressed there, contact your state's consumer protection agency. Valid or not, be advised that a landlord who expects tenants to be bound by the owner's last-minute decisions and short notice periods is probably one to avoid.

What happens if you give less than the required amount of notice? It's simple: You can leave, but you pay rent for those days, anyway. For example, if you suddenly move out of a month-to-month unit where 30 days' notice is required, the landlord will probably simply deduct from your security deposit the amount of rent you would have paid if you had delivered the required notice.

What If You Change Your Mind?

Notice is notice—there's no retraction period. Once you have delivered your termination notice, that's it. Your landlord is entitled to hold you to it and need not even listen to you as you attempt to explain why circumstances now make it impossible or unwise for you to move.

If you decide to stay put and hope that your landlord will simply forget about the notice you gave, think carefully. If your landlord has rented your place to someone else after you've given notice, but then you decide to stay on ("hold over"), there's the problem of the tenant who expected to take your place. You can be liable for the new tenant's temporary housing costs incurred while the landlord evicts you.

There's more. If the disappointed tenant walks away in disgust, your landlord will have a pile of rental expenses occasioned by your expected departure (advertisements, applicant screening costs, time spent showing your unit) that now appear to be a waste of time and money.

The landlord will have an easy time deducting these expenses from your security deposit and then suing you in small claims court if you don't replenish the deposit. In short, don't announce that you're leaving until you're really sure that's your plan.

Bailing Out of a Bad Place

If your landlord seriously violates the rental agreement or fails to fulfill legal responsibilities—for example, by not correcting serious health or safety problems—you might be able to move out legally, with no responsibility for future rent, before the official end of the tenancy. In legalese, the landlord has effected a "constructive eviction," by allowing or maintaining intolerable living conditions (for example, no heat for an extended period in the winter). For all intents and purposes, these conditions have "evicted" you as much as a lockout or a utility shutoff.

The conditions that constitute a constructive eviction vary slightly under state law. Generally, if the landlord is on notice that a rental unit has serious habitability problems for an extended time, you're entitled to move out on short notice or, in extreme cases, without giving notice. (See Chapter 7, which explains all of your options when faced with an unlivable unit, for more information.)

What Happens When Your Lease Runs Out

A lease lasts for a fixed term, typically one year, then simply ends of its own accord at the end of the term. Your landlord doesn't have to give you notice of the end of the lease, because you already know (or should remember!) that the time is up. At this point, you must either:

- move
- sign a new lease, with the same or different terms, or
- stay on as a month-to-month tenant *with your landlord's approval.* In most states, the terms and conditions of the old lease (such as the rent amount and a no-pets clause) will carry over into your new, oral month-to-month tenancy.

If you do none of these things and your landlord wants you to move on, you are considered a "holdover" tenant and will probably be evicted. The landlord can file an eviction lawsuit within a very few days of your failure to move out, and you'll have little chance of winning unless you can show that the refusal to renew was illegal because it was discriminatory (see Chapter 5) or an act of retaliation (see Chapter 11). If your intent in staying on is to buy time, forget it—eviction lawsuits for holdovers are fast affairs. And if your lease has an "attorneys' fees" clause in it (see Chapter 2), you'll be on the hook for your landlord's lawyer and court costs. Even if you capitulate on the courthouse steps, these costs will stick—as will the notation on your credit report that an eviction suit was filed against you. Far better to negotiate for a little more time, as suggested above.

Breaking a Lease and Leaving Early

For all sorts of reasons—a job transfer, an invitation to move in with someone else, or deciding that you just don't like the place—you might want to leave before your lease ends. If you're lucky, your landlord will agree to let you go—a response most likely if your landlord is a decent sort or there is a shortage of rental housing and hordes of eager applicants—or, ironically, if the landlord considers you a pain in the neck and would be delighted to say good-bye. But what if you don't have your landlord's official *bon voyage*? Like lots of legal answers, it depends, mostly on your state law and your landlord's opinion about how easily you can be replaced with a quality, financially sound new tenant.

The explanation that follows applies to situations in which you do not have a legally justified reason for leaving. Justified reasons for breaking a lease or moving out early include the landlord's failure to maintain a fit and habitable rental or substantial destruction of the property (topics covered in Chapter 7), and the landlord's persistent violation of your rights to privacy (the focus of Chapter 8). And depending on your situation, state law might allow you to leave early if you need to move because of a new job, domestic violence, being called up for active military duty, or for health or age reasons.

Most Landlords Must Rerent

Let's start with the basics: Your lease is a contract, obligating you to pay rent for the entire term. The fact that you pay in monthly installments doesn't change the fact that you owe the landlord for the entire amount. So if you split early, what's to stop the landlord from suing you for the remaining months' rent?

Fortunately, in most states landlords cannot simply sit back and wait for the term to end, then sue you for the months you weren't there. They must take reasonable steps to rerent the place and credit that rent to your debt. This duty goes by a mouthful of words—"the landlord's duty to mitigate damages." The chart "Landlord's Duty to Rerent" in Appendix B notes which states require landlords to mitigate. This tenant-friendly rule has some limitations, however:

- You might still be responsible for the costs of advertising and showing the unit.
- Landlords must take *reasonable* steps to rerent, not heroic ones. They needn't put your unit at the top of their list of properties to rent, and they don't have to offer it for a song.
- Landlords needn't accept any applicant who walks in the door. They're entitled to be as choosy with the next tenant as they were with you.

Unfortunately, many landlords are unaware of their duty to rerent for the benefit of the departing tenant. And even if they are aware of the rule, the notion that they must make an effort to minimize the financial hit to people who broke their lease is often tough for them to swallow. Their response is to keep the security deposit at least and often to send a threatening letter demanding the balance of the rent. If this sounds like what happened to you, read on.

When Your Landlord Hasn't Hustled for a New Tenant

If you've broken your lease and taken off, expect to lose a month's rent even if state law requires your landlord to mitigate—most judges will give the landlord a month of rent as damages, no matter how quickly the landlord advertised and showed the unit—or how quickly it *could* have rented if the landlord had tried. Your landlord will take this month's rent out of your security deposit.

But being asked to pony up the rest of the rent due under your lease is something else entirely. If your landlord sends you a righteous letter demanding the balance due under your lease, a polite letter, citing your state's law, might disabuse the landlord of this "right" to sit idle and collect on an empty apartment. The sample letter below shows how one tenant has done this. With luck, your landlord will back off.

But what if your letter doesn't produce the desired result? If you are sued for an enormous amount of rent or have a sizable deposit sitting in the landlord's bank account, you'll be headed for court—either as a defendant if the landlord sues you, or as a plaintiff if you sue to recover some of your deposit.

If the courthouse is on the horizon, you'll have to have some proof that the landlord failed to mitigate. Be smart and, after you leave, collect evidence of the landlord's efforts to rerent (or ask a friend in the area to do so). Find out whether the landlord advertised (check the rental ads for a month or so), showed the unit (ask the neighbors), rented comparable units but not yours, or in fact rented the unit and is now attempting to double-dip. In some states, if you end up in court arguing that the landlord failed to take steps to rerent, you can't sit back and wait for the landlord to produce proof that he diligently tried to rerent. Instead, you will have to supply the proof of the landlord's laziness, in the form of screen shots, for example, of rental sites that do not include your unit.

Although you should weigh the risks carefully before deciding to break a lease, keep in mind that few landlords will want to keep a unit vacant (especially a single-family home) while they chase down the departed tenant. Vacant properties are targets for vandalism, and attempting to collect from a tenant with modest means (particularly one who has moved out of state) can be futile. Most landlords will keep the entire security deposit, rerent the unit, and give you a dismal reference when contacted by any of your future landlords.

Sample Letter Alerting Landlord to the Duty to Mitigate

June 21, 20xx

Bill C. Lecter
90 Maple Avenue
Monroe, CA 90000

Dear Mr. Lecter:

Until recently, I rented your flat at 78 Oak Street in Monroe. Unfortunately, a job transfer made it necessary for me to move to Harding, some 100 miles away. As I explained in late May, I had no choice but to break my year's lease on June 1, 20xx. The lease had six months left. I left owing no rent for the time that I lived there.

I was disappointed to receive your letter dated June 18, 20xx, in which you informed me that you expect me to pay you for the remaining six months' rent. You stated that you will keep my entire security deposit (two months' rent) and have demanded that I pay you for the remaining four months.

May I direct your attention to California Civil Code Section 1951.2, which requires a landlord to use reasonable efforts to rerent after a tenant has broken the lease. As you know, rentals are scarce in this town, and I would think that you could rerent my flat, which is quite nice, fairly quickly. While I am prepared to cover one month while you prepare, advertise, and show the unit, I am certainly not willing to pay further rent on an apartment that you have purposely left empty.

Please reimburse me for the one month's rent that you withheld from my deposit.

Yours truly,
Tom Tenant
23 Seventh Avenue
Harding, CA 90000
209-555-4567

NEGOTIATE

Offer your landlord a replacement tenant. If you can find a sub who is likely to pass your landlord's screening criteria, offer that tenant when (or before) you break the lease. Ideally, the landlord will accept the sub (you've really saved the owner a lot of time and hassles), and you, too, will end up not being liable for any unrented months. In addition, a landlord who unreasonably refuses an acceptable would-be tenant will have a hard time arguing in court that reasonable efforts to find a replacement were fruitless.

Domestic Violence Situations

Many states extend special protections to tenants who are victims of domestic violence. If you are facing a domestic violence situation (including stalking) and want to move, check first with local law enforcement or a battered women's shelter regarding special laws that might apply. Your state might have rules for tenant-victims like the following (see "State Laws in Domestic Violence Situations," in Appendix B, for specific laws and additional protections).

Antidiscrimination status and eviction protection. Many states make it illegal to discriminate against someone who is a victim of domestic violence. This means that landlords cannot refuse to rent (or terminate) solely because the person is a victim of domestic violence.

Early termination rights. In many states, a victim of domestic violence can end a lease with notice (often 30 days). States typically require that the tenant provide proof (such as a protective order) of the tenant's status as a domestic violence victim.

Limits on rental clauses. Some states prohibit clauses that allow the landlord to terminate the tenancy if a tenant calls for police help in a domestic violence situation, or that make tenants pay for the cost of such calls.

More Help From Restraining Orders

All states have a process by which victims of domestic or workplace violence can go to court to get a restraining order against the aggressor. These "stay away" orders prohibit the abuser from coming physically near the victim, no matter where the victim happens to be. So, when a cotenant is the aggressor, the victim tenant can use the restraining order to keep the cotenant away from the rental property. If the object of the restraining order violates it, the victim can call the police to remove the aggressor.

Restraining orders operate independently of any protective law directed specifically at landlords and tenants. For that reason, we do not list them in our "State Laws in Domestic Violence Situations" chart in Appendix B. For information on obtaining restraining orders, contact local law enforcement.

If your state has no law giving victims of domestic violence early termination rights or other domestic violence protections, don't automatically assume that you're stuck (consider getting a restraining order, as explained above). First, if you want to move, appeal to your landlord's bottom line: The last thing any landlord wants on the property is a disruptive, potentially violent situation. Letting you out of the lease might be just want the landlord wants, too—what the landlord loses in rent might pale in comparison with what the repair costs may be if the property is damaged, not to speak of the fallout from negative publicity if the situation escalates.

Even if your state gives some special protections to domestic violence victims, these accommodations do not prevent landlords from terminating, if necessary, for nonpayment of rent. Unfortunately, all too often the abuser will leave the property but the remaining victim struggles to pay the rent. Landlords can legally terminate the tenancy of a domestic violence victim who falls behind in the rent, just as they would any tenant who hasn't paid.

The Landlord's Bankruptcy

If your landlord declares bankruptcy, the bankruptcy court will appoint a trustee to take over the landlord's business operations. Your lease will not automatically end, and it's possible that very little will change for you (you might even be instructed to continue to pay rent to the landlord). And your security deposit (which is your money, not the landlord's) will be safe from the clutches of eager creditors.

However, the bankruptcy trustee does have the right to "reject" your lease, which simply means that if this happens, you can, if you choose, treat the lease as terminated and move out without liability for future rent. You can also decide to stay put and retain all your rights under the original lease.

If you decide to remain after the lease has been rejected, you'll need to be aware that your normal remedies for dealing with a landlord who fails to maintain the property (repair-and-deduct, and rent withholding, to the extent they are recognized in your state) will be replaced by the bankruptcy code. Instead of withholding rent, you'll need to go to the bankruptcy judge and obtain an offset against the rent, to compensate you for the substandard conditions. This can all be rather tricky, and you might need the help of a lawyer.

If the property is sold, you'll end up with a new owner/landlord, who must honor the terms and conditions of your lease.

Foreclosure

All too often, tenants find their rented home the subject of a foreclosure. In a nutshell, this is what you need to know:

- **Rent.** Unless instructed otherwise by the lender or bank, tenants should continue to pay the rent to the landlord, or at the very least, set up an escrow account for their rent payments.
- **Maintenance.** Defaulting owners are not excused from their continuing duty to maintain fit and habitable rental property,

though many stop doing so. On the other hand, the lender who started the foreclosure probably has no legal duty to take over for the owner at this point. If you decide to avail yourself of a tenant remedy, such as rent withholding, be sure to follow the steps set out by your state law very carefully.

- **Foreclosure.** If the property is taken by foreclosure, your lease will survive unless an individual (or individuals) purchase the property at the foreclosure sale and intend to live there as their principal place of residence (in that case, the purchaser can terminate your lease on 90 days' notice). If you are a month-to-month tenant, you can be asked to leave with 90 days' notice.
- **Maintenance postforeclosure.** Lenders who end up owning rental properties are notorious for not understanding that they are now landlords, subject to the same rules that their former borrower (your landlord) had to respect. Some states (including California) specifically impose maintenance duties, but this is the exception. If you need to use a tenant remedy, be sure to follow the procedure precisely.

Rules to Rent By

- **Understand how much notice (advance warning) your landlord must give you before terminating or changing your rental agreement.** Know how much notice you, too, must give before moving out.
- **Insist that important changes to leases or rental agreements be put to writing, and signed by you and the landlord.**
- **If you need to break a lease and move early, try to find a replacement tenant who has the same good credit and rental history that you did (or better).**

CHAPTER

10

Getting Your Deposit Back

It's a rare departing tenant who doesn't have some hassle with the landlord over the return of the deposit. Some landlords don't know the law, and many haven't set up their business to make it clear from the outset what they expect, in the way of cleanliness, when their tenants move out. You can do a lot both to educate the landlord and to establish some reasonable guidelines for having your deposit returned.

TIP

Inspect and photograph the rental unit before you move in. Without objective proof of the condition of the unit when you moved in, it will be difficult to effectively counter a landlord's claim that you caused damage that, in fact, was there when you took over. Pictures don't lie. (See our move-in tips in Chapter 2.)

How Your Landlord Can Use Your Deposit

Legally, a landlord can use the deposit for any cleaning or repairs necessary to restore the rental unit to its condition at the beginning of the tenancy (minus ordinary wear and tear), and to cover unpaid back rent (and a reasonable amount of future rent if you break a lease and leave early). We emphasize that the landlord may not use your security deposit for the cost of remedying the results of ordinary use. This means that if the paint is ruined because your toddler mistook the wall for an easel, expect to be charged; but if the carpet needs to be replaced because it's ten years old and is simply worn out, it's the landlord's responsibility.

Unfortunately, it's not always easy to decide what constitutes ordinary wear and tear or how clean your rental unit must be when you move out. Here are some guidelines:

- You shouldn't be charged for damage that was there when you moved in.
- You shouldn't be expected to leave the unit any cleaner than it was when you moved in.
- Your landlord should not charge you the replacement cost of a broken item if it can be repaired without diminishing its function or appearance.

- The longer you've lived in a place, the greater the amount of wear and tear.
- If you've paid a nonrefundable cleaning fee (some states allow them in addition to security deposits), you shouldn't be charged for additional cleaning.

The Final Blow to Worn Furnishings

Red wine on a brand-new white carpet? Face it, you'll pay for this one. But what about stains on an old, worn carpet; or scratches from your dog's paws on a floor already marred by water damage; or major nail holes on a wall that hasn't been painted in years? Should you be expected to pay the full cost for refurbishing these worn, yet still-usable items, simply because your error was the last straw?

Of course not. Still, many a landlord will try to stick a tenant with the entire bill because the tenant's goof prematurely ended the life of the carpet, floor, or paint job. Unfortunately, there is practically no clear law on the subject. You caused the early demise of the rug, floor, or wall, but how much should you fairly pay?

The answer begins by remembering that normal wear and tear must be covered by the landlord, which means that replacement costs of worn-out items are borne by the landlord, too. So, suppose that the carpet with a stain the size of Texas originally cost $1,000 and had an expected life of ten years. At the end of these ten years, the carpet would be worth $0 (its value decreases by $100 per year), and the landlord would have to shell out the money to replace it. If your mishap occurs in the fifth year, your landlord will lose $500 worth of use. Arguably, you owe that amount.

This method of calculating damage costs is not accepted by everyone. And it is subject to some very big variables. For example, the useful life of a carpet in the home of a fastidious single tenant will be longer than the life of the same carpet used by a family of four. Nevertheless, it's one way to approach being charged for the entire amount. If you use this method, be sure to collect information on the "useful life" of the item you're being charged for and its original cost. If you go to small claims court to argue for the return of your deposit, you'll need this proof.

The Mechanics of Getting the Deposit Back

Depending on the state, landlords generally have from 14 to 30 days after you leave—whether voluntarily or by eviction—to return all or part of your deposit. (State laws are in Appendix B.) The landlord must mail either of the following to your last known address (or forwarding address, if known):

- Your entire deposit, with interest if required (the chart in Appendix B lists state laws requiring interest).
- A written, itemized statement as to how the deposit has been applied toward back rent and costs of cleaning and damage repair, together with whatever is left of the deposit, including any interest that is required. In most states, landlords must send the itemization along with any deposit balance. A few states add an additional step that gives tenants time to respond to proposed deductions before they are actually made.

If your landlord is slow in returning your deposit, a reminder letter is in order. (In some states, deliberate or "bad faith" retention of the deposit subjects the landlord to sizable penalties.) Ask for the amount to be refunded, cite your state or local law regarding deposits, send the letter certified, and keep a copy. Known as a "demand letter," you'll need to show it to the judge if you end up in court attempting to collect your deposit. (In Chapter 2, see "Using Email for Notice or a Letter of Understanding," for information on how to use email to deliver written requests.)

Sample Letter Demanding Return of Security Deposit

July 15, 20xx

Sandy Beach
5 Lake View Drive
Washburn, Illinois 12345

Dear Ms. Beach:

As you know, until May 30, 20xx, I rented Apartment #4 at 1492 Columbus Avenue. I gave 30 days' notice on May 1, and moved out owing no rent. The apartment was not damaged in any way.

As of today, I have received neither my $750 security deposit nor any accounting from you for that money. Under Illinois law (Ill. Rev. Stat. Ch. 765 para. 710, 715), I was entitled to receive my deposit, including an itemization of any deductions, 30 days after my tenancy ended—that is, by June 30, 20xx. You are now over two weeks late.

Please return the deposit to me immediately. If I do not receive my money by July 25, I will regard your retention of my deposit as showing bad faith and will sue you in small claims court for $1,500, which is double the amount of my deposit, as allowed under Illinois law.

I look forward to receiving my deposit forthwith at the address below.

Yours truly,

Andrew Noble
76 Noview Drive
Evanston, Illinois 12345
847-555-2234

Avoiding Fights Over Deposits

Most deposit hassles involve disputes over "How clean is clean?" or "What's wear and tear?" Disputes over back rent or replacements are less common. Unfortunately, no statute or court opinion will give you a universally accepted standard for cleanliness or "normal" wear and tear. Smart landlords announce their own definitions, usually in a set of rules and regulations or in a letter that follows the receipt or sending of a termination notice. These are perfectly legal as long as they are reasonable. Examples include:

- floors swept and thoroughly cleaned
- carpets professionally steam-cleaned (more than just a thorough vacuuming)
- windows and mirrors washed
- refrigerator emptied of food and cleaned inside and out, and
- all trash and personal belongings removed (don't expect the landlord to dispose of your castoffs).

If you don't know your landlord's expectations for move-out cleaning, ask. When your departure date nears, send your landlord a letter explaining what you intend to do to ensure the return of your entire deposit (there's a sample below). You'll be on solid footing if you set your goals to correspond to the condition of the place when you moved in—after all, the law requires no more.

What's the advantage of this procedure? If you remember the value of a letter of understanding (covered in Chapter 2), you'll recognize how nicely you've just prepared your landlord. Landlords who do not object in writing will be locked in, legally speaking, to your plans. Assuming your plans are fair and you do a decent job (you should take photos or video, or have a witness willing to testify about the condition of the unit when you left), it will be hard for the landlord to argue in court that you didn't do what was expected or did it poorly.

Sample Letter Explaining Tenant's Cleaning Plans

May 15, 20xx

Mr. Rusty Shaque
5 Leisure Lane
Lakeport, Illinois 60600

Dear Mr. Shaque,

As you know, I gave notice on April 30, 20xx, that I intend to terminate my tenancy effective May 30, 20xx. I intend to leave the apartment clean and undamaged, in the same condition it was in when I moved in a year ago, minus normal wear and tear. In particular, I intend to:

- vacuum all floors and carpets, and clean the linoleum floor in the kitchen
- wash bathroom floors and wall tiles
- clean all bathroom and kitchen appliances and counters with cleaning products designed for these areas; clean oven and turn off and clean refrigerator
- cold-water wash the cotton drapes in the kitchen and bathroom
- vacuum drapes in living room and bedroom
- wash the interior surfaces of the windows, and
- remove all rubbish and personal items.

I believe that thoroughly accomplishing these tasks will satisfy my obligations under Illinois law to leave my rental unit clean. And because my apartment has not been damaged and I owe no back rent, I expect a full and prompt refund of my $750 security deposit. Please let me know in writing within five days of your receipt of this letter if my cleaning plan is not acceptable to you. If I don't hear from you, I'll assume that you agree with it.

Yours truly,

P.T. Smart
11256 Seventh Avenue
Chicago, Illinois 60600
312-555-8887

In most cases, most landlords will be so delighted that you intend to put some elbow grease into cleaning your unit that they wouldn't dream of objecting.

Suing to Get the Deposit Back

If your landlord has unfairly kept your deposit by making improper deductions or failing to return it within the time specified by your state's law, it's time to shift gears. You should send the landlord a letter (return receipt requested) asking for the return of your deposit or what you think your landlord owes you. In the letter, concisely review the main facts, ask for exactly what you want, and explain your legal rights. Conclude by stating that you will promptly sue in small claims court if necessary. (In Chapter 2, see "Using Email for Notice or a Letter of Understanding," for information on how to use email to deliver written requests.)

Hopefully, you've taken some of the suggestions throughout this chapter (such as nailing down what's expected in the way of cleaning and taking photos when you leave) so that you can head for court armed with helpful evidence. (For more information on small claims court, see Chapter 13.)

Rules to Rent By

- **Before you move out, find out exactly what the landlord expects in the way of cleaning.** If you get no answer, announce a cleaning plan of your own, designed to return the place to its condition (minus ordinary wear and tear) at the start of your tenancy. Unless the landlord objects, follow through with your plan.
- **Ask the landlord to inspect when you leave, and take your own photos.** You don't want to run the risk that you'll be charged for damage caused by the next tenant.
- **Be sure to write a demand letter before going off to court.**

CHAPTER

11

Landlord Retaliation

Rare are the tenants who, having asserted their rights, have not been hit with a landlord's payback—whether in the form of petty harassment, a rent hike, or an all-out termination and eviction. The good news is that landlord retaliation is illegal in most states—landlords who engage in it can be stopped and sued, sometimes for big bucks. The bad news is that asserting your rights can be a hassle, involving court fights and lots of time. Rather than have to react to bad landlord behavior, it's far better to be proactive by choosing your landlord wisely in the first place, as we advise in Chapter 1.

Sometimes, though, despite your best efforts to pick a well-run building managed by professionals, you can find that your request for repairs has been met with the sudden loss of your parking spot; or your efforts to organize other tenants into complaining about security have earned you a termination notice. In this chapter, we'll explain what you can do when you're faced with similar types of landlord retaliation.

Tenant Traps

Read this chapter to find out why you should:

- **Never challenge your landlord without being fully aware of your state's laws (or lack thereof) on landlord retaliation.** You won't want to take certain actions without knowing whether your state will protect you if the landlord strikes back. Some state laws do not, and some protect only certain actions. Without knowing your state's rules, you might come to regret your righteousness. Make sure you choose your battles wisely.
- **Never attempt to nail your landlord for illegal retaliation when there's a skeleton or two in your own closet.** Lots of information gets out in a legal fight, and your own record as a renter might be examined.
- **Never go after your landlord without carefully weighing the pros and cons,** especially whether you would be better served by spending the time and energy looking for another place rather than inviting a legal battle.

But suppose now that, despite your best efforts to live in a well-run building managed by businesspeople of integrity, your request for repairs has been met with the sudden loss of your parking spot; or your efforts to organize other tenants into complaining about security have earned you a termination notice. In this chapter, we'll explain what you can do about it.

Where Does the Law Protect You?

The laws of most states will protect you from landlord revenge when you have acted within your tenant rights—in other words, you can expect legal protection if you are blameless and it's the landlord who began the shoving match. In almost all states, you cannot be retaliated against if you have:

- complained to a building inspector, fire department, health inspector, or other governmental department about unsafe or illegal living conditions
- assembled and presented your views collectively, as in joining or organizing a tenant union, or
- availed yourself of self-help strategies allowed by your state or local law, such as deducting money from the rent and using it to fix defects in the rental unit, or even withholding the rent entirely for an uninhabitable unit. (See Chapter 7.)

Additionally, some states have passed laws preventing landlords from retaliating against tenants due to their status as victims of domestic violence (check the chart "State Laws in Domestic Violence Situations" in Appendix B).

Only six states—Indiana, Louisiana, Missouri, North Dakota, Oklahoma, and Wyoming—do not have statutes or court decisions protecting tenants against retaliation.

Differences in State Laws

It's important to understand that the antiretaliation laws will shield you *only* for those activities that are mentioned in your state's statute. Not all states protect tenants for each of the types of actions mentioned above. (Check your state's range by referring to "State Laws Prohibiting Landlord Retaliation" in Appendix B.) For example, in Washington, D.C., a tenant who circulates a petition demanding better services cannot be retaliated against; but that same activity would not be protected in Illinois, because "exercise of a legal right" isn't included in the Illinois statute.

Don't Push Your Luck

Don't think that you can abuse the system and still avoid your landlord's wrath. You must exercise your legal rights in good faith in order to be protected. If you withhold rent with no valid reason; circulate a patently scurrilous petition about your landlord; or file endless, groundless complaints with government inspectors, no judge will prevent a landlord from taking appropriate action (such as not renewing your lease or terminating your rental agreement).

You Don't Have to Be Perfect

An honest mistake made during an otherwise valid attempt to exercise your rights usually won't deprive you of the protection of your state's antiretaliation statute. For example, suppose that in response to a broken heater in the winter you withhold rent without complying strictly with your state's notice requirement. Your angry landlord is likely to call you on your error and demand the rent. If you pay it, can the owner then terminate your tenancy? Assuming that the heater was truly broken and your mistake relatively minor, you'll be in a good position to argue that you still deserve the benefit of your state law. Of course, you'd be far better off to follow the withholding rules carefully, as we counsel in Chapter 7.

What Is Retaliation?

Now that you know what *you* can do, let's turn to what your landlord *cannot* do. The kinds of retaliatory acts covered by state statutes include:

- terminating a month-to-month tenancy or refusing to renew a lease, and following up with an eviction lawsuit if you decide to stay and fight
- increasing the rent, and
- decreasing services, such as locking the laundry room, draining the pool, removing cable access, or canceling the security service or doorman.

Of course, few landlords are dumb enough to announce a retaliatory plan. Chances are that they will cloak their real motives in a cover-up, such as the sudden need to rent to a long-lost aunt or their financial inability to keep up with the just-decreased service. It's up to you to expose the truth, as explained below in "Proving That It's Retaliation."

Responding to Retaliation

If you're the object of your landlord's nasty moves, two responses are possible, depending on what the landlord has done:

- If the retaliation consists of a termination and eviction, you might want to stay and fight, defending yourself against eviction by proving to the judge that the real reason for the termination was illegal.
- If the retaliation is a rent hike, a reduction in services, or any other negative treatment, you might want to take the offensive by filing suit in small claims court. In your suit, you'd ask the judge to prohibit the rent hike, order the services reinstated (or a rent reduction to compensate you for the loss), or take other appropriate measures.

Is the Retaliation a Big Deal?

If you think a rent hike or other negative treatment is motivated by your assertion of a tenant's legal right, you might decide to fight back. But before you do, ask yourself the following questions:

- **Are you covered?** Check your state statutes to make sure that you have antiretaliation protection for what you've done.
- **How soon after your action did the rent increase or negative treatment come?** Obviously, the shorter the interval between your exercise of a legal right and the date of the increase, the more suspicious it becomes.
- **How large was the increase; how onerous was the mean move?** Judges are more likely to view a large rent increase (rather than a small one) as the landlord's way to punish or drive away a troublesome tenant. Ditto with reductions in services.
- **Does the rent increase or nasty move affect you alone, or does it apply to many others?** Your chances of proving a retaliatory motive will be greatly increased if you can show that you alone, but not tenants in similar units, received the negative treatment.
- **Is your landlord known for repeatedly and seriously trampling on tenants' rights?** Your landlord's reputation is certainly a relevant factor if you contemplate challenging a rent increase. You can learn whether the landlord is a frequent visitor to landlord-tenant or small claims court by asking the local tenants' organization or even your fellow tenants. The judge might tell you that this information is irrelevant and won't be considered—but you might want to share it anyway, then listen politely while the judge gives you a little lecture on the rules of evidence.
- **How disruptive or expensive, from the landlord's point of view, was your exercise of a legal right?** It's easier to win the cases in which you can convince a judge that the landlord has a strong motive to get even. Did you cause the landlord considerable time, expense, aggravation, or embarrassment? For example, if you complained to the local health department that your housing is uninhabitable because the roof leaked, and the department ordered your landlord

Is the Retaliation a Big Deal? (continued)

to put on a new roof, that's an expensive job that your landlord might resent highly. This anger could well prompt a retaliatory rent hike, you'll claim. Similarly, an accusation of discrimination against your landlord, even if it's ultimately defeated, could easily generate strong feelings of bitterness and retaliation. On the other hand, your isolated request for a necessary and inexpensive repair is far less likely in the eyes of a judge to motivate serious landlord revenge.

Sometimes you'll have a choice. For example, if the retaliation consists of a rent increase, you could refuse to pay and force the landlord to terminate and evict, banking on your antiretaliation statute as your defense. Or, you could immediately file suit in small claims court as soon as you get notice of the increase, hoping to resolve the issue before the increase kicks in. We strongly advise choosing the latter course whenever possible—if you lose, you can leave on your own terms, when and if you want to, without an eviction lawsuit going onto your credit report. On the other hand, if you force an eviction lawsuit and lose, your credit report will include this fact. Even if you win, an eviction in your past is not good news for most prospective landlords.

By far the most common kind of retaliation, however, is of the petty sort. Before filing papers in small claims court, ask yourself if the issue is really worth your time and money to fight. And, unfortunately, many intensely annoying ploys are just not that big a deal to a judge, either.

Proving That It's Retaliation

If you're determined to fight back by filing suit or hunkering down and defending against an eviction, there's one more issue you need to think about. How do you prove your landlord is trying to retaliate against you? In the real world, landlords are rarely so foolish as to say directly, "If you complain to the housing department, I'll evict you!" Instead, they're likely to stick it to you for a trumped-up reason, hoping to mask the fact that the real motive is to get rid of a tenant whom they regard as a troublemaker. Common examples of cover-ups that are really retaliations are:

- an unexplained termination that follows hard on the heels of a long-term tenant's legitimate decision to withhold the rent
- a refusal to renew a lease following a tenant's complaint to the health department, and
- sending a termination notice alleging misuse of common facilities after a tenant has used the common room to bring tenants together to fight a proposed rent increase.

Fortunately, however, many states give tenants an edge when it comes to unmasking illegal reasons to end a tenancy. In many states, the landlord is presumed to be retaliating against you if a tenancy is ended (or services decreased) within a certain amount of time after your exercise of a legal right, typically six months but sometimes 90 days or one year. This means that it will be up to the landlord to prove to the judge, should you end up in court, that his motives were *not* retaliatory.

Rules to Rent By

- **Make sure you know what your state or local law prohibits in the way of landlord retaliation.** Don't assume that everything you do is protected.
- **Whenever possible, respond to retaliation by taking the offensive (filing in small claims court) rather than refusing to go along and risking an eviction.** That way, you avoid the notation on your credit record that you were involved in an eviction lawsuit, which will be damaging if you lose.
- **Enlist the support of fellow tenants.** Landlords will hesitate to strike back if they know that they're facing a solid group, not just one individual. Banding together is especially important if your state gives you little or no antiretaliation protection.

CHAPTER

12

Rent Control

Some states, cities, and counties have laws that limit the amount of rent landlords can charge. Some of these ordinances also restrict the circumstances under which landlords can terminate month-to-month rental agreements or decide not to renew leases. Rent control laws and ordinances (also called "rent stabilization" or "maximum rent regulation" laws) are now in effect statewide in Oregon, New York, and California, as well as some of the country's largest cities, including Washington, D.C., and Newark, New Jersey.

Where to Get Information About Rent Control

If you are protected by a rent control ordinance, get straight information from these resources:

- **Your state's housing agency.** If you live in a state with statewide rent control, visit your state's official website, and locate the division that oversees housing or rent control in the state. This might be the state's housing agency, the courts, or human services agency.
- **A local tenants' organization.** Virtually every city or state with a rent control ordinance or law has at least one active and vocal tenants' group. (In many cases, the pressure from these groups is why the state or city has rent control in the first place.) These organizations typically are vigorous watchdogs of the rent board and monitor court decisions and any political goings-on that might affect the ordinance (such as proposed ballot amendments). Most importantly, tenant organizations can usually provide a written explanation of the ordinance and how it works, and many have volunteer staff available to explain ambiguous or complex facets of the ordinance. Some even provide free or low-cost legal services or assistance.
- **Local attorneys who specialize in landlord/tenant law.** If you have difficulty finding attorneys who will represent tenants (many lawyers are interested in representing landlords only), ask for referrals from a tenants' organization or any legal aid office. (See Chapter 13 for advice on finding an attorney.)

Tenant Traps

Read this chapter to find out why you should:

- **Never assume that all rent control is alike.** Ordinances vary considerably, and the only way you can know whether you're protected in any particular situation is to read your local ordinance.
- **Never exercise any tenant right you may have under state law without checking to see whether your local rent control speaks to the issue, too.** While local ordinances can only add to—not decrease—your rights under state law, it's not wise to take action without knowing your local law on the issue. Many ordinances go beyond the regulation of rent and termination and have detailed provisions on other issues, such as security deposits.
- **Never agree with your landlord to circumvent the rent control law without giving it careful thought.** Once you've gone down that road, you may end up in worse shape.
- **Never bring in a roommate without your landlord's knowledge and consent.** Your adherence to the terms of the lease or rental agreement protects you from eviction under rent control laws. When you bring in an unauthorized roommate, your landlord could seize this opportunity to evict both of you and raise the rent for the next tenant.

Rent control ordinances vary widely. Some have real teeth, while others (without eviction protection) are practically useless. Many states' laws restrict local rent control rules or bans them altogether; more than 30 states have laws prohibiting local rent control ordinances.

Because rent control ordinances are often extremely complex, we cannot give you a complete rundown of every feature. "Where to Get Information About Rent Control," above, suggests further resources.

We can, however, explain common features found in most laws and ordinances. Generally, these rules enhance tenant-protection provisions of already existing laws on landlord-tenant issues such as security deposits and evictions. Be sure to read the main chapter on each topic in conjunction with the rent control information here. For example, take a look at Chapter 4, "Security Deposits," along with the text below, explaining how rent control ordinances often add requirements and protections to a state's security deposit law.

Property Subject to Rent Control

Even when a state or city has rent control laws, some rental housing is exempt from the rules. Most rent control statutes exempt:

- new buildings
- owner-occupied buildings with no more than three or four units, and
- single-family houses and luxury units that rent for more than a certain amount.

To find out whether your building is too new to fall within the statute, you'll need to look at the certificate of occupancy, issued after construction is complete and the inspectors have approved the work, on file in the local building inspector's office.

Limits on Rent

Rent control comes in two basic styles: one that protects only the present tenant, and one that regulates rent over the long term, regardless of turnover. In rent control jargon, these varieties are known respectively as "vacancy decontrol" (rent restrictions turn off when there's a new tenant) and "vacancy control" (rent restrictions remain in place when the unit rerents).

Vacancy Decontrol Statutes: Protecting Current Tenants

Rent control might not be as great as you think—in most rent control areas, landlords can raise rent as much as they want when one tenant moves out and a new one moves in. This feature, called "vacancy decontrol" or "vacancy rent ceiling adjustment," means that rent control applies to a particular rental unit only as long as a particular tenant (or tenants) stays there. If a tenant voluntarily leaves or, in some cities, is evicted for a legal or "just" cause (discussed below), the rental unit is not subject to rent control again until the landlord sets the new (and presumably higher) rent. In short, in a "vacancy decontrol" city, don't expect to pay the same rent as the prior tenant.

In addition to built-in annual increases, most rent control boards allow landlords to petition for a rent hike based on an increase in costs, such as taxes or capital improvements like remodeling or bringing the building up to code.

Vacancy Control Statutes: Protecting Future Tenants

These rent control ordinances lock in the rent even when a unit turns over. The rent board sets a base rent for each rental unit, taking into account several factors, including the rent that was charged before rent control took effect, the landlord's operating and maintenance expenses, inflation, and housing supply and demand. The base rent can be raised during the tenancy under certain circumstances, such as an increase in inflation. When the tenant moves out, a landlord cannot raise the rent to market level. Rent stays controlled, subject to the formula of the rent control ordinance.

Evictions in Rent Control Areas

Tenancies normally end by their own accord: either at the end of a lease or after the proper amount of notice has been given in a month-to-month tenancy. As long as the landlord is not acting with discriminatory or retaliatory motives (see Chapters 5 and 11) the landlord can decide to call it quits, no reasons needed.

But for rent control to work—especially if the ordinance allows rents to rise when a tenant leaves—there must be added restrictions on eviction. Otherwise, landlords could throw out current tenants in order to get a chance to increase the rent. Recognizing this, many local ordinances require landlords to have a "just cause"—that is, a good reason—to evict. Acceptable reasons usually include:

- violating a significant term of the lease or rental agreement—for example, if you fail to pay rent or allow unauthorized people to live in the rental unit
- engaging in illegal activities on the premises, including drug dealing, substantial disturbance to the neighbors, or intentional damage to property
- a landlord's desire to move into the rental unit or give it to an immediate family member, and
- a landlord's desire to substantially remodel the property, which could not be done with people living there. Sometimes, a landlord must offer you another similar unit or give you first chance to move back in after the remodeling.

Landlords who violate these restrictions on evicting tenants often face stiff civil and even criminal penalties. Nonetheless, landlords in vacancy decontrol areas are fairly notorious for devising creative "just causes" to evict tenants—especially long-term ones—in order to get a chance to raise the rent to market rates. Sometimes it's easy for a landlord to find a reason to justify the eviction, such as pointing to a just-arrived unauthorized pet that the tenant insists on keeping. Other times, landlords try to turn a trivial offense into a just cause for the eviction, such as pointing to a single instance of rent arriving a day late as justification for a termination notice.

To prevent these types of disingenuous evictions, some rent control ordinances require that the stated reason for eviction be the landlord's "dominant motive." In other words, if you can prove that your one-day-late rent isn't the landlord's dominant motive, and that a desire to raise the rent is the true purpose behind the eviction, you might prevail in court. Of course, proving this—sometimes called a "bad faith eviction"—is often no easy task, and, even if you win, you'll undoubtedly have to devote precious time and money to defend yourself.

If you're facing a just cause eviction that you feel is a mere excuse for the landlord to raise the rent, one strategy is to fight aggressively to prevent the eviction lawsuit from being filed at all, starting with your first notice of the impending suit. Research the applicable law and heed the advice of many tenants before you: Hire a lawyer. When the stakes are high (perhaps your landlord can double the rent if you lose), you can be sure the landlord will hire counsel. Because rent control laws and court procedures are complex and often confusing, you'll almost certainly be outmatched by a professional on the other side.

If you decide to handle the matter yourself, make it clear to your landlord in writing that you do not believe the eviction is legal, and that you plan to defend yourself to the full extent of the law. Emphasize whatever penalties exist for violating the rent control law, and send copies of your correspondence to any governing rent board. In some areas such as San Francisco, you can file a complaint against your landlord with the rent board for wrongful eviction. While most rent control boards don't have the power to stop an eviction lawsuit filed in court, they might be able to dissuade a landlord from pursuing an eviction that has little merit by reminding the landlord of the law—and the potential penalties for violating it.

NEGOTIATE

Rent control hearings can be time-consuming, expensive, and awful. Knowing how difficult a rent hearing can be, don't head for one if you have a weak case or none at all. Instead, consider trading your right to bring the landlord's eviction attempt before the rent board for a little extra time. For example, if you are being asked to move because of the impending arrival of the landlord's relative, you might well get an extension of a month or two in exchange for your promise not to challenge the legitimacy of the relative move-in. However, if you suspect an eviction is truly bogus, don't negotiate away your right to challenge it.

Interest Payments on Security Deposits

Local rent control ordinances sometimes impose rules regarding security deposits that supplement those set out by state law. For example, in Los Angeles and San Francisco, landlords are required to put security deposits in interest-bearing bank accounts, something not required under California state law. Check your ordinance to see whether similar protections apply to you. (Chapter 4 discusses interest payments on security deposits.)

Special Notice Requirements

State laws typically require landlords to give a specified amount of notice when it comes to raising the rent or terminating the tenancy. (Notice requirements in general are explained in Chapter 9.) In rent control situations, however, the notice requirements are often tighter in two situations:

- **Raising the rent.** State law often requires a 30-day notice for a rent increase. A local rent control law might also require the notice to inform the tenant that the rent control board can verify that the new rental amount is legal under the ordinance.

- **Terminating the tenancy.** Some rent control ordinances forbid the landlord from terminating (or refusing to renew) a tenancy without a "just cause," as explained above. Laws typically require the landlord to list the just cause that underlies the termination. And where the landlord does have a just cause, the termination or nonrenewal period is often longer than that required under general state law.
- **Where to go for help.** Some rent control ordinances require the landlord to tell the tenant where to get information, such as from the local rent board or other administrative agency.

Bypassing the Rent Control Ordinance

Why do landlords generally hate rent control? They don't like being told how to run their business, and they are sure that they would be making more money if they could set the rent at will. But they probably know better than to defy the ordinance directly. So how can landlords get around rent control?

One typical landlord dodge is simply to reduce their operating expenses, thereby increasing their profit (if they turn off the sauna or forgo a needed paint job, that's money saved). Many rent control ordinances address this ploy (under a doctrine known as "decrease in services") and allow you to challenge it directly by bringing it to the attention of the rent board. But there's another way a landlord can work this approach: Many landlords will barter needed maintenance for under-the-table rent. Or they will condition their approval of a perfectly reasonable request (such as giving approval for a new roommate or a sublet for the summer) on some added cash. Desperate for needed services or someone to share the rent, tenants often go along with the deal.

The consequences of playing outside the rules can be serious. For example, if you agree to pay under-the-table rent and are later evicted for failure to pay that rent, you *might* be able to survive the eviction by bringing to light the landlord's illegal circumvention of the rent control law. But you cannot know for sure whether a court will step in and save you from your foolishness and refuse to uphold your waiver. (If your midnight deal with the landlord is especially outrageous and offensive, your chances go up that a judge will throw it out.) In short, you might find yourself injured by your own bad deal.

So think carefully before agreeing to your landlord's scheme. Instead, bring the situation (lack of needed maintenance or a refusal to deal in good faith with your reasonable request for a roommate) to the attention of your rent board. If that proves futile and you agree to the deal, realize that there might be little you can do if the landlord reneges.

Rules to Rent By

- **Get a copy of your rent control laws and study them.** Rent control laws are often complex. Don't assume your landlord understands rent control any better than you do.
- **Contact a local tenants' advocacy group.** Most rent-controlled states and cities have one or more enthusiastic and savvy tenant-oriented community organizations . You can get a lot of information on what goes on "under the hood" from them.
- **Watch out for landlord attempts to get around the ordinance.** Landlords frequently ask tenants to waive their rights under rent control, by asking for more money "under the table" in exchange for service or privileges. If you partake in one of these deals, understand that it's like making a pact with the devil—you might have nowhere to turn if the landlord doesn't come through.

CHAPTER

13

Getting Help With Your Dispute

Chances are, you picked up this book because you're in (or think you soon will be in) a dispute with your landlord. Hopefully, we've been able to give you the legal information you need to figure out whether you or the landlord has the stronger legal position. But knowing the law is one thing; knowing how to use it to your advantage is sometimes another.

It's rarely a good idea to go marching off to a lawyer's office or small claims court the minute you run up against an illegal rental policy or sneaky landlord move, no matter how legally correct your position might be. Negotiation, stressed repeatedly throughout this book, is cheaper and usually less stressful, and often results in solutions that last. However, we are not so naive as to think that every spat can be talked out over coffee and doughnuts. Sometimes you need help. Mediation and, if necessary, suing in small claims court are the next levels of engagement. And in some cases, such as a complicated discrimination lawsuit or a battle involving rent control, you'll need an attorney's help.

TIP

Contact groups that are concerned with tenants' rights. Some communities have citywide tenant associations that can furnish technical and legal advice if you have a dispute with your landlord. A good place to start is the HUD website at HUD.gov. Search "[name of your state] rental help" for a list of state and local tenants' rights groups.

How to Negotiate a Settlement

When you try to resolve a dispute with your landlord, you'll almost always increase your chances for success if you focus on exactly what you want the landlord to do, rather than fighting for the principle involved. Berating your landlord for insensitivity or ignorance might give you a sense of righteous vindication, but won't necessarily bring better results.

Here are some helpful pointers for negotiating with your landlord:

- **Figure out ahead of time exactly what you want to happen.** Do you want to stay, or do you want out of your lease? Will you be satisfied with a sincere apology and pledge to do better, and can you trust the landlord to stick to that promise? Are you willing to compromise? What's your bottom line?
- **Set up an appointment to discuss the problem.** Arrange a quiet time and place, preferably in a neutral location, where you can both express your concerns and work out an agreement.
- **Let the landlord vent.** Once the landlord starts talking, listen closely and don't interrupt, even if some points are not true or some opinions are inflammatory. Whenever you're in a negotiation, listening to the other side's version indicates that you are willing to listen—an essential first step toward an eventual understanding.
- **State that you understand and respect the landlord's key points.** Even if you strongly disagree with your landlord's position, it's often a good idea to restate the other person's concerns as accurately as you can. This should discourage your landlord from endlessly repeating the same point.
- **Avoid personal attacks.** Even if true, suggesting that your landlord is a slumlord or is profiteering at the expense of tenants will only raise the level of hostility and make settlement more difficult. Equally important, it's usually best to stay calm and not to react impulsively or emotionally to your landlord's misstatements.
- **Be courteous, but not weak.** If the law is on your side or you have the firm backing of most other tenants, let the landlord know that you're coming from a position of strength. Make it clear that you prefer negotiating an agreement but, if necessary, you have the resources and evidence to fight and win. If the issue concerns the landlord's failure to follow a state or local code, consider equipping yourself with a copy of the law, which you can bring to the meeting.

- **Emphasize problem solving.** Try to structure the negotiation as a mutual attempt to solve a problem. For instance, if you're complaining about a landlord's policy of entering tenants' apartments unannounced to make repairs, seek solutions that recognize the interests of both parties—for example, an understanding that repairs are necessary and even desirable but that the timing for most can be prearranged (and is required by law in most states).
- **Put yourself in the landlord's shoes.** How would you want to work with unhappy tenants if roles were reversed? Your answer might be something like, "I'd want to feel that I've won." As it turns out, this is a great insight—the best settlements are often those in which both sides feel they've won, or at least have not given up anything fundamental.
- **If you reach an understanding with your landlord, promptly write it down and sign it.** You should volunteer to prepare the first draft—not because you're a glutton for work, but because (as any savvy lawyer will tell you) the person who drafts the document has the upper hand. If you agree to pay the landlord some money as part of the settlement, make it clear that the payment fully satisfies the landlord's claim: "Tenant's $200 payment on August 1, 20xx, fully satisfies any claim Landlord has against Tenant regarding damaged patio furniture."

Using a Mediator

If you're unsuccessful negotiating a settlement with your landlord, or relations are so strained that no meeting seems possible, you might feel ready to give up on the idea of negotiation. This would be a mistake. Instead, the best approach is often to enlist the help of a neutral third-party mediator. Even if your landlord won't speak to you on the phone, a skilled and experienced mediator might be able to convince everyone to come to the negotiating table.

Many people confuse mediation with arbitration, a different legal tool that's seldom, if ever, used in residential landlord-tenant disputes. While both are nonjudicial ways to resolve disputes, there's a huge difference between them: Arbitration, like a lawsuit, results in a binding decision handed down by the arbitrator, who's like a judge. Mediators, by contrast, have no power to impose a decision. Their job is simply to help the parties work out a mutually acceptable solution to their dispute. Put another way, if you and your landlord don't agree on a solution, there is no solution. However, if both sides desire to craft a resolution that *both* want to be binding, they can do so.

Mediation can make especially good sense if:

- Your landlord doesn't realize what a poor job the resident manager or management company has been doing, and you want the opportunity to bring this up.
- You are dealing with a good or at least halfway decent landlord, and you think there's hope for resolution.
- You think the landlord is savvy enough to want to avoid a protracted court battle.

TIP

Mediation can also help resolve roommate disputes. If you and your roommate disagree about noise, overnight guests, or some other issue, consider trying mediation.

Many skeptics are surprised to learn that mediation really does work. One big reason is the cooperative spirit that emerges. By agreeing to mediate a dispute in the first place, you and the landlord implicitly agree to solve your own problems. Also, the fact that no judge or arbitrator has the power to impose what might be an unacceptable solution reduces fear and defensiveness on both sides. This, in turn, often means both landlord and tenant take less extreme—and more conciliatory—positions.

The success of mediation in such a wide range of situations doesn't mean that it's always the right solution, however—sometimes, mediation isn't the best approach. For example, if your landlord has discriminated against you based on your race, your sex, or some other illegal reason, you should probably file a fair housing complaint or a lawsuit, as explained in Chapter 5.

How to Find a Mediation Service

Many cities offer free or low-cost community mediation programs that handle landlord-tenant disputes. For information, call your mayor's or city manager's office and ask for the staff member who handles landlord-tenant mediation matters or housing disputes. That person should refer you to the public office or community group that attempts to resolve landlord-tenant disputes informally—and at little or no cost—before they reach the court stage. You can also get referrals for mediators from the American Arbitration Association (you'll see a list of regional offices by visiting their website at www.adr.org) or a neighborhood dispute resolution center. Colleges and universities often offer mediation services through their housing offices, especially when there is a large student population living in a relatively small town and the school has taken steps to address the quality of student-community relations.

How Mediation Works

Mediation in landlord-tenant disputes is fairly informal. More likely than not, the mediator will have you and your landlord sit down together. Each side is usually asked to discuss all issues they consider important—even emotional ones. This process of airing the entire dispute often cools people off considerably and can lay the foundation for a fairly quick compromise.

If the dispute is not resolved easily, the mediator might suggest ways to resolve the problem, or might even keep everyone talking long enough to realize that the real problem goes deeper than the one being mediated. Typically this is helped along through a process called caucusing, in which each side occupies a separate, private room, with the mediator shuttling back and forth with offers and counteroffers. When settlement appears near, everyone gets back together and the mediator helps guide the parties to an agreement everyone approves.

For example, assume you and your landlord are in a tussle because you have threatened to withhold rent due to a serious defect in the premises, such as a broken heater. In a regular court hearing, this issue would be the only issue considered. In contrast, in the looser mediation process it might come to light that a major part of your grievance is that the manager has been slow to make all types of repairs, and the broken heater is simply the final straw.

You're not the only one who will have a chance to discuss peripheral issues. You might discover that your landlord is angry at you for letting your kids run wild and ruin the garden, or is sick and tired of getting calls from the police responding to noise complaints filed by your neighbors. Once all of this is on the table, a compromise solution might fall easily into place: You could agree to provide better supervision of your kids and cut out overly loud parties in exchange for the manager getting the heat fixed and doing other repairs quickly.

RESOURCE

For more information on the mediation process, see *Mediate, Don't Litigate: Strategies for Successful Mediation,* by Peter Lovenheim and Lisa Guerin (Nolo), which explains mediation from start to finish, including how to get the other side to the mediation table (even if they oppose the idea), prepare for mediation, and draft a legally enforceable agreement. This eBook is available at Nolo.com.

Small Claims Court

If all else fails and you're ready to file a lawsuit, start with small claims court. Unlike regular trial courts, these courts use simplified procedures that are easy for people to handle without lawyers (in fact, in some states lawyers aren't even allowed to represent clients in small claims court).

Small claims court is most appropriate for disputes involving money, rather than disputes in which one side wants a judge to order the other to change his or her behavior. For example, arguments over security deposit refunds are prime candidates for small claims: There is a dispute as to whether the tenant damaged the property, left it a mess, or owes rent, and there is a sum of money at issue. The judge decides whose argument is more credible and orders the money returned or not. If the money isn't returned as ordered, the victor can use that judgment (the official name for the judge's decision) to attach the loser's bank account or garnish the loser's wages.

A case whose resolution involves more than the payment of money, however, isn't always so neatly resolved. For instance, sexual harassment cases often result in orders that the harasser pay the victim damages and that the illegal behavior stop (often some counseling is required, too). If the harasser doesn't obey the judge's orders, the victim has to go back to court and ask the judge to enforce the decision (a judge might do this by slapping the loser with a contempt of court fine). Regular trial courts are often involved in enforcing their decisions, but small claims courts are not set up to do follow-up work. Consequently, small claims judges will hesitate to make orders that, if disobeyed, will land the parties back in their court again.

This said, there are still many landlord-tenant disputes that have monetary resolutions and are appropriate for small claims court. And often when a landlord learns (the hard way) that the consequences of bad behavior are a stiff money judgment, the landlord will change that behavior. For instance, a landlord who fails to adequately maintain the property might get sued by a tenant who is injured by defective conditions. After being ordered to pay the tenant for medical bills and lost work, the landlord is likely to take care of business in the future.

If your case falls within the financial limits on small claims cases (in most states, you can't sue for more than a few thousand dollars), this route is a practical alternative to regular trial court. You can use small claims court to:

- force a landlord to follow through with promises in rental ads
- pressure a landlord to do minor repairs
- comply with an ordinance requiring the payment of interest on security deposits, and
- get your security deposit back.

Learning the Rules

Small claims court procedures are relatively simple and easy to master. Basically, you pay a small fee, file your lawsuit with the court clerk, see to it that the papers are served on your landlord (this can often be done by mail), show up on the appointed day, tell the judge your story, and present any witnesses and other evidence. Often judges will announce their decisions from the bench, or mail them to you within a short time.

Court rules that cover such things as where you file your lawsuit, how legal papers must be delivered to your opponent ("service of process"), and how promptly you must sue are usually available from the small claims clerk or online. In addition, clerks in small claims court are expected to explain procedures to you. In some states, they might even help you fill out the necessary forms, which are quite simple anyhow. If necessary, be persistent in your requests for assistance. If you ask enough questions, you'll get the answers you need to handle your own case comfortably. Also, in some states such as California, you can consult a free small claims court adviser.

Financial Caps on Small Claims Cases

Exactly how much can you sue for in small claims court? The maximum varies from state to state, from $4,000 to $15,000. Call your local court clerk and ask for the small claims division, or look online.

Keep in mind that it might make sense to scale back your claim to fit within the small claims limit, rather than suing for the entire amount in regular trial court. By the time you pay your lawyer and court costs in regular trial court, you might find that you would have come out ahead had you chosen small claims in the first place.

How to Win

Showing up with persuasive evidence that supports your story is the way to win in small claims court. For example, if you are suing your landlord to get your security deposit returned, you'll want to have photographs of a clean and undamaged apartment and the convincing testimony of someone who helped you clean up.

Luckily, you don't have to be a Harvard-trained lawyer to present your evidence, either. People in small claims court aren't usually held to the picky and difficult-to-understand rules of formal court. For example, a judge might be willing to listen to your account of what a repairman had to say about the condition of the furnace in your frigid flat—in formal court, you'd hardly get the words out before the other side would yell "Hearsay!" and shut you down. That's not to say, however, that the judge will necessarily *believe* that the repairperson in fact said what you claim. It's far better to have a written, signed statement from the repairperson, which dispels any suggestion that you are making it all up.

RESOURCE

***Everybody's Guide to Small Claims Court,* by Cara O'Neill (Nolo),** provides detailed advice on bringing or defending a small claims court case, preparing evidence and witnesses for court, and collecting your money judgment when you win. Especially if you have never been to small claims court, you'll want to closely study the material on how to present your testimony and witnesses in court. *Everybody's Guide to Small Claims Court* will also be useful in defending yourself against a landlord who sues you in small claims court—for example, claiming that you owe money for damage to the premises. California tenants should use *Everybody's Guide to Small Claims Court in California,* by Cara O'Neill (Nolo).

When and How to Find a Lawyer

In some instances an attorney's advice or services might be useful—usually in disputes that involve lots of money or are very complicated. For example, if you become involved in a lawsuit over housing discrimination, or claim that your landlord's wrongful acts resulted in your being seriously injured, or face what you feel is an unjustified eviction, you'll likely benefit from a lawyer's help.

The best way to find a suitable attorney is through one or more of these sources:

- **A local tenants' rights organization.** For a list of state and local tenants' rights group, go to the HUD website (HUD.gov) and search "[name of your state] tenant rights."
- **Organizations that focus on a particular area of the law or special interest groups.** Fair housing groups (you'll find a list for your state at HUD.gov) can give referrals for discrimination cases; women's organizations might recommend attorneys who handle sexual harassment cases; and so on.
- **Local legal aid (legal services) office.** Legal aid usually has lawyers who will represent tenants. If you have a limited income, you might be eligible for their services. Even if you are not eligible, the legal aid office might be able to refer you to a good tenants' rights attorney.

Be sure to check a lawyer's experience, references, and fees before signing an engagement letter.

TIP

Disputes over a term of your lease or rental agreement. If your lease or rental agreement has an "attorneys' fees" clause, and your position appears to be a solid winner, the landlord will end up paying for your lawyer if you win. This provision might make your case more attractive to a lawyer.

Rules to Rent By

If you and your landlord are at odds, plan your approach carefully. Keep in mind:

- **You'll catch more flies with honey than with vinegar.** Unless you're facing someone with a Neanderthal's sensitivity, start with a willingness to listen to the landlord's position, however much you disagree. Then explain your side and the (hopefully) persuasive legal reasons you have to back you up.
- **Try mediation before hustling off to court.** Even if the landlord refuses, it's to your advantage to be able to say later to a judge, "I tried to get the landlord to participate but he wouldn't budge."
- **Document every move in a landlord-tenant dispute as if it is, in fact, heading for court.** For example, save copies of letters (and send them certified), take photos, and memorialize conversations in letters of understanding. (See Chapter 2.) If you don't need to go to court, fine; but if all else fails, you will appreciate knowing that you've amassed helpful evidence.
- **If you and the landlord reach a decision, write it down and ask the landlord to review your draft and sign it.**

APPENDIX

A

How to Find Landlord-Tenant Laws Online

Every landlord-tenant relationship is covered by state, local, and federal law. Sometimes, the laws passed by these levels of government overlap—for example, most states and localities have passed their own antidiscrimination laws. When there's overlap on a certain topic, the stricter laws will apply. In practical terms, this usually means that the laws that give tenants the most protection (rights and remedies) will prevail over less-protective laws.

The text of every federal and state statute is available online, free of charge. Rules put out by federal and state regulatory agencies are often available, too. We list below some of the many websites where you can get your hands on legal information. When looking up statutes online, though, consider the source: Many websites don't update content on a regular basis, so you'll need to confirm that you are reading the most recent version of any statute, ordinance, or law.

State Laws

Tenants are primarily concerned with state law. State statutes cover many aspects of the landlord-tenant relationship, including deposits, privacy, discrimination, housing standards, rent rules, repair and maintenance rights and responsibilities, and eviction procedures. We include citations for the major state landlord-tenant laws in Appendix B so that you can do additional research. You'll find more detail on these and other state-by-state laws in the Tenants' section of Nolo.com.

You can easily find state statutes online at Nolo's website: www.nolo.com/legal-research. Under "How to Find a Law," you'll see a link to the Library of Congress's legal research site, where you can click on the name of the state to find a directory of its statutes.

Don't forget to check your state consumer protection agency or attorney general's office—many provide useful publications explaining state laws that affect tenants (but check the publication date closely—some informational booklets are many years old). To find yours, go to USA.gov. Also, be sure to see the links to tenants' rights guides by state in the Tenants' section of Nolo.com.

Local Ordinances

Local ordinances, such as rent control rules, noise regulations, health and safety standards, and antidiscrimination rules also affect tenants. Many municipalities have local ordinances online. Many municipalities have websites—just search for the name of a particular city, and then look for a link to its codes and ordinances when you're on the city's official site. You can also go to State & Local Government on the Net (www.statelocalgov.net) or Municode.com and locate your state and city under the "Code Library" menu link.

Finally, your local public library or office of the city attorney, mayor, or city manager can provide information on local ordinances that affect tenants.

If your rental unit is rent-regulated, be sure to get a copy of the ordinance, as well as all rules issued by the rent board covering rent increases and hearings.

Federal Statutes and Regulations

Congress has enacted laws, and federal agencies such as the U.S. Department of Housing and Urban Development (HUD) have adopted regulations covering discrimination and other issues affecting tenants, such as disclosure of environmental health hazards. We include citations for some of the key federal laws affecting tenants throughout this book. The U.S. Code is the starting place for most federal statutory research. To access the U.S. Code online, visit the Cornell Legal Information Institute's website at www.law.cornell.edu. You can also find the U.S. Code on the U.S. Government Publishing Office's website at www.govinfo.gov.

The Basics of Legal Research

Nolo's Legal Research page at www.nolo.com/legal-research provides a wealth of information on understanding and researching law, including links to state and federal laws, advice on finding local ordinances and court cases, and more. If you want to go further, we recommend *Legal Research: How to Find & Understand the Law*, by the Editors of Nolo (Nolo). This nontechnical book gives easy-to-use step-by-step instructions on how to find legal information.

APPENDIX

B

State Landlord-Tenant Laws

How to Use the State Landlord-Tenant Law Charts

The State Landlord-Tenant Law charts are comprehensive, 50-state charts that give you two kinds of information:

- citations for key statutes and cases, which you can use if you want to read the law yourself or look for more information, and
- the state rules themselves, such as notice periods and deposit limits—in other words, what the statutes and cases say.

When you're looking for information for your state, simply find your state along the left-hand list on the chart, and read to the right—you'll see the statute or case, and the rule.

Your state's landlord-tenant rules might not apply to *your* tenancy. Many states exempt some types of tenancies from their landlord-tenant statutes. In other words, the rules in the following charts might not apply to your rental situation. For example, your state might excuse landlords from applying these rules to the tenancy of a resident property manager. To learn whether your tenancy is exempt from the rules in your state's landlord-tenant statutes, you'll need to review the statutes (our "State Landlord-Tenant Statutes" chart lists them). If your state exempts certain tenancies from its landlord-tenant laws, the exemptions will likely be in a statute whose title contains the word "exclusions," "exemptions," "application," or "applicability."

For more detailed information on the state laws included in Appendix B, as well as information on other state laws, such as those covering abandoned-property and small claims court limits, see the "State Landlord-Tenant Laws" section in the Landlords & Tenants area of Nolo.com.

COVID-Related Emergency Laws and Orders Might Affect These Statutes

The federal government, plus state and local governments, have all passed emergency laws and orders in response to the COVID-19 pandemic. Many of these laws directly affect the landlord-tenant relationship by addressing issues such as evictions, late rent fees, and tenant screening. Emergency laws passed by the federal government (such as the CARES Act) apply to landlords and tenants in all states.

Along with any applicable laws passed by the federal government, landlords and tenants must also follow the laws, orders, and regulations that apply in the state (and city or county) where their rental is located. Each state is handling the situation differently. In some states, governors are issuing emergency orders, while in others the state court or the state legislature (or a combination of any of these branches of government) are creating emergency rules.

As this book went to press, these laws, regulations, and orders were changing daily. Printing in these charts what we know today would be misleading to you when you refer to the chart tomorrow. That's because even when you have a starting point (the first instance of the law or order), it can be very difficult to pin down the most recent version. For example, a governor might have issued an emergency order on April 1, 2020 that laid out details about when landlords can and cannot charge late fees for unpaid rent. However, that April 1, 2020 order might have been amended in August 2020. Most of the time, when you look at the April 1, 2020 order online, there is no indication that it has been amended or repealed.

Because of the rapidly changing nature of these COVID-related laws, there's no way we can accurately and fully address how they affect the charts we provide here in Appendix B. However, we can provide you with some tips and hints about how to find COVID-related emergency laws that might apply to your situation.

COVID-Related Emergency Laws and Orders Might Affect These Statutes (continued)

- **Start by going to your state's designated COVID-19 website.** Every state has one, and you can find it by searching the Internet for your state's name and "official COVID-19 website." From this page, you might be able to access quite a few official COVID-related emergency rules and regulations.
- **Read your state's emergency declaration.** Nearly every state has declared a state of emergency due to the pandemic. Even if the declaration doesn't address landlord-tenant matters, it can provide a launching point for additional research. Most states' emergency declarations can be found on the state's official COVID-19 website or on the governor's official website.
- **Visit your state governor's official website.** Governors' executive orders are the most likely source of regulations that will apply to the landlord-tenant relationship. Look for "emergency orders" or "executive orders." If your state governor's website has a separate category for COVID-related orders, look there first for applicable orders. Regardless, you should also use the website's search function (if it has one), to search for terms such as "rent," "landlord," "tenant," "evict," and "renter" to find relevant orders. Be creative with the terms you search for; not all states use the same terminology.
  - Be warned: Many titles of executive orders consist of only a number or date of when they were issued—the titles usually do not contain other information about the topic of or substance of the order. Also, many executive orders are amended, extended, or repealed by subsequent orders that refer to the original order by nothing more than the original order's number or date—which means that a search of a keyword such as "rent" might not help in finding all the relevant orders. You might have to read through many orders to find any that apply to your situation.

COVID-Related Emergency Laws and Orders Might Affect These Statutes (continued)

- It's helpful to find the very first order that addresses your situation, then read subsequent ones to find out the current status of the original order. If you're still having difficulty, try searching the Internet for your governor's name and the topic you're interested in—many times, this will reveal a press release or news report that will indicate the date when your governor issued the relevant order.

- **Visit your state judicial branch's website.** If the state's highest court has issued any orders relating to COVID-19, the information will likely be linked from the judicial branch's home page. Often, a state's judicial branch will step in with landlord-tenant COVID-19 orders after being directed to do so by the governor. For example, at one point during the pandemic, Virginia's governor encouraged the state's highest court to extend the eviction moratorium, and the court then issued an order doing so.
- **Visit your state legislature's website.** If your state's legislature has passed emergency COVID-related laws, you will most likely find them linked from the legislature's home page. At press time, only a few states' legislatures have passed COVID-19 laws. However, the longer the pandemic drags on, the more likely it is that state legislatures will step in and pass more long-term COVID-related statutes.
- **Search the Internet for news on the issue.** Try searching for your exact question. Most search engines will recognize plain-language queries, and will display relevant results with dates. For example, if you're wondering whether landlords in your state can charge late fees during the pandemic, you could search for "Can landlords charge a late fee in [your state] during COVID-19?"—Look for the most recent posts. Attorney blogs, legal aid websites, news outlet articles, landlord organizations' websites, and tenant rights' groups' websites often have the most accurate and up-to-date information. As with any Internet research project, be sure to evaluate whether the source of the information is a reputable one, and try to find a second or third source to confirm the content.

State Landlord-Tenant Statutes

Here are some of the key statutes pertaining to landlord-tenant law in each state. Your state might exempt certain tenancies from these statutes. If so, you'll likely find any exemption law within the ranges of statutes given in this chart: Look for a statute with the word "exclusions," "exemptions," "application," or "applicability" in the title. In some states, important legal principles are contained in court opinions, not codes or statutes. Court-made law is not reflected in this chart. Also listed below are statutes regulating rent stabilization—rent control—in each state. When a state does not have an applicable statute, the space is left blank.

Alabama	Ala. Code §§ 35-9-1 to 35-9-100; 35-9A-101 to 35-9A-603
Alaska	Alaska Stat. §§ 34.03.010 to 34.03.380
Arizona	Ariz. Rev. Stat. Ann. §§ 12-1171 to 12-1183; 33-301 to 33-381; 33-1301 to 33-1381; 36-1637
Arkansas	Ark. Code Ann. §§ 18-16-101 to 18-16-306; 18-16-501 to 18-16-509; 18-17-101 to 18-17-913
California	Cal. Civ. Code §§ 827; 1925 to 1934; 1940 to 1954.05; 1954.50 to 1954.605; 1961 to 1995.340; 2079.10a; 2924.85; Cal. Health & Safety Code §§ 25400.28; 26147 to 26148; Cal. Bus. & Prof. Code § 8538; Cal. Govt Code § 8589.45
Colorado	Colo. Rev. Stat. §§ 13-40-101 to 13-40-123; 13-40.1-101 to 13-40.1-102; 38-12-101 to 38-12-104; 38-12-301 to 38-12-1007; 38-12-1201 to 38-12-1205
Connecticut	Conn. Gen. Stat. Ann. §§ 47a-1 to 47a-74
Delaware	Del. Code Ann. tit. 25, §§ 5101 to 5907
Dist. of Columbia	D.C. Code Ann. §§ 42-3201 to 42-3651.08; D.C. Mun. Regs., tit. 14, §§ 300 to 399
Florida	Fla. Stat. Ann. §§ 83.40 to 83.683; 404.056; 715.10 to 715.111
Georgia	Ga. Code Ann. §§ 44-1-16; 44-7-1 to 44-7-81
Hawaii	Haw. Rev. Stat. §§ 521-1 to 521-82
Idaho	Idaho Code §§ 6-301 to 6-324; 55-208 to 55-308
Illinois	425 Ill. Comp. Stat. § 60/3; 430 Ill. Comp. Stat. § 135/10; 735 Ill. Comp. Stat. §§ 5/9-201 to 5/9-321; 765 Ill. Comp. Stat. §§ 705/0.01 to 742/30; 750/1 to 750/35; 755/1 to 755/999
Indiana	Ind. Code Ann. §§ 8-1-2-1.2; 32-31-1-1 to 32-31-9-15; 36-1-24.2-1 to 36-1-24.2-4
Iowa	Iowa Code Ann. §§ 562A.1 to 562A.37
Kansas	Kan. Stat. Ann. §§ 58-2501 to 58-2573; 58-25,127; 58-25,137
Kentucky	Ky. Rev. Stat. Ann. §§ 224.1-410; 383.010 to 383.715; 902 Ky. Admin. Regs. 47:200

State Landlord-Tenant Statutes (continued)	
Louisiana	La. Rev. Stat. Ann. §§ 9:3251 to 9:3261.1; La. Civ. Code Ann. Art. 2002; 2668 to 2729
Maine	Me. Rev. Stat. Ann. tit. 14, §§ 6000 to 6046
Maryland	Md. Code Ann. [Real Prop.] §§ 8-101 to 8-604
Massachusetts	Mass. Gen. Laws Ann. ch. 111, § 127L; ch. 186, §§ 1A to 30; ch. 186a, §§ 1 to 6; ch. 239, § 8A
Michigan	Mich. Comp. Laws §§ 125.530; 554.131 to 554.201; 554.601 to 554.641
Minnesota	Minn. Stat. Ann. §§ 504B.001 to 504B.471
Mississippi	Miss. Code Ann. §§ 89-7-1 to 89-8-29
Missouri	Mo. Rev. Stat. §§ 441.005 to 441.920; 442.055; 535.010 to 535.300
Montana	Mont. Code Ann. §§ 70-24-101 to 70-27-117; 75-10-1305
Nebraska	Neb. Rev. Stat. §§ 76-1401 to 76-1449
Nevada	Nev. Rev. Stat. Ann. §§ 40.215 to 40.425; 118A.010 to 118A.530
New Hampshire	N.H. Rev. Stat. Ann. §§ 477:4-g; 540:1 to 540:29; 540-A:1 to 540-A:8; 540-B:1 to 540-B:10
New Jersey	N.J. Stat. Ann. §§ 2A:18-51 to 2A:18-61.67; 2A:42-1 to 2A:42-96; 46:8-1 to 46:8-51; N.J.A.C. §§ 5:10-5.1
New Mexico	N.M. Stat. Ann. §§ 47-8-1 to 47-8-51; N.M. Admin. Code § 20.4.5.13
New York	N.Y. Real Prop. Law §§ 220 to 238; Real Prop. Acts §§ 701 to 853; Mult. Dwell. Law (all); Mult. Res. Law (all); Gen. Oblig. Law §§ 7-101 to 7-109; N.Y. Envtl. Conserv. Law § 27-2405; N.Y. Penal Law §§ 241.00 to 241.05; N.Y. Unconsol. Law §§ 8581 to 8597 (Emergency Housing Rent Control Law); 8601 to 8617 (Local Emergency Housing Rent Control Act); 8621 to 8634 (Emergency Tenant Protection Act)
North Carolina	N.C. Gen. Stat. §§ 42-1 to 42-14.2; 42-25.6 to 42-76
North Dakota	N.D. Cent. Code §§ 23-13-15; 47-06-04; 47-16-01 to 47-16-41; 47-17-01 to 47-17-05
Ohio	Ohio Rev. Code Ann. §§ 5321.01 to 5321.19
Oklahoma	Okla. Stat. Ann. tit. 41, §§ 101 to 136; 201; tit. 74, § 324.11a
Oregon	Or. Rev. Stat. §§ 90.100 to 90.228; 90.243 to 90.265; 90.295 to 90.493; 105.005 to 105.168; 105.190; 479.270 to 479.280
Pennsylvania	68 Pa. Cons. Stat. Ann. §§ 250.101 to 399.18
Rhode Island	R.I. Gen. Laws §§ 34-18-1 to 34-18-57

State Landlord-Tenant Statutes (continued)	
South Carolina	S.C. Code Ann. §§ 5-25-1330; 27-40-10 to 27-40-940
South Dakota	S.D. Codified Laws Ann. §§ 43-32-1 to 43-32-36
Tennessee	Tenn. Code Ann. §§ 66-7-101 to 66-7-102; 66-7-104; 66-7-106 to 66-7-107; 66-7-109 to 66-7-111; 66-28-101 to 66-28-521
Texas	Tex. Prop. Code Ann. §§ 91.001 to 92.355
Utah	Utah Code Ann. §§ 57-17-1 to 57-17-5; 57-22-1 to 57-22-7; 57-27-201; 78B-6-801 to 78B-6-816
Vermont	Vt. Stat. Ann. tit. 9, §§ 4451 to 4469a; 4471 to 4475
Virginia	Va. Code Ann. §§ 54.1-2108.1; 55.1-1200 to 55.1-1259
Washington	Wash. Rev. Code Ann. §§ 59.04.010 to 59.18.912
West Virginia	W.Va. Code §§ 37-6-1 to 37-6A-6; 64-92-6
Wisconsin	Wis. Stat. Ann. §§ 704.01 to 704.95; Wis. Admin. Code ATCP §§ 134.01 to 134.10
Wyoming	Wyo. Stat. §§ 1-21-1001 to 1-21-1016; 1-21-1201 to 1-21-1211; 1-21-1301 to 1-21-1304; 34-2-128 to 34-2-129

State Rent Rules

Here are citations for statutes that set out rent rules in each state. When a state has no statute, the space is left blank. (See the "Notice Required to Change or Terminate a Month-to-Month Tenancy" chart in this appendix for citations to laws about raising rent.)

State	When Rent Is Due	Grace Period	Where Rent Is Due	Late Fees
Alabama	Ala. Code § 35-9A-161 (c)		Ala. Code § 35-9A-161(c)	
Alaska	Alaska Stat. § 34.03.020(c)		Alaska Stat. § 34.03.020(c)	
Arizona	Ariz. Rev. Stat. Ann. §§ 33-1314(C), 33-1368(B)		Ariz. Rev. Stat. Ann. § 33-1314(C)	Ariz. Rev. Stat. Ann. § 33-1368(B) [1]
Arkansas	Ark. Code Ann. § 18-17-401	Ark. Code Ann. §§ 18-17-701 & 18-17-901	Ark. Code Ann. § 18-17-401	
California	Cal. Civ. Code § 1947		Cal. Civ. Code § 1962	*Orozco v. Casimiro*, 121 Cal.App.4th Supp. 7 (2004) [2]
Colorado				
Connecticut	Conn. Gen. Stat. Ann. § 47a-3a	Conn. Gen. Stat. Ann. § 47a-15a	Conn. Gen. Stat. Ann. § 47a-3a	Conn. Gen. Stat. Ann. §§ 47a-4(a)(8), 47a-15a [3]
Delaware	Del. Code Ann. tit. 25, § 5501(b)		Del. Code Ann. tit. 25, § 5501(b)	Del. Code Ann. tit. 25, § 5501(d) [4]
Dist. of Columbia		D.C. Code Ann. § 42-3505.31		D.C. Code Ann. § 42-3505.31 [5]
Florida	Fla. Stat. Ann. § 83.46(1)			
Georgia [6]				

1 Late fees must be set forth in a written rental agreement and be reasonable. (Arizona)

2 Late fees will be enforced only if specified language is included in a written lease or rental agreement. (California)

3 Landlords may not charge a late fee until 9 days after rent is due. (Connecticut)

4 To charge a late fee, landlord must maintain an office in the county where the rental unit is located, where tenants can pay rent. If a landlord doesn't have a local office for this purpose, tenant has 3 extra days (beyond the rent due date) to pay rent before the landlord can charge a late fee. Late fee cannot exceed 5% of rent and cannot be imposed until the rent is more than 5 days late. (Delaware)

5 Fee policy (including a statement of the maximum amount of late fees that may be charged) must be stated in the lease, and cannot exceed 5% of rent due or be imposed until rent is five days late (or later, if lease so provides). Landlord cannot evict for failure to pay late fee (may deduct unpaid fees from security deposit at end of tenancy). During a declared public emergency, landlords may not impose a late fee. (District of Columbia)

6 Although there is no specific statute regarding late fees, Georgia law states that all contracts for rent bear interest from the time rent is due. (Georgia)

State Rent Rules (continued)

State	When Rent Is Due	Grace Period	Where Rent Is Due	Late Fees
Hawaii	Haw. Rev. Stat. § 521-21(b)		Haw. Rev. Stat. § 521-21(b)	Haw. Rev. Stat. § 521-21(f) [7]
Idaho				
Illinois	735 Ill. Comp. Stat. Ann. § 5/9-218		735 Ill. Comp. Stat. Ann. § 5/9-218	
Indiana	*Watson v. Penn,* 108 Ind. 21 (1886), 8 N.E. 636 (1886)			
Iowa	Iowa Code Ann. § 562A.9(3)		Iowa Code Ann. § 562A.9(3)	Iowa Code Ann. § 562A.9(4) [8]
Kansas	Kan. Stat. Ann. § 58-2545(c)		Kan. Stat. Ann. § 58-2545(c)	
Kentucky	Ky. Rev. Stat. Ann. § 383.565(2)		Ky. Rev. Stat. Ann. § 383.565(2)	
Louisiana	La. Civ. Code Ann. art. 2703		La. Civ. Code Ann. art. 2703	
Maine		Me. Rev. Stat. Ann. tit. 14, § 6028		Me. Rev. Stat. Ann. tit. 14, § 6028 [9]
Maryland				Md. Code Ann. [Real Prop.] § 8-208(d)(3) [10]
Massachusetts		Mass. Gen. Laws Ann. ch. 186, § 15B(1)(c); ch. 239, § 8A		Mass. Gen. Laws Ann. ch. 186, § 15B(1)(c) [11]
Michigan	*Hilsendegen v. Scheich,* 21 N.W. 894 (1885)			

7 Late charge cannot exceed 8% of the amount of rent due. (Hawaii)

8 When rent is $700 per month or less, late fees cannot exceed $12 per day, or a total amount of $60 per month; when rent is more than $700 per month, fees cannot exceed $20 per day or a total amount of $100 per month. (Iowa)

9 Late fees cannot exceed 4% of the amount due for 30 days. Landlord must notify tenants, in writing, of any late fee at the start of the tenancy, and cannot impose it until rent is 15 days late. (Maine)

10 Late fees cannot exceed 5% of the rent due. (Maryland)

11 Late fees, including interest on late rent, may not be imposed until the rent is 30 days late. So long as the act providing for an eviction moratorium (Chapter 65 of the Acts of 2020) is in force, landlords may not impose late fees if, within 30 days of the rent due date, tenants provide documentation that the nonpayment was due to a financial impact from COVID-19. (Massachusetts)

State Rent Rules (continued)

State	When Rent Is Due	Grace Period	Where Rent Is Due	Late Fees
Minnesota				Minn. Stat. Ann. § 540B.177 [12]
Mississippi				
Missouri	Mo. Rev. Stat. § 535.060			
Montana	Mont. Code Ann. § 70-24-201(2)(c)		Mont. Code Ann. § 70-24-201(2)(b)	
Nebraska	Neb. Rev. Stat. § 76-1414(3)		Neb. Rev. Stat. § 76-1414(3)	
Nevada	Nev. Rev. Stat. Ann. § 118A.210		Nev. Rev. Stat. Ann. § 118A.200	Nev. Rev. Stat. Ann. §§ 118A.200, 118A.210(4) [13]
New Hampshire				N.H. Rev. Stat. § 540:8 [14]
New Jersey		N.J. Stat. Ann. § 2A:42-6.1	N.J. Stat. Ann. § 2A:42-6.1	N.J. Stat. Ann. § 2A:42-6.1 [15]
New Mexico	N.M. Stat. Ann. § 47-8-15(B)		N.M. Stat. Ann § 47-8-15(B)	N.M. Stat. Ann. § 47-8-15(D) [16]
New York		N.Y. Real Prop. Law § 238-a		N.Y. Real Prop. Law § 238-a [17]

[12] Late fee policy must be agreed to in writing, and may not exceed 8% of the overdue rent payment. The "due date" for late fee purposes does not include a date earlier than the usual rent due date, by which date a tenant earns a discount. (Minnesota)

[13] A court will presume that there is no late fee provision unless it is included in a written rental agreement, but the landlord can offer evidence to overcome that presumption. Landlord may charge a reasonable late fee as set forth in the rental agreement, but it cannot exceed 5% of the amount of the periodic rent, and the maximum amount of the late fee must not be increased based upon a late fee that was previously imposed. (Nevada)

[14] Landlord cannot demand an amount greater than the the whole rent in arrears when rent is late. (New Hampshire)

[15] Landlord must wait 5 business days before charging a late fee, but only when the premises are rented or leased by senior citizens receiving Social Security Old Age Pensions, Railroad Retirement Pensions, or other governmental pensions in lieu of Social Security Old Age Pensions; or when rented by recipients of Social Security Disability Benefits, Supplemental Security Income, or benefits under Work First New Jersey. (New Jersey)

[16] Late fee policy must be in the lease or rental agreement and may not exceed 10% of the rent specified per rental period. Landlord must notify the tenant of the landlord's intent to impose the charge no later than the last day of the next rental period immediately following the period in which the default occurred. (New Mexico)

[17] Landlord must wait five days after the rent due date before imposing a late fee. A late fee may not be more than $50 or 5% of the rent, whichever is less. (New York)

State Rent Rules (continued)

State	When Rent Is Due	Grace Period	Where Rent Is Due	Late Fees
North Carolina		N.C. Gen. Stat. § 42-46		N.C. Gen. Stat. § 42-46 [18]
North Dakota	N.D. Cent. Code § 47-16-20			
Ohio				
Oklahoma	Okla. Stat. Ann. tit. 41, § 109	Okla. Stat. Ann. tit. 41, § 132(B)	Okla. Stat. Ann. tit. 41, § 109	*Sun Ridge Investors, Ltd. v. Parker*, 956 P.2d 876 (1998) [19]
Oregon	Or. Rev. Stat. § 90.220	Or. Rev. Stat. § 90.260	Or. Rev. Stat. § 90.220	Or. Rev. Stat. § 90.260 [20]
Pennsylvania				
Rhode Island	R.I. Gen. Laws § 34-18-15(c)	R.I. Gen. Laws § 34-18-35	R.I. Gen. Laws § 34-18-15(c)	
South Carolina	S.C. Code Ann. § 27-40-310(c)		S.C. Code Ann. § 27-40-310(c)	
South Dakota	S.D. Codified Laws Ann. § 43-32-12			
Tennessee	Tenn. Code Ann. § 66-28-201(c)	Tenn. Code Ann. § 66-28-201(d)	Tenn. Code Ann. § 66-28-201(c)	Tenn. Code Ann. § 66-28-201(d) [21]
Texas		Tex. Prop. Code Ann. § 92.019		Tex. Prop. Code Ann. §§ 92.019, 92.0191 [22]

18 Late fee when rent is due monthly cannot be higher than $15 or 5% of the rental payment, whichever is greater (when rent is due weekly, may not be higher than $4.00 or 5% of the rent, whichever is greater); and may not be imposed until the rent is 5 days late. A late fee may be imposed only one time for each late rental payment. A late fee for a specific late rental payment may not be deducted from a subsequent rental payment so as to cause the subsequent rental payment to be in default. (North Carolina)

19 Preset late fees are invalid. (Oklahoma)

20 Landlord must wait 4 days after the rent due date before imposing a late fee, and must disclose the late fee policy in the rental agreement. A flat fee must be "reasonable." A daily late fee may not be more than 6% of a reasonable flat fee, and cannot add up to more than 5% of the monthly rent. (Oregon)

21 Landlord can't charge a late fee until the rent is 5 days late (the day rent is due is counted as the first day). If day five is a Sunday or legal holiday, landlord cannot impose a fee if the rent is paid on the next business day. Fee can't exceed 10% of the amount past due. (Tennessee)

22 Late fee provision must be included in a written lease and cannot be imposed until the rent remains unpaid two full days after the date it is due. The fee must be reasonable: For properties that have four or fewer units, it cannot be more than 12% of the rent; for properties that have more than four units, it cannot be more than 10% of the rent; OR it must be related to the late payment of rent (such as expenses, costs, and overhead associated with the collection of late payment). Landlord may charge an initial fee and a daily fee for each day the rent is late—the combined fees are considered a single late fee. Tenants can ask landlords to provide statement of whether they owe late fees. (Texas)

State Rent Rules (continued)

State	When Rent Is Due	Grace Period	Where Rent Is Due	Late Fees
Utah				
Vermont	Vt. Stat. Ann. tit. 9, § 4455			
Virginia	Va. Code Ann. § 55.1-1204	Va. Code Ann. § 55.1-1204	Va. Code Ann. § 55.1-1204	Va. Code Ann. § 55.1-1204 [23]
Washington		Wash. Rev. Code Ann. § 59.18.170		Wash. Rev. Code Ann. § 59.18.285 [24]
West Virginia				
Wisconsin				
Wyoming				

[23] Landlords cannot charge a tenant a late fee unless it is provided for in a written rental agreement or lease. No late charge shall exceed the lesser of 10% of the periodic rent or 10% of the remaining balance due and owed by the tenant. (Virginia)

[24] Nonrefundable fees must be described in lease or rental agreement; otherwise, they will be considered to be deposits. Landlords may not impose late fees until the rent is more than five days late. The fee may commence as of the first day the rent is overdue, and landlords may serve a notice to pay rent or quit as soon as the rent is overdue. If tenants can demonstrate in writing that their primary source of income is a regular, monthly source of governmental assistance that is not received until after the date rent is due in the rental agreement, landlords must adjust rental due date (to no more than five days after the date specified in the rental agreement). (Washington)

Notice Required to Change or Terminate a Month-to-Month Tenancy

Except where noted, the amount of notice a landlord must give to increase rent or change another term of the rental agreement in a month-to-month tenancy is the same as that required to end a month-to-month tenancy. Be sure to check state and local rent control laws, which might have different notice requirements.

State	Tenant	Landlord	Statute	Comments
Alabama	30 days	30 days	Ala. Code § 35-9A-441	No state statute on the amount of notice required to change rent or other terms.
Alaska	30 days	30 days	Alaska Stat. § 34.03.290(b)	No state statute on the amount of notice required to change rent or other terms.
Arizona	30 days	30 days	Ariz. Rev. Stat. Ann. §§ 33-1342, 33-1375	Landlords may adopt new rules and regulations that don't substantially modify the rental agreement after giving the tenant 30 days' notice.
Arkansas	30 days	30 days	Ark. Code Ann. § 18-17-704	No state statute on the amount of notice required to change rent or other terms.
California	30 days	30 days to terminate; 30-60+ days to change terms or increase rent, depending on size of increase	Cal. Civ. Code §§ 827, 1946	At least 30 days' notice to change rental terms, but if the change is a proposed rent increase of more than 10% of the rental amount charged to that tenant at any time during the 12 months prior to the effective date of the increase, either in and of itself or when combined with any other rent increases for the 12 months prior to the effective date of the increase, then an additional 30 days' notice is required.
Colorado	21 days	21 days	Colo. Rev. Stat. § 13-40-107	No state statute on the amount of notice required to change rent or other terms.

Notice Required to Change or Terminate a Month-to-Month Tenancy (continued)

State	Tenant	Landlord	Statute	Comments
Connecticut		3 days	Conn. Gen. Stat. Ann. §§ 47a-9, 47a-23	Landlord must provide 3 days' notice to terminate tenancy. Landlord is not required to give a particular amount of notice of a proposed rent increase unless prior notice was previously agreed upon. If landlord makes a new rule or regulation resulting in a substantial modification of the rental agreement, it is not valid unless tenant agrees to it in writing.
Delaware	60 days	60 days	Del. Code Ann. tit. 25, §§ 5106, 5107	For termination, the 60-day notice period begins on the first day of the month following the day of actual notice. For change of terms, upon receiving notice of landlord's proposed change of terms tenant has 15 days to terminate tenancy. Otherwise, changes will take effect as announced.
Dist. of Columbia	30 days	30 days	D.C. Code Ann. §§ 42-3202, 42-3509.04(b)	No rent increases shall be effective until the first day on which rent is normally paid occurring more than 30 days after notice of the increase is given to the tenant.
Florida	15 days	15 days	Fla. Stat. Ann. § 83.57	No state statute on the amount of notice required to change rent or other terms.
Georgia	30 days	60 days	Ga. Code Ann. §§ 44-7-6 & 44-7-7	No state statute on the amount of notice required to change rent or other terms.
Hawaii	28 days	45 days	Haw. Rev. Stat. §§ 521-71, 521-21(d)	Landlord shall not increase rent without written notice given 45 consecutive days prior to the effective date of the increase. The landlord may terminate the rental agreement by notifying the tenant, in writing, at least 45 days in advance of the anticipated termination. The tenant may terminate the rental agreement by notifying the landlord, in writing, at least 28 days in advance of the anticipated termination.

Notice Required to Change or Terminate a Month-to-Month Tenancy (continued)

State	Tenant	Landlord	Statute	Comments
Idaho	One month	15 or 30 days	Idaho Code §§ 55-208, 55-307	A "month" means a calendar month. For landlords: 30 days' notice to increase rent or end tenancy; 15 days' notice to change terms of lease other than rent.
Illinois	30 days	30 days	735 Ill. Comp. Stat. § 5/9-207	No state statute on the amount of notice required to change rent or other terms.
Indiana	One month	One month	Ind. Code Ann. §§ 32-31-1-1, 3 2-31-5-4	Unless agreement states otherwise, landlord must give 30 days' written notice to modify written rental agreement.
Iowa	30 days	30 days	Iowa Code Ann. §§ 562A.34, 562A.13(5)	To end or change a month-to-month agreement, landlord must give written notice at least 30 days before the next time rent is due (not including any grace period). Each tenant shall be notified, in writing, of any rent increase at least 30 days before the effective date. Such effective date shall not be sooner than the expiration date of original rental agreement or any renewal or extension thereof.
Kansas	30 days	30 days	Kan. Stat. Ann. §§ 58-2556, 58-2570	After the tenant enters into the rental agreement, if a rule or regulation that effects a substantial modification of the rental agreement is adopted, such rule or regulation isn't enforceable against the tenant unless the tenant consents to it in writing.
Kentucky	30 days	30 days	Ky. Rev. Stat. Ann. §§ 383.610, 383.695	If a rule or regulation is adopted after the tenant enters into the rental agreement that works a substantial modification of the bargain, it is not valid unless the tenant consents to it in writing.
Louisiana	10 days	10 days	La. Civ. Code art. 2728	No state statute on the amount of notice required to change rent or other terms.

Notice Required to Change or Terminate a Month-to-Month Tenancy (continued)

State	Tenant	Landlord	Statute	Comments
Maine	30 days	30 days	Me. Rev. Stat. Ann. tit. 14 §§ 6002, 6015	Landlord must provide 45 days' notice to increase rent.
Maryland	One month	One month	Md. Code Ann. [Real Prop.] § 8-402(b)(3), (b)(4)	Two months' notice required in Montgomery County (single-family rentals excepted) and Baltimore City.
Massachusetts	See comments	See comments	Mass. Gen. Laws Ann. ch. 186, § 12	Interval between days of payment or 30 days, whichever is longer.
Michigan	One month	One month	Mich. Comp. Laws § 554.134	No state statute on the amount of notice required to change rent or other terms.
Minnesota	See comments	See comments	Minn. Stat. Ann. § 504B.135	For terminations, interval between time rent is due or three months, whichever is less; no state statute on the amount of notice required to change rent or other terms.
Mississippi	30 days	30 days	Miss. Code Ann. § 89-8-19	No state statute on the amount of notice required to change rent or other terms.
Missouri	One month	One month	Mo. Rev. Stat. § 441.060	No state statute on the amount of notice required to change rent or other terms.
Montana	30 days	30 days	Mont. Code Ann. §§ 70-24-441, 70-26-109	Landlord may change terms of tenancy with 15 days' notice.
Nebraska	30 days	30 days	Neb. Rev. Stat. §§ 76-1422, 76-1437	A rule or regulation adopted after the tenant enters into the rental agreement is enforceable if the landlord gives reasonable notice to tenant of its adoption and if it doesn't substantially modify the rental agreement.

Notice Required to Change or Terminate a Month-to-Month Tenancy (continued)

State	Tenant	Landlord	Statute	Comments
Nevada	30 days	30 days	Nev. Rev. Stat. Ann. §§ 40.251, 118A.300	Landlords must provide 45 days' notice to increase rent. Tenants 60 years old or older, or physically or mentally disabled, may request an additional 30 days' possession, but only if they have complied with basic tenant obligations as set forth in Nev. Rev. Stat. Chapter 118A (termination notices must include this information).
New Hampshire	30 days	30 days	N.H. Rev. Stat. Ann. §§ 540:2, 540:3, 540:11	Landlord may terminate only for just cause. Tenant's termination: If the date of termination given in the notice does not coincide with the rent due date, tenant is responsible for the rent for the entire month in which the notice expires, up to the next rent due date, unless the terms of the rental agreement provide otherwise.
New Jersey	One month	One month	N.J. Stat. Ann. §§ 2A:18-56, 2A:18-61.1	Landlord may terminate only for just cause. The landlord may increase the rent only at the beginning of the term of the agreement. The landlord cannot increase the rent while an agreement exists. The landlord must offer the tenant the option of entering into a new agreement, at the increased rental rate, after the old agreement expires. If the tenant doesn't sign the new agreement and doesn't move at the expiration of the old agreement, and has been given a valid notice to quit and notice of rent increase, a new tenancy is automatically created at the increased rental rate. New Jersey landlords should check local ordinances, as they might have different rules regarding rent increase notice.

Notice Required to Change or Terminate a Month-to-Month Tenancy (continued)

State	Tenant	Landlord	Statute	Comments
New Mexico	30 days	30 days	N.M. Stat. Ann. §§ 47-8-37, 47-8-15(F)	Landlord must deliver rent increase notice at least 30 days before rent due date.
New York	One month, within NYC and statewide	Within NYC and statewide, 30 to 90 days for terminations and rent increases of 5% or more	N.Y. Real Prop. Law §§ 226-c, 232-b	Terminations and rent increases of 5% over existing rent: Tenants occupying for a year or having a lease of at least one year: 30 days' notice. Tenants occupying from one to two years and lease holders of one- to two-year leases: 60 days' notice. Tenants occupying more than two years or having leases of two years or more: 90 days' notice.
North Carolina	7 days	7 days	N.C. Gen. Stat. § 42-14	No state statute on the amount of notice required to change rent or other terms.
North Dakota	One calendar month	One calendar month	N.D. Cent. Code §§ 47-16-07, 47-16-15	Landlord may change the terms of the lease to take effect at the expiration of the month upon giving notice in writing at least 30 days before the expiration of the month. Tenant may terminate with 25 days' notice if landlord has changed the terms of the agreement.
Ohio	30 days	30 days	Ohio Rev. Code Ann. § 5321.17	No state statute on the amount of notice required to change rent or other terms.
Oklahoma	30 days	30 days	Okla. Stat. Ann. tit. 41, § 111	No state statute on the amount of notice required to change rent or other terms.

Notice Required to Change or Terminate a Month-to-Month Tenancy (continued)				
State	**Tenant**	**Landlord**	**Statute**	**Comments**
Oregon	30 days, or 72 hours (lack of bedroom exit only)	Termination: 30 days within the first year; 90 days after that, only for cause. Rent increase: See comments	Or. Rev. Stat. §§ 90.275, 90.323, 90.427, 90.460, 91.070	When the rental is in the same building or on the same property as the landlord's residence, and the property has no more than two dwelling units, unique termination periods and notice requirements apply. Temporary occupants are not entitled to notice. No rent increase during the first year of the tenancy. After that, 90 days, and rent cannot be increased more than 7% plus the consumer price index (CPI) above the existing rent during any 12-month period. Landlords are excepted from the 7%+CPI increase limit if either: the unit's first certificate of occupancy was issued less than 15 years from the date of the rent increase notice, or landlord accepts reduced rent as part of a federal, state, or local program or subsidy.
Pennsylvania		15 days	68 Pa. Stat. Ann. § 250.501	At the end of the term or due to a breach of the lease landlord must give 15 days' notice to terminate. If notice to terminate is due to tenant's failure to pay rent, notice required is 10 days.
Rhode Island	30 days	30 days	R.I. Gen. Laws §§ 34-18-16.1, 34-18-37	Landlord must provide 30 days' notice to increase rent if tenant is age 62 or younger; if tenant is over 62 years old, landlord must provide 60 days' notice.
South Carolina	30 days	30 days	S.C. Code Ann. §§ 27-40-520, 27-40-770	Rules or regulations adopted after a tenant enters into a rental agreement do not apply to a tenant if the rules or regulations substantially modify the tenant's agreement with landlord and, after receiving notice upon adoption of the right to object, the tenant objects in writing to the landlord within 30 days after the rules are made.

Notice Required to Change or Terminate a Month-to-Month Tenancy (continued)				
State	**Tenant**	**Landlord**	**Statute**	**Comments**
South Dakota	One month	One month	S.D. Codified Laws Ann. §§ 43-8-8, 43-32-13	If tenant (or spouse or minor child) is in active duty in the military, landlord must give two months' notice (unless there is tenant misconduct, a sale of the property, or the property has passed into the landlord's estate). Landlord must give at least 30 days' notice to modify lease (including rent amount). Tenant may terminate lease within 15 days of receipt of the notice of modification.
Tennessee	30 days	30 days	Tenn. Code Ann. §§ 66-28-402, 66-28-512	A rule or regulation adopted after the tenant enters into the rental agreement is enforceable against the tenant if reasonable notice of its adoption is given to the tenant and it does not work a substantial modification of the rental agreement.
Texas	One month	One month	Tex. Prop. Code Ann. §§ 91.001, 92.013	Landlord and tenant may agree in writing to different notice periods, or none at all. No state statute on the amount of notice required to change rent or other terms. A landlord shall give prior written notice to a tenant regarding a landlord rule or policy change that is not included in the lease agreement and that will affect any personal property owned by the tenant that is located outside the tenant's dwelling.
Utah		15 days	Utah Code Ann. § 78B-6-802	No state statute on the amount of notice required to change rent or other terms.
Vermont	One rental period, unless written lease says otherwise	30 days	Vt. Code Ann. tit. 9, §§ 4456(d), 4467	If there is no written rental agreement, for tenants who have continuously resided in the unit for two years or less, 60 days' notice to terminate; for those who have resided longer than two years, 90 days. If there is a written rental agreement, for tenants who have lived continuously in the unit for two years or less, 30 days; for those who have lived there longer than two years, 60 days.

Notice Required to Change or Terminate a Month-to-Month Tenancy (continued)

State	Tenant	Landlord	Statute	Comments
Virginia	30 days	30 days	Va. Code Ann. §§ 55.1-1204, 55.1-1253	Rental agreement may provide for a different notice period. By operation of law, month-to-month tenant who does not have a written agreement has a 12-month lease, whose terms and conditions cannot be changed except by agreement of the parties.
Washington	20 days; tenants who are members of the armed forces (as well as their spouses and dependents) may give less than 20 days' notice if they receive permanent change of station or deployment orders that don't allow a 20-day written notice.	20 days; when landlord plans to convert apartments to condominiums that are separately owned, or plans to demolish, substantially remodel, or change the use of the premises, the landlord shall provide tenants with at least 120 days' written notice of termination.	Wash. Rev. Code Ann. §§ 59.18.140, 59.18.200	Landlord must give 60 days' notice to change rent, and any increase in rent may not become effective before the end of the term of the rental agreement, but if the rental is a subsidized tenancy, landlord can give 30 days' notice. If the landlord plans to change rental agreement to exclude children, the landlord shall give tenant at least 90 days' notice. All other changes require 30 days' written notice.
West Virginia	One month	One month	W.Va. Code § 37-6-5	No state statute on the amount of notice required to change rent or other terms.
Wisconsin	28 days	28 days	Wis. Stat. Ann. § 704.19	No state statute on the amount of notice required to change rent or other terms.
Wyoming			No statute	

State Security Deposit Rules

Here are the statutes and rules that govern a landlord's collection and retention of security deposits. Many states require landlords to disclose, at or near the time they collect the deposit, information about how deposits may be used, as noted in the Disclosure or Requirement section.

Alabama

Ala. Code § 35-9A-201

Limit: One month's rent, except for pet deposits, deposits to cover undoing tenant's alterations, and deposits to cover tenant activities that pose increased liability risks.

Deadline for Landlord to Itemize and Return Deposit: 60 days after termination of tenancy and delivery of possession.

Alaska

Alaska Stat. § 34.03.070

Limit: Two months' rent, unless rent exceeds $2,000 per month. Landlord may ask for an additional month's rent as deposit for a pet that is not a service animal, but may use it only to remedy pet damage.

Disclosure or Requirement: Orally or in writing, landlord must disclose the conditions under which landlord may withhold all or part of the deposit.

Separate Account: Required (but may commingle prepaid rent with security deposits).

Advance notice of deduction: Not required.

Deadline for Landlord to Itemize and Return Deposit: 14 days if the tenant gives proper notice to terminate tenancy; 30 days if the tenant does not give proper notice or if landlord has deducted amounts needed to remedy damage caused by tenant's failure to maintain the property (Alaska Stat. § 34.03.120).

Arizona

Ariz. Rev. Stat. Ann. § 33-1321

Limit: One and one-half months' rent.

Disclosure or Requirement: If landlord collects a nonrefundable fee, its purpose must be stated in writing. All fees not designated as nonrefundable are refundable.

Advance notice of deduction: Not required.

Deadline for Landlord to Itemize and Return Deposit: 14 days; tenant has the right to be present at final inspection.

Arkansas

Ark. Code Ann. §§ 18-16-301 to 18-16-305

Exemption: Security deposit rules do not apply to the following unless the management of the rental (including rent collection) is performed by a third party for a fee: Dwellings owned by an individual, if the individual, the individual's spouse and minor children, and any and all partnerships, corporations, or other legal entities formed for the purpose of renting dwelling units and of which they are officers, owners, or majority shareholders own, or collectively own, five or fewer units.

Limit: Two months' rent.

Advance notice of deduction: Not required.

Deadline for Landlord to Itemize and Return Deposit: 60 days.

State Security Deposit Rules (continued)

California

Cal. Civ. Code §§ 1940.5(g), 1950.5

Limit: Two months' rent (unfurnished); 3 months' rent (furnished). If the tenant is an active service member, no more than one month's rent (unfurnished) or two months' rent (furnished). Add extra one-half month's rent for waterbed.

Advance notice of deduction: Required.

Deadline for Landlord to Itemize and Return Deposit: 21 days.

Colorado

Colo. Rev. Stat. §§ 38-12-102 to 38-12-104

Limit: No statutory limit.

Advance notice of deduction: Not required.

Deadline for Landlord to Itemize and Return Deposit: One month, unless lease agreement specifies longer period of time (which may be no more than 60 days); 72 hours (not counting weekends or holidays) if a hazardous condition involving gas equipment requires tenant to vacate.

Connecticut

Conn. Gen. Stat. Ann. § 47a-21

Limit: Two months' rent (tenant under 62 years of age); one month's rent (tenant 62 years of age or older). Tenants who paid a deposit in excess of one month's rent, who then turn 62 years old, are entitled, upon request, to a refund of the amount that exceeds one month's rent.

Separate Account: Required.

Interest Payment: Interest payments must be made annually (or credited toward rent, at the landlord's option) and no later than 30 days after termination of tenancy. The interest rate must be equal to the average rate paid on savings deposits by insured commercial banks, rounded to the nearest 0.1%, as published by the Federal Reserve Board Bulletin.

Advance notice of deduction: Not required.

Deadline for Landlord to Itemize and Return Deposit: 30 days, or within 15 days of receiving tenant's forwarding address, whichever is later.

Delaware

Del. Code Ann. tit. 25, §§ 5311, 5514

Limit: One month's rent on leases for one year or more. For month-to-month tenancies, no limit for the first year, but after that, the limit is one month's rent (at the expiration of one year, landlord must give tenant a credit for any deposit held by the landlord that is in excess of one month's rent). No limit for furnished units. Tenant may offer to supply a surety bond in lieu of or in conjunction with a deposit, which landlord may elect to receive.

Separate Account: Required. Orally or in writing, the landlord must disclose to the tenant the location of the security deposit account.

Advance notice of deduction: Not required.

Deadline for Landlord to Itemize and Return Deposit: 20 days.

State Security Deposit Rules (continued)

District of Columbia

D.C. Code Ann. § 42-3502.17; D.C. Mun. Regs. tit. 14, §§ 308 to 310

Exemption: Landlords cannot demand or receive a security deposit from a tenant in a rental unit occupied by the tenant as of July 17, 1985, when no security deposit had been required prior to that date.

Limit: One month's rent.

Disclosure or Requirement: In the lease, rental agreement, or receipt, landlord must state the terms and conditions under which the security deposit was collected (to secure tenant's obligations under the lease or rental agreement).

Separate Account: Required.

Interest Payment: Interest payments at the prevailing statement savings rate must be made at termination of tenancy.

Advance notice of deduction: Not required.

Deadline for Landlord to Itemize and Return Deposit: 45 days.

Florida

Fla. Stat. Ann. §§ 83.43(12), 83.49

Limit: No statutory limit.

Disclosure or Requirement: Within 30 days of receiving the security deposit, the landlord must disclose in writing whether it will be held in an interest- or non-interest-bearing account; the name of the account depository; and the rate and time of interest payments. Landlord who collects a deposit must include in the lease the disclosure statement contained in Florida Statutes § 83.49.

Separate Account: Landlord may post a security bond securing all tenants' deposits instead.

Interest Payment: Interest payments, if any (account need not be interest-bearing) must be made annually and at termination of tenancy. However, no interest is due a tenant who wrongfully terminates the tenancy before the end of the rental term.

Advance notice of deduction: Required.

Deadline for Landlord to Itemize and Return Deposit: 15 to 60 days depending on whether tenant disputes deductions.

Georgia

Ga. Code Ann. §§ 44-7-30 to 44-7-37

Exemption: Landlord who owns ten or fewer rental units, unless these units are managed by an outside party, need not supply written list of preexisting damage, nor place deposit in an escrow account. Rules for returning the deposit still apply.

Limit: No statutory limit.

Disclosure or Requirement: Landlord must give tenant a written list of preexisting damage to the rental before collecting a security deposit.

Separate Account: Required. Landlord must place the deposit in an escrow account in a state- or federally regulated depository, and must inform the tenant of the location of this account. Landlord may post a security bond securing all tenants' deposits instead.

State Security Deposit Rules (continued)

Advance notice of deduction: Required.

Deadline for Landlord to Itemize and Return Deposit: 30 days

Hawaii

Haw. Rev. Stat. § 521-44

Limit: One month's rent. Landlord may require an additional one month's rent as security deposit for tenants who keep a pet.

Advance notice of deduction: Not required.

Deadline for Landlord to Itemize and Return Deposit: 14 days.

Idaho

Idaho Code § 6-321

Limit: No statutory limit.

Advance notice of deduction: Not required.

Deadline for Landlord to Itemize and Return Deposit: 21 days, or up to 30 days if landlord and tenant agree.

Illinois

765 Ill. Comp. Stat. 710/1; 715/1 to 715/3

Limit: No statutory limit.

Disclosure or Requirement: If a lease specifies the cost for repair, cleaning, or replacement of any part of the leased premises; or the cleaning or repair of any component of the building or common area that will not be replaced, the landlord may withhold the dollar amount specified in the lease. Landlord's itemized statement must reference the specified dollar amount(s) and include a copy of the lease clause.

Interest Payment: Landlords who rent 25 or more units in either a single building or a complex located on contiguous properties must pay interest on deposits held for more than six months. The interest rate is the rate paid for minimum deposit savings accounts by the largest commercial bank in the state, as of December 31 of the calendar year immediately preceding the start of the tenancy. Within 30 days after the end of each 12-month rental period, landlord must pay any interest that has accumulated to an amount of $5 or more, by cash or credit applied to rent due, except when the tenant is in default under the terms of the lease. Landlord must pay all interest that has accumulated and remains unpaid, regardless of the amount, upon termination of the tenancy.

Advance notice of deduction: Not required.

Deadline for Landlord to Itemize and Return Deposit: For properties with 5 or more units, 30 to 45 days, depending on whether tenant disputes deductions or if statement and receipts are furnished.

Indiana

Ind. Code Ann. §§ 32-31-3-9 to 32-31-3-19

Exemption: Does not apply to rental agreements entered into before July 1, 1989.

Limit: No statutory limit.

State Security Deposit Rules (continued)

Advance notice of deduction: Not required.

Deadline for Landlord to Itemize and Return Deposit: 45 days.

Iowa

Iowa Code Ann. § 562A.12

Limit: Two months' rent.

Separate Account: Required.

Interest Payment: Interest payment, if any (account need not be interest-bearing) must be made at termination of tenancy. Interest earned during first five years of tenancy belongs to landlord.

Advance notice of deduction: Not required.

Deadline for Landlord to Itemize and Return Deposit: 30 days.

Kansas

Kan. Stat. Ann. §§ 58-2548, 58-2550

Limit: One month's rent (unfurnished); one and one-half month's rent (furnished); for pets, add extra one-half month's rent.

Advance notice of deduction: Not required.

Deadline for Landlord to Itemize and Return Deposit: 30 days.

Kentucky

Ky. Rev. Stat. Ann. § 383.580

Limit: No statutory limit.

Disclosure or Requirement: Orally or in writing, landlord must disclose where the security deposit is being held and the account number.

Before accepting a security deposit, landlords must give tenants a list of pre-existing damage that would justify a charge against the deposit, including the amount of the charge. Tenants have the right to inspect before taking possession. Both parties must sign the list, and if tenants disagree with its accuracy, they must state in writing the basis for their disagreement and sign the statement of dissent. A mutually signed listing is conclusive proof of the listed defects, but not as to latent (unobservable) defects.

Separate Account: Required.

Advance notice of deduction: Required.

Deadline for Landlord to Itemize and Return Deposit: 30 to 60 days depending on whether tenant disputes deductions.

Louisiana

La. Rev. Stat. Ann. § 9:3251

Limit: No statutory limit.

Advance notice of deduction: Not required.

Deadline for Landlord to Itemize and Return Deposit: One month.

State Security Deposit Rules (continued)

Maine

Me. Rev. Stat. Ann. tit. 14, §§ 6031 to 6038

Exemption: Entire security deposit law does not apply to rental unit that is part of structure with five or fewer units, one of which is occupied by landlord.

Limit: Two months' rent.

Disclosure or Requirement: Upon request by the tenant, landlord must disclose orally or in writing the account number and the name of the institution where the security deposit is being held.

Separate Account: Required.

Advance notice of deduction: Not required.

Deadline for Landlord to Itemize and Return Deposit: 30 days (if written rental agreement) or 21 days (if tenancy at will).

Maryland

Md. Code Ann. [Real Prop.] §§ 8-203, 8-203.1, 8-208

Limit: Two months' rent.

Disclosure or Requirement: Landlord must provide a receipt that describes tenant's rights to move-in and move-out inspections (and to be present at each), and right to receive itemization of deposit deductions and balance, if any; and penalties for landlord's failure to comply. Landlord must include this information in the lease.

Separate Account: Required. Landlord may hold all tenants' deposits in secured certificates of deposit, or in securities issued by the federal government or the State of Maryland.

Interest Payment: For security deposits of $50 or more, when landlord has held the deposit for at least six months: Within 45 days of termination of tenancy, interest must be paid at the daily U.S. Treasury yield curve rate for 1 year, as of the first business day of each year, or 1.5% a year, whichever is greater, less any damages rightfully withheld. Interest accrues monthly but is not compounded, and no interest is due for any period less than one month. (See the Department of Housing and Community Development website for a calculator.) Deposit must be held in a Maryland banking institution.

Advance notice of deduction: Required.

Deadline for Landlord to Itemize and Return Deposit: 45 days.

Massachusetts

Mass. Gen. Laws Ann. ch. 186, § 15B

Exemption: Security deposit rules do not apply to any lease, rental, occupancy, or tenancy of 100 days or less in duration which lease or rental is for a vacation or recreational purpose.

Limit: One month's rent.

Disclosure or Requirement: At the time of receiving a security deposit, landlord must furnish a receipt indicating the amount of the deposit; the name of the person receiving it, and, if received by a property manager, the name of the lessor for whom the security deposit is received; the date on which it is received; and a description of the premises leased or rented. The receipt must be signed by the person receiving the security deposit.

State Security Deposit Rules (continued)

Separate Account: Required. Within 30 days of receiving security deposit, landlord must disclose the name and location of the bank in which the security deposit has been deposited, and the amount and account number of the deposit.

Interest Payment: Landlord must pay tenant 5% interest per year or the amount received from the bank (which must be in Massachusetts) that holds the deposit. Interest should be paid yearly, and within 30 days of termination date. Interest will not accrue for the last month for which rent was paid in advance.

Advance notice of deduction: Not required.

Deadline for Landlord to Itemize and Return Deposit: 30 days.

Michigan

Mich. Comp. Laws §§ 554.602 to 554.616

Limit: One and one-half months' rent.

Disclosure or Requirement: Within 14 days of tenant's taking possession of the rental, landlord must furnish in writing the landlord's name and address for receipt of communications, the name and address of the financial institution or surety where the deposit will be held, and the tenant's obligation to provide in writing a forwarding mailing address to the landlord within 4 days after termination of occupancy. The notice shall include the following statement in 12-point boldface type that is at least 4 points larger than the body of the notice or lease agreement: "You must notify your landlord in writing within 4 days after you move of a forwarding address where you can be reached and where you will receive mail; otherwise your landlord shall be relieved of sending you an itemized list of damages and the penalties adherent to that failure."

Separate Account: Required. Landlord must place deposits in a regulated financial institution, and may use the deposits as long as the landlord deposits with the secretary of state a cash or surety bond.

Advance notice of deduction: Required. Not a typical advance notice provision: Tenants must dispute the landlord's stated deductions within 7 days of receiving the itemized list and balance, if any, or give up any right to dispute them.

Deadline for Landlord to Itemize and Return Deposit: 30 days.

Minnesota

Minn. Stat. Ann. §§ 504B.151, 504B.175, 504B.178, & 504B.195

Limit: No statutory limit. If landlord collects a "prelease deposit" and subsequently rents to tenant, landlord must apply the prelease deposit to the security deposit.

Disclosure or Requirement: Before collecting rent or a security deposit, landlord must provide a copy of all outstanding inspection orders for which a citation has been issued, pertaining to a rental unit or common area, specifying code violations that threaten the health or safety of the tenant, and all outstanding condemnation orders and declarations that the premises are unfit for human habitation. Citations for violations that do not involve threats to tenant health or safety must be summarized and posted in an obvious place. With some exceptions, landlord who has received notice of a contract for deed cancellation or notice of a mortgage foreclosure sale must so disclose before entering a lease, accepting rent, or accepting a security deposit; and must furnish the date on which the contract cancellation period or the mortgagor's redemption period ends.

State Security Deposit Rules (continued)

Interest Payment: Landlord must pay 1% simple, noncompounded interest per year. (Deposits collected before 8/1/03 earn interest at 3%, up to 8/1/03, then begin earning at 1%.) Any interest amount less than $1 is excluded.

Advance notice of deduction: Not required.

Deadline for Landlord to Itemize and Return Deposit: Three weeks after tenant leaves and landlord receives forwarding address; five days if tenant must leave due to building condemnation.

Mississippi

Miss. Code Ann. § 89-8-21

Limit: No statutory limit.

Advance notice of deduction: Not required.

Deadline for Landlord to Itemize and Return Deposit: 45 days.

Missouri

Mo. Ann. Stat. § 535.300

Limit: Two months' rent.

Advance notice of deduction: Not required.

Deadline for Landlord to Itemize and Return Deposit: 30 days.

Montana

Mont. Code Ann. §§ 70-25-101 to 70-25-206

Limit: No statutory limit.

Disclosure or Requirement: Before signing a lease, landlords must give tenants a signed statement of the physical condition of the premises, including a statement (if applicable) that the premises have never been leased. Upon request, landlords must furnish a separate written statement of the damage and cleaning charges of the departing tenants. Landlords who fail to comply may not deduct any sums for damage or cleaning unless the landlord can establish by "clear and convincing evidence" that the tenant, tenant's family, licensees, or invitees were responsible.

Advance notice of deduction: Required. Tenant is entitled to advance notice of cleaning charges, but only if such cleaning is required as a result of tenant's negligence and is not part of the landlord's cyclical cleaning program.

Deadline for Landlord to Itemize and Return Deposit: 30 days; 10 days if no deductions.

Nebraska

Neb. Rev. Stat. § 76-1416

Limit: One month's rent (no pets); one and one-quarter months' rent (pets).

Advance notice of deduction: Not required.

Deadline for Landlord to Itemize and Return Deposit: 14 days.

Nevada

Nev. Rev. Stat. Ann. §§ 118A.240 to 118A.250

Limit: Three months' rent; if both landlord and tenant agree, tenant may use a surety bond for all or part of the deposit.

State Security Deposit Rules (continued)

Disclosure or Requirement: Lease or rental agreement must explain the conditions under which the landlord will refund the deposit.

Advance notice of deduction: Not required.

Deadline for Landlord to Itemize and Return Deposit: 30 days.

New Hampshire

N.H. Rev. Stat. Ann. §§ 540-A:5 to 540-A:8; 540-B:10

Exemption: Entire security deposit law does not apply to landlord who leases a single-family residence and owns no other rental property, or landlord who leases rental units in an owner-occupied building of five units or fewer (exemption does not apply to any individual unit in owner-occupied building that is occupied by a person 60 years of age or older).

Limit: One month's rent or $100, whichever is greater; when landlord and tenant share facilities, no statutory limit.

Disclosure or Requirement: Unless tenant has paid the deposit by personal or bank check, or by a check issued by a government agency, landlord must provide a receipt stating the amount of the deposit and the institution where it will be held. Regardless of whether a receipt is required, landlord must inform tenant that if tenant finds any conditions in the rental in need of repair, tenant may note them on the receipt or other written instrument, and return either within five days.

Separate Account: Required. Upon request, landlord must disclose the account number, the amount on deposit, and the interest rate. Landlord may post a bond covering all deposits instead of putting deposits in a separate account.

Interest Payment: Landlord who holds a security deposit for a year or longer must pay interest at a rate equal to the rate paid on regular savings accounts in the New Hampshire bank, savings & loan, or credit union where it's deposited. If a landlord mingles security deposits in a single account, the landlord must pay the actual interest earned proportionately to each tenant. A tenant may request the interest accrued every three years, 30 days before that year's tenancy expires. The landlord must comply with the request within 15 days of the expiration of that year's tenancy.

Advance notice of deduction: Not required.

Deadline for Landlord to Itemize and Return Deposit: 30 days; for shared facilities, if the deposit is more than 30 days' rent, landlord must provide written agreement acknowledging receipt and specifying when deposit will be returned—if no written agreement, 20 days after tenant vacates.

New Jersey

N.J. Stat. Ann. §§ 46:8-19 to 46:8-26

Exemption: Security deposit law does not apply to owner-occupied buildings with not more than two rental units where the tenant has failed to provide 30 days' written notice to the landlord invoking the law.

Limit: One and one-half months' rent. Any additional security deposit, collected annually, may be no greater than 10% of the current security deposit.

Separate Account: Required. Within 30 days of receiving the deposit and every time the landlord pays the tenant interest, landlord must disclose the name and address of the banking organization where the deposit is being held, the type of account, current rate of interest, and the amount of the deposit.

State Security Deposit Rules (continued)

Interest Payment: Landlord with 10 or more units must invest deposits as specified by statute or place deposit in an insured money market fund account, or in another account that pays quarterly interest at a rate comparable to the money market fund. Landlords with fewer than 10 units may place deposit in an interest-bearing account in any New Jersey financial institution insured by the FDIC. All landlords must pay tenants interest earned on account annually or credit toward payment of rent due.

Advance notice of deduction: Not required.

Deadline for Landlord to Itemize and Return Deposit: 30 days; five days in case of fire, flood, condemnation, or evacuation.

New Mexico

N.M. Stat. Ann. § 47-8-18

Limit: One month's rent (for rental agreement of less than one year); no limit for leases of one year or more.

Interest Payment: Landlord who collects a deposit larger than than one month's rent on a year's lease must pay interest, on an annual basis, equal to the passbook interest.

Advance notice of deduction: Not required.

Deadline for Landlord to Itemize and Return Deposit: 30 days.

New York

N.Y. Gen. Oblig. Law §§ 7-103 to 7-108

Limit: One month's limit for units other than those subject to the City Rent and Rehabilitation Law or the Emergency Housing Rent Control Law.

Disclosure or Requirement: If deposit is placed in a bank, landlord must disclose the name and address of the banking organization where the deposit is being held, and the amount of such deposit.

Separate Account: Statute requires that deposits not be commingled with landlord's personal assets, but does not explicitly require placement in a banking institution (however, deposits collected in buildings of six or more units must be placed in New York bank accounts).

Interest Payment: Landlord who rents out nonregulated units in buildings with five or fewer units need not pay interest. Interest must be paid at the prevailing rate on deposits received from tenants who rent units in buildings containing six or more units. The landlord in every rental situation may retain an administrative fee of 1% per year on the sum deposited. Interest can be subtracted from the rent, paid at the end of the year, or paid at the end of the tenancy according to the tenant's choice.

Advance notice of deduction: Yes.

Deadline for Landlord to Itemize and Return Deposit: 14 days.

North Carolina

N.C. Gen. Stat. §§ 42-50 to 42-56

Exemption: Not applicable to rentals of single rooms.

Limit: One and one-half months' rent for month-to-month rental agreements; two months' rent if term is longer than two months; may also charge a reasonable, nonrefundable pet deposit.

State Security Deposit Rules (continued)

Disclosure or Requirement: Within 30 days of the beginning of the lease term, landlord must disclose the name and address of the banking institution where the deposit is located or the name of the insurance company providing the bond.

Separate Account: Required. The landlord may choose to furnish a bond from an insurance company licensed to do business in N.C. rather than deposit the security deposit in a trust account.

Advance notice of deduction: Not required.

Deadline for Landlord to Itemize and Return Deposit: 30 days; if landlord's claim against the deposit cannot be finalized within that time, landlord may send an interim accounting and a final accounting within 60 days of the tenancy's termination.

North Dakota

N.D. Cent. Code § 47-16-07.1

Limit: One month's rent. If tenant has a pet, an additional pet deposit of up to $2,500 or two months' rent, whichever is greater. To encourage renting to persons with records of felony convictions, landlords may charge these applicants up to two months' rent as security. Applicants who have had court judgments entered against them "for violating the terms of a previous rental agreement" can also be charged up to two months' rent (this appears to refer to prior evictions and might not apply to evictions based on conduct not prohibited by the rental agreement).

Separate Account: Required.

Interest Payment: Landlord must pay interest if the period of occupancy is at least nine months. Money must be held in a federally insured interest-bearing savings or checking account for benefit of the tenant. Interest must be paid upon termination of the lease.

Advance notice of deduction: Not required.

Deadline for Landlord to Itemize and Return Deposit: 30 days.

Ohio

Ohio Rev. Code Ann. § 5321.16

Limit: No statutory limit.

Interest Payment: Any deposit in excess of $50 or one month's rent, whichever is greater, must bear interest on the excess at the rate of 5% per annum if the tenant stays for six months or more. Interest must be paid annually and upon termination of tenancy.

Advance notice of deduction: Not required.

Deadline for Landlord to Itemize and Return Deposit: 30 days.

Oklahoma

Okla. Stat. Ann. tit. 41, § 115

Limit: No statutory limit.

Separate Account: Required.

Advance notice of deduction: Not required.

Deadline for Landlord to Itemize and Return Deposit: 45 days.

State Security Deposit Rules (continued)

Oregon

Or. Rev. Stat. § 90.300

Limit: No statutory limit. Landlord may not impose or increase deposit within first year unless parties agree to modify the rental agreement to allow for a pet or other cause, and the imposition or increase relates to that modification.

Disclosure or Requirement: Landlord must provide a receipt for any security deposit the tenant pays.

Advance notice of deduction: Not required.

Deadline for Landlord to Itemize and Return Deposit: 31 days.

Pennsylvania

68 Pa. Cons. Stat. Ann. §§ 250.511a to 250.512

Limit: Two months' rent for first year of renting; one month's rent during second and subsequent years of renting.

Disclosure or Requirement: For deposits over $100, landlord must deposit them in a federally or state-regulated institution, and give tenant the name and address of the banking institution and the amount of the deposit.

Separate Account: Required. Instead of placing deposits in a separate account, landlord may purchase a bond issued by a bonding company authorized to do business in the state.

Interest Payment: Tenant who occupies rental unit for two or more years is entitled to interest beginning with the 25th month of occupancy. Landlord must pay tenant interest (minus 1% fee) at the end of the third and subsequent years of the tenancy.

Advance notice of deduction: Not required.

Deadline for Landlord to Itemize and Return Deposit: 30 days.

Rhode Island

R.I. Gen. Laws § 34-18-19

Limit: One month's rent (unfurnished); if furnished, separate furniture security deposit up to one month's rent if furnishings' replacement value at the start of the tenancy is $5,000 or more.

Advance notice of deduction: Not required.

Deadline for Landlord to Itemize and Return Deposit: 20 days.

South Carolina

S.C. Code Ann. § 27-40-410

Limit: No statutory limit.

Advance notice of deduction: Not required.

Deadline for Landlord to Itemize and Return Deposit: 30 days.

State Security Deposit Rules (continued)

South Dakota

S.D. Codified Laws Ann. §§ 43.32-6.1, 43-32-24

Limit: One month's rent (higher deposit may be charged if special conditions pose a danger to maintenance of the premises).

Advance notice of deduction: Not required.

Deadline for Landlord to Itemize and Return Deposit: Two weeks, and must supply reasons if withholding any portion; 45 days for a written, itemized accounting, if tenant requests it.

Tennessee

Tenn. Code Ann. § 66-28-301

Limit: No statutory limit.

Separate Account: Orally or in writing, landlord must disclose the location of the separate account (but not the account number) used by landlord for the deposit.

Advance notice of deduction: Required.

Deadline for Landlord to Itemize and Return Deposit: No statutory deadline.

Texas

Tex. Prop. Code Ann. §§ 92.101 to 92.110

Limit: No statutory limit.

Disclosure or Requirement: If a security deposit isn't required by the lease or rental agreement, but the tenant is liable for damage or rent when they leave, the landlord must notify the tenant in writing about the claim before reporting the claim. Landlords who don't provide notice forfeit the right to collect damages and charges from the tenant.

Advance notice of deduction: Not required.

Deadline for Landlord to Itemize and Return Deposit: 30 days. If landlord wants to condition the refund of the security deposit on the tenant's giving advance notice of surrender, landlord must put this condition in the lease, and it must be either underlined or printed in conspicuous bold print.

Utah

Utah Code Ann. §§ 57-17-1 to 57-17-5

Limit: No statutory limit.

Disclosure or Requirement: For written leases or rental agreements only, if part of the deposit is nonrefundable, landlord must disclose this feature.

Advance notice of deduction: Not required.

Deadline for Landlord to Itemize and Return Deposit: 30 days.

State Security Deposit Rules (continued)

Vermont

Vt. Stat. Ann. tit. 9, § 4461

Limit: No statutory limit.

Advance notice of deduction: Not required.

Deadline for Landlord to Itemize and Return Deposit: 14 days; 60 days if the rental is seasonal and not intended as the tenant's primary residence.

Virginia

Va. Code Ann. §§ 55.1-1204, 55.1-1206, 55.1-1208, 55.1-1226

Limit: Two months' rent. Alternatively, landlord may permit a tenant to provide damage insurance coverage in an amount not more than two months' rent in lieu of the payment of a security deposit. (Landlord may also require a mix of a deposit and insurance.) The damage insurance coverage must meet the requirements listed in Virginia Code Annotated sections 55.1-1226(I)-(K).

Advance notice of deduction: Not required.

Deadline for Landlord to Itemize and Return Deposit: 45 days; 30 days to itemize any deductions to be made during the course of the tenancy (45 days if the deductions exceed the amount of the security deposit). Lease can provide for expedited processing at the end of the tenancy and specify an administrative fee for such processing, which will apply only if tenant requests it with a separate written document. Landlord must give tenant written notice of tenants right to be present at a final inspection.

Washington

Wash. Rev. Code Ann. §§ 59.18.0001; 59.18.260 to 59.18.285

Limit: Landlords must allow tenants to pay the deposit and fees in installments (does not apply if the deposit and any nonrefundable fees are less than 25% of the monthly rent, or the landlord has not demanded the last month's rent). Tenants with tenancies of three months or more may pay in three equal and consecutive installments, beginning at the start of the tenancy; two installments for shorter tenancies. Installment schedules must be written and signed. Does not apply to holding deposits (which may not be more than 25% of the first month's rent).

Disclosure or Requirement: In the lease, landlord must disclose the circumstances under which all or part of the deposit may be withheld. No deposit may be collected unless the rental agreement is in writing and a written checklist or statement specifically describing the condition and cleanliness of or existing damages to the premises and furnishings is provided to the tenant at the start of the tenancy. The landlord must provide tenant with a written receipt for the deposit and provide the name, address, and location of where the deposit will be kept; if location changes, landlord must notify tenant. Nonrefundable fees must be identified as such in a written rental agreement. If landlords fail to provide a written agreement, tenants are entitled to the return of the fee. If the written agreement does not specify that the fee is refundable, it must be treated as a refundable deposit.

Separate Account: Required.

Advance notice of deduction: Not required.

Deadline for Landlord to Itemize and Return Deposit: 21 days.

State Security Deposit Rules (continued)

West Virginia

W. Va. Code §§ 37-6A-1 to 37-6A-6

Exemption: Agreements for the payment of security deposits entered into before June 10, 2011.

Limit: No statutory limit.

Deadline for Landlord to Itemize and Return Deposit: 60 days from the date the tenancy has terminated, or within 45 days of the occupancy of a subsequent tenant, whichever is shorter. If the damage exceeds the amount of the security deposit and the landlord has to hire a contractor to fix it, the notice period is extended 15 days.

Wisconsin

Wis. Admin. Code ATCP 134.04, 134.06, Wis. Stat. § 704.28

Exemption: Security deposit rules do not apply to a dwelling unit occupied, under a contract of sale, by the purchaser of the dwelling unit or the purchaser's successor in interest; or to a dwelling unit that the landlord provides free to any person, or that the landlord provides as consideration to a person whom the landlord currently employs to operate or maintain the premises.

Limit: No statutory limit.

Disclosure or Requirement: Before accepting the deposit, landlord must inform tenant of tenant's inspection rights, disclose all habitability defects, and show tenant any outstanding building and housing code violations, inform tenant of the means by which shared utilities will be billed, and inform tenant if utilities are not paid for by landlord.

Advance notice of deduction: Not required.

Deadline for Landlord to Itemize and Return Deposit: 21 days.

Wyoming

Wyo. Stat. §§ 1-21-1207, 1-21-1208

Limit: No statutory limit.

Disclosure or Requirement: Lease or rental agreement must state whether any portion of a deposit is nonrefundable, and landlord must give tenant written notice of this fact when collecting the deposit.

Advance notice of deduction: Not required.

Deadline for Landlord to Itemize and Return Deposit: 30 days, when applying it to unpaid rent (or within 15 days of receiving tenant's forwarding address, whichever is later); additional 30 days allowed for deductions due to damage.

State Laws on Rent Withholding and Repair-and-Deduct Remedies

State	Statute or case on rent withholding	Statute or case on repair-and-deduct
Alabama	Ala. Code § 35-9A-164	Ala. Code § 35-9A-164
Alaska	Alaska Stat. §§ 34.03.100, 34.03.180(a)(3), 34.03.190	Alaska Stat. §§ 34.03.100, 34.03.180
Arizona	Ariz. Rev. Stat. Ann. §§ 33-1364 and 33-1365	Ariz. Rev. Stat. Ann. §§ 33-1363 and 1364
Arkansas	No statute	No statute
California	Cal. Civ. Code § 1174.2; *Green v. Superior Court*, 10 Cal. 3d 616 (1974)	Cal. Civ. Code § 1942
Colorado	Colo. Rev. Stat. § 38-12-507	Colo. Rev. Stat. § 38-12-507
Connecticut	Conn. Gen. Stat. Ann. §§ 47a-13 to -14h	Conn. Gen. Stat. Ann. § 47a-13
Delaware	Del. Code Ann. tit. 25, § 5308	Del. Code Ann. tit. 25, §§ 5307, 5308
District of Columbia	D.C. Mun. Regs. § 14-4303; *Javins v. First Natl Realty Corp.*, 428 F.2d 1071 (D.C. Cir. 1970)	No statute
Florida	Fla. Stat. Ann. § 83.60	Fla. Stat. Ann. § 83.60
Georgia	No statute	Not addressed by statute, but Georgia courts recognize a tenant's right to this remedy. See *Georgia Landlord Tenant Handbook*, 2020, Georgia Department of Community Affairs; and see *Abrams v. Joel*, 108 Ga. App. 662, 134 S.E.2d 480 (1963).
Hawaii	Haw. Rev. Stat. § 521-78	Haw. Rev. Stat. § 521-64
Idaho	No statute	No statute on repair and deduct generally, but if a landlord won't make repairs, tenant must provide landlord with a written notice with a list of violations. Landlord then has three days to fix; failure to repair allows the tenant to sue the landlord to force compliance. (Idaho Code § 6-320.) Repair and deduct is available specifically (and only) for failure to install and/or maintain smoke detectors. (Idaho Code § 6-320(a)(6).)
Illinois	765 Ill. Comp. Stat. §§ 735/2, 735/2.2 (applies only when a court has appointed a receiver to collect rents, following landlord's failure to pay for utilities)	765 Ill. Comp. Stat. § 742/5

State Laws on Rent Withholding and Repair and Deduct Remedies (continued)

State	Statute or case on rent withholding	Statute or case on repair and deduct
Indiana	No statute	No statute on repair and deduct, but once tenant gives landlord notice of landlords need to repair, landlord has reasonable amount of time to remedy. If landlord doesn't remedy, tenant can sue for enforcement and might obtain actual and consequential damages, as well as attorneys' fees and court costs. (Ind. Code Ann. § 32-31-8-6.)
Iowa	Iowa Code Ann. § 562A.24	Iowa Code Ann. § 562A.23
Kansas	Kan. Stat. Ann. § 58-2561	No statute
Kentucky	Ky. Rev. Stat. Ann. § 383.645	Ky. Rev. Stat. Ann. §§ 383.635, 383.640
Louisiana	No statute	La. Civ. Code Ann. art. 2694
Maine	Me. Rev. Stat. Ann. tit. 14, § 6021	Me. Rev. Stat. Ann. tit. 14, § 6026
Maryland	Md. Code Ann. [Real Prop.] §§ 8-211, 8-211.1	No statute
Massachusetts	Mass. Gen. Laws Ann. ch. 239, § 8A	Mass. Gen. Laws Ann. ch. 111, § 127L
Michigan	Mich. Comp. Laws § 125.530	*Rome v. Walker*, 198 N.W.2d 850 (1972); Mich. Comp. Laws § 554.139
Minnesota	Minn. Stat. Ann. §§ 504B.215(3)(d), 504B.385	Minn. Stat. Ann. § 504B.425
Mississippi	No statute	Miss. Code Ann. § 89-8-15
Missouri	Mo. Ann. Stat. §§ 441.570, 441.580; *Kohner Properties, Inc. v. Johnson*, 553 S.W.3d 280 (Mo. Sup. Ct. 2018)	Mo. Ann. Stat. § 441.234
Montana	Mont. Code Ann. § 70-24-421	Mont. Code Ann. §§ 70-24-406 to -408
Nebraska	Neb. Rev. Stat. § 76-1428	Neb. Rev. Stat. § 76-1427
Nevada	Nev. Rev. Stat. Ann. § 118A.490	Nev. Rev. Stat. Ann. §§ 118A.360, 118A.380
New Hampshire	N.H. Rev. Stat. Ann. § 540:13-d	No statute
New Jersey	*Berzito v. Gambino*, 63 N.J. 460 (1973)	*Marini v. Ireland*, 265 A.2d 526 (1970)
New Mexico	N.M. Stat. Ann. § 47-8-27.2	No statute
New York	N.Y. Real Prop. Law § 235-b, *Semans Family Ltd. Partnership v. Kennedy*, 675 N.Y.S.2d 489 (N.Y. City Civ. Ct.,1998)	For emergency repairs (such as broken door lock) only: N.Y. Real Prop. Law § 235-b; *Jangla Realty Co. v. Gravagna*, 447 N.Y.S. 2d 338 (Civ. Ct., Queens County, 1981)

State Laws on Rent Withholding and Repair and Deduct Remedies (continued)

State	Statute or case on rent withholding	Statute or case on repair and deduct
North Carolina	No statute	No statute
North Dakota	No statute	N.D. Cent. Code §§ 47-16-13, 47-16-13.1
Ohio	Ohio Rev. Code Ann. § 5321.07 (does not apply to student tenants; or when landlord owns three or fewer rental units, as long as landlord has given written notice to tenant)	No statute
Oklahoma	Okla. Stat. Ann. tit. 41, § 121	Okla. Stat. Ann. tit. 41, § 121
Oregon	Or. Rev. Stat. § 90.365	Or. Rev. Stat. § 90.365
Pennsylvania	68 Pa. Cons. Stat. Ann. § 250.206; 35 Pa. Cons. Stat. Ann. § 1700-1	*Pugh v. Holmes*, 405 A.2d 897 (1979)
Rhode Island	R.I. Gen. Laws § 34-18-32	R.I. Gen. Laws §§ 34-18-30 to -31
South Carolina	S.C. Code Ann. § 27-40-640	S.C. Code Ann. § 27-40-630
South Dakota	S.D. Codified Laws Ann. § 43-32-9	S.D. Codified Laws Ann. § 43-32-9
Tennessee	Tenn. Code Ann. § 68-111-104	Tenn. Code Ann. § 66-28-502
Texas	No statute	Tex. Prop. Code Ann. §§ 92.056, 92.0561
Utah	No statute	Utah Code Ann. § 57-22-6
Vermont	Vt. Stat. Ann. tit. 9, § 4458	Vt. Stat. Ann. tit. 9, § 4459
Virginia	Va. Code Ann. § 55.1-1244	Va. Code Ann. § 55.1-1244.1
Washington	Wash. Rev. Code Ann. §§ 59.18.110, 59.18.115	Wash. Rev. Code Ann. §§ 59.18.100, 59.18.110
West Virginia	*Teller v. McCoy*, 253 S.E.2d 114 (W.Va. 1978)	*Teller v. McCoy*, 253 S.E.2d 114 (W.Va. 1978)
Wisconsin	Wis. Stat. Ann. § 704.07(4)	No statute
Wyoming	Wyo. Stat. § 1-21-1206	No statute

State Laws in Domestic Violence Situations

Many states extend special protections to tenants who are victims of domestic violence, governing what the landlord can and cannot do in response to the situation. Most states also have procedures whereby tenants can obtain restraining orders against perpetrators; often the effect of these orders is to ban the perpetrator-tenant from the rental property (these laws are not cited in this chart). For information on obtaining restraining orders, contact local law enforcement.

Alabama

No statute

Alaska

No statute

Arizona

Ariz. Rev. Stat. Ann. §§ 33-1315, 33-1318, 33-1414

- Lease cannot include a waiver of some or all DV rights
- Landlord entitled to proof of DV status
- Early termination right for DV victim
- Lease cannot prohibit calling the police in a DV situation or otherwise penalize DV victim
- DV victim has the right to have the locks changed
- Penalty for falsely reporting domestic violence (including obtaining early termination)
- Perpetrator of DV liable to landlord for resulting damages.

Miscellaneous provisions: Enumerated rights apply to victims of domestic violence and victims of a sexual assault in the tenant's residence.

Arkansas

Ark. Code Ann. § 18-16-112

- Landlord entitled to proof of DV status
- Landlord cannot refuse to rent to victim of DV
- Landlord cannot terminate a victim of DV
- Lease cannot prohibit calling the police in a DV situation or otherwise penalize DV victim
- DV victim has the right to have the locks changed
- Perpetrator of DV liable to landlord for resulting damages
- Landlord or court may modify the lease by terminating only the perpetrator.

California

Cal. Civ. Code §§ 1941.5, 1941.6, 1946.7; Cal. Code Civ. Proc. §§ 1161, 1161.3

- Landlord entitled to proof of DV status
- Landlord cannot refuse to rent to victim of DV
- Landlord cannot terminate a victim of DV
- Early termination right for DV victim
- DV is an affirmative defense to an eviction lawsuit

State Laws in Domestic Violence Situations (continued)

- DV victim has the right to have the locks changed
- Landlord or court may modify the lease by terminating only the perpetrator
- Landlord has limited right to evict the DV victim.

Miscellaneous provisions: Protection against termination has been expanded to include elder or dependent adults.

Colorado

Colo. Rev. Stat. §§ 13-40-104 (4), 13-40-107.5 (5), 38-12-401, 38-12-402, 38-12-503

- Lease cannot include a waiver of some or all DV rights
- Landlord entitled to proof of DV status
- Landlord cannot terminate a victim of DV
- Early termination right for DV victim
- Lease cannot prohibit calling the police in a DV situation or otherwise penalize DV victim.

Miscellaneous provisions: Legal protections extend to victims of unlawful sexual behavior and stalking, as well as domestic violence. Landlords may not disclose that tenants were victims of such acts, except with permission or as required by law. If tenant terminates lease because of these acts, and the tenant provides the landlord with a new address, the landlord may not disclose the new address to any person except with permission or as required by law.

Connecticut

Conn. Gen. Stat. Ann. § 47a-11e

- Landlord entitled to proof of DV status
- Early termination right for DV victim.

Delaware

Del. Code Ann. tit. 25, §§ 5141(7), 5314(b), 5316

- Landlord entitled to proof of DV status
- Landlord cannot terminate a victim of DV
- Early termination right for DV victim.

District of Columbia

D.C. Code Ann. §§ 2-1402.21, 42-3505.07, 42-3505.08

- Lease cannot include a waiver of some or all DV rights
- Landlord entitled to proof of DV status
- Landlord cannot refuse to rent to victim of DV
- Early termination right for DV victim
- DV is an affirmative defense to an eviction lawsuit
- Lease cannot prohibit calling the police in a DV situation or otherwise penalize DV victim
- DV victim has the right to have the locks changed
- Landlord or court may modify the lease by terminating only the perpetrator.

State Laws in Domestic Violence Situations (continued)

Miscellaneous provisions: Landlord must make reasonable accommodation in restoring or improving security and safety measures that are beyond the landlord's duty of ordinary care and diligence, when such accommodation is necessary to ensure the tenant's security and safety (tenant may be billed for the cost).

Florida

No statute

Georgia

Ga. Code Ann. § 44-7-23

- Lease cannot include a waiver of some or all DV rights
- Landlord entitled to proof of DV status
- Early termination right for DV victim.

Miscellaneous provisions: Tenant can terminate without penalty with 30 days' written notice. The notice shall include a copy of the civil family violence order or criminal family violence order, as well as a police report if the order was an ex parte temporary protective order.

Hawaii

Haw. Rev. Stat. §§ 521-80 to 521-82

- Landlord entitled to proof of DV status
- Early termination right for DV victim
- DV victim has the right to have the locks changed
- Penalty for falsely reporting domestic violence (including obtaining early termination)
- Landlord or court may modify the lease by terminating only the perpetrator.

Miscellaneous provisions: Landlord may not disclose information gathered with respect to tenant's exercise of rights under these laws, unless the tenant consents in writing, the information is required or relevant in a lawsuit, or the disclosure is required by law.

Idaho

No statute

Illinois

735 Ill. Comp. Stat. 5/9-106.2; 765 Ill. Comp. Stat. 750/1 through 750/35

- Landlord entitled to proof of DV status
- Early termination right for DV victim
- DV is an affirmative defense to an eviction lawsuit
- DV victim has the right to have the locks changed
- Landlord or court may modify the lease by terminating only the perpetrator.

Miscellaneous provisions: Landlord may not disclose to others that a tenant has exercised a right under the law; violations expose landlord to damages that result up to $2,000, as well as the tenant's attorneys' fees and costs.

State Laws in Domestic Violence Situations (continued)

Indiana

Ind. Code Ann. §§ 32-31-9-1 through 32-31-9-15

- Landlord entitled to proof of DV status
- Landlord cannot refuse to rent to victim of DV
- Landlord cannot terminate a victim of DV
- Early termination right for DV victim
- Lease cannot prohibit calling the police in a DV situation or otherwise penalize DV victim
- DV victim has the right to have the locks changed.

Iowa

Iowa Code §§ 562A.27A, 562A.27B, 562B.25A (3)

- Lease cannot include a waiver of some or all DV rights
- Landlord entitled to proof of DV status
- Landlord cannot terminate a victim of DV
- Landlord has limited right to evict the DV victim
- Lease cannot prohibit calling the police in a DV situation or otherwise penalize DV victim.

Miscellaneous provisions: Landlord can recover from the tenant the cost to repair damage caused by emergency responders called by tenant. Cities cannot impose penalties against residents or landlords, including fines, permit or license revocations, and evictions, when they had a reasonable belief that emergency assistance was necessary, and it was in fact needed.

Kansas

Kan. Stat. Ann. § 58-25,137

- Lease cannot include a waiver of some or all DV rights
- Landlord entitled to proof of DV status
- Landlord cannot refuse to rent to victim of DV
- Landlord cannot terminate a victim of DV
- Early termination right for DV victim
- DV is an affirmative defense to an eviction lawsuit
- Penalty for falsely reporting domestic violence (including obtaining early termination)
- Landlord or court may modify the lease by terminating only the perpetrator.

Miscellaneous provisions: Protections extend to victims (within the past twelve months) of domestic violence, sexual assault, human trafficking, and stalking. Landlord may impose a reasonable termination fee for victims who seek early termination, but only if this provision is included in the terms of the rental agreement or lease. Court may impose statutory damages of $1,000 and reasonable attorneys' fees and costs on landlords who violate the statute.

State Laws in Domestic Violence Situations (continued)

Kentucky

Ky. Rev. Stat. Ann. §§ 383.300, 383.302

- Lease cannot include a waiver of some or all DV rights
- Landlord entitled to proof of DV status
- Landlord cannot refuse to rent to victim of DV
- Landlord cannot terminate a victim of DV
- Early termination right for DV victim
- DV is an affirmative defense to an eviction lawsuit
- DV victim has the right to have the locks changed
- Perpetrator of DV liable to landlord for resulting damages
- Landlord or court may modify the lease by terminating only the perpetrator.

Louisiana

La. Rev. Stat. Ann. § 9:3261.1

- Lease cannot include a waiver of some or all DV rights
- Landlord entitled to proof of DV status
- Landlord cannot refuse to rent to victim of DV
- Landlord cannot terminate a victim of DV
- Early termination right for DV victim
- Lease cannot prohibit calling the police in a DV situation or otherwise penalize DV victim.

Miscellaneous provisions: Statute applies only to multifamily housing of six or more units; does not apply if building has ten or fewer units and one is occupied by the owner.

Maine

Me. Rev. Stat. Ann. tit. 14, §§ 6000, 6001, 6002, 6025

- Landlord entitled to proof of DV status
- Landlord cannot terminate a victim of DV
- Early termination right for DV victim
- DV victim has the right to have the locks changed
- Perpetrator of DV liable to landlord for resulting damages
- Landlord or court may modify the lease by terminating only the perpetrator.

Miscellaneous provisions: Landlord may terminate and/or bifurcate the lease with 7 days' notice when a tenant perpetrates domestic violence, sexual assault, or stalking (against another tenant, a tenant's guest, or the landlord or landlord's employee or agent), and the victim is also a tenant.

Maryland

Md. Code Ann. [Real Prop.] §§ 8-5A-01 through 8-5A-06

- Landlord entitled to proof of DV status
- Early termination right for DV victim.
- DV is an affirmative defense to an eviction lawsuit.

State Laws in Domestic Violence Situations (continued)

Massachusetts

Mass Gen. Laws ch. 186, §§ 24, 25, 26, and 28; ch. 239, § 2A

- Lease cannot include a waiver of some or all DV rights
- Landlord entitled to proof of DV status
- Landlord cannot refuse to rent to victim of DV
- Early termination right for DV victim
- DV is an affirmative defense to an eviction lawsuit
- DV victim has the right to have the locks changed.

Michigan

Mich. Comp. Laws § 554.601b

- Landlord entitled to proof of DV status
- Early termination right for DV victim
- Landlord or court may modify the lease by terminating only the perpetrator.

Minnesota

Minn. Stat. Ann. §§ 504B.205, 206

- Lease cannot include a waiver of some or all DV rights
- Landlord entitled to proof of DV status
- Landlord cannot terminate a victim of DV
- Early termination right for DV victim
- DV is an affirmative defense to an eviction lawsuit
- Lease cannot prohibit calling the police in a DV situation or otherwise penalize DV victim.

Miscellaneous provisions: Landlord must keep information about the domestic violence confidential. In a multitenant situation, termination by one tenant terminates the lease of all, though other tenants may reapply to enter into a new lease. All of the security deposit is forfeited.

Mississippi

No statute

Missouri

Mo. Rev. Stat. § 441.920

- Landlord entitled to proof of DV status
- Landlord cannot refuse to rent to victim of DV
- Landlord cannot terminate a victim of DV
- Early termination right for DV victim
- DV is an affirmative defense to an eviction lawsuit
- Penalty for falsely reporting domestic violence (including obtaining early termination).

Miscellaneous provisions: Landlord may impose a reasonable termination fee on a tenant who desires to terminate a lease before the expiration of the date of the lease due to status as a DV victim.

State Laws in Domestic Violence Situations (continued)

Montana

No statute

Nebraska

Neb. Rev. Stat. § 76-1431

- Landlord has limited right to evict the DV victim.

Miscellaneous provisions: Landlord's right to unconditionally terminate the lease following on-site criminal acts, sale of illegal substances, or any act that threatens health and safety does not apply if tenant has sought a protective order against the perpetrator or has asked for police help in an effort to bring charges against the perpetrator.

Nevada

Nev. Rev. Stat. Ann. §§ 118A.345, 118A.347, 118A.510

- Lease cannot include a waiver of some or all DV rights
- Landlord entitled to proof of DV status
- Landlord cannot terminate a victim of DV
- Early termination right for DV victim
- DV victim has the right to have the locks changed
- Perpetrator of DV liable to landlord for resulting damages.

Miscellaneous provisions: Protections extend to victims of harassment, sexual assault, and stalking, as well as domestic violence. Landlord may not disclose the fact of a tenant's early termination to a prospective landlord; nor may a prospective landlord require an applicant to disclose any prior early terminations. Antiretaliation protection extended to tenants who are domestic violence victims or who have terminated a rental agreement pursuant to law.

New Hampshire

N.H. Rev. Stat. Ann. § 540:2.VII

- Landlord entitled to proof of DV status
- Landlord cannot terminate a victim of DV
- DV victim has the right to have the locks changed
- Landlord or court may modify the lease by terminating only the perpetrator.

New Jersey

N.J. Stat. Ann. §§ 46:8-9.5 through 46:8-9.12

- Lease cannot include a waiver of some or all DV rights
- Landlord entitled to proof of DV status
- Early termination right for DV victim.

Miscellaneous provisions: Landlord may not disclose information provided by a tenant that documents domestic violence.

State Laws in Domestic Violence Situations (continued)

New Mexico

N.M. Stat. Ann. § 47-8-33(J)

- DV is an affirmative defense to an eviction lawsuit
- Landlord or court may modify the lease by terminating only the perpetrator.

New York

N.Y. Real Prop. Law §§ 227-c(2) and 227–d; N.Y. Real Prop. Acts. Law § 744; N.Y. Crim. Proc. Law § 530.13(1); N.Y. Dom. Rel. Law § 240(3)

- Landlord entitled to proof of DV status
- Landlord cannot refuse to rent to victim of DV
- Landlord cannot terminate a victim of DV
- Early termination right for DV victim
- DV is an affirmative defense to an eviction lawsuit
- Penalty for falsely reporting domestic violence (including obtaining early termination).

Miscellaneous provisions: Victim must follow statutory requirements in order to take advantage of right of early termination. Anti-discrimination protection and eviction protection do not apply to owner-occupied buildings with two or fewer units.

North Carolina

N.C. Gen. Stat. §§ 42-40, 42-42.2, 42-42.3, 42-45.1

- Landlord entitled to proof of DV status
- Landlord cannot refuse to rent to victim of DV
- Early termination right for DV victim
- DV victim has the right to have the locks changed.

North Dakota

N.D. Cent. Code §§ 42-45.1, 47-16-17.1

- Landlord entitled to proof of DV status
- Landlord cannot refuse to rent to victim of DV
- Landlord cannot terminate a victim of DV
- Early termination right for DV victim.

Miscellaneous provisions: Landlord may not disclose information provided by a tenant that documents domestic violence. Landlords who violate the provisions providing early termination are subject to damages including actual damages, $1,000, reasonable attorneys' fees, costs, and disbursements. Perpetrators who have been excluded from the dwelling by court order, as well as any remaining tenants, remain jointly and severally liable for rent and damages.

Ohio

No statute

State Laws in Domestic Violence Situations (continued)

Oklahoma

No statute

Oregon

Or. Rev. Stat. §§ 90.449, 90.453, 90.456, 90.459

- Landlord entitled to proof of DV status
- Landlord cannot refuse to rent to victim of DV
- Landlord cannot terminate a victim of DV
- Early termination right for DV victim
- DV is an affirmative defense to an eviction lawsuit
- Lease cannot prohibit calling the police in a DV situation or otherwise penalize DV victim
- DV victim has the right to have the locks changed
- Landlord or court may modify the lease by terminating only the perpetrator
- Landlord has limited right to evict the DV victim.

Pennsylvania

53 Pa.C.S.A. § 304

Miscellaneous provisions: The state law shields residents, tenants, and landlords from penalties that could otherwise be levied under a local ordinance or regulation when police or emergency services respond to a residence or tenancy to assist a victim of abuse or crime. Does not give domestic violence victims direct protection, nor does it impose duties or restrictions on landlords. However, the City of Philadelphia Fair Housing Ordinance offers some protections for Philadelphia residents.

Rhode Island

R.I. Gen. Laws §§ 34-37-1 through 34-37-4

- Landlord cannot refuse to rent to victim of DV
- Landlord cannot terminate a victim of DV
- Landlord or court may modify the lease by terminating only the perpetrator.

South Carolina

No statute

South Dakota

S.D. Codified Laws §§ 43-32-18.1, 43-32-19.1

- Lease cannot include a waiver of some or all DV rights
- Landlord entitled to proof of DV status
- Early termination right for DV victim.

Miscellaneous provisions: When tenants exercise early termination rights and provide the landlord with a forwarding address or other contact information, the landlord may not disclose the new address or information to any person unless the tenant gives permission or as required by law.

State Laws in Domestic Violence Situations (continued)

Tennessee

Tenn. Code Ann. §§ 66-7-109(e), 66-28-517(g)

- Landlord entitled to proof of DV status
- Landlord cannot terminate a victim of DV
- Landlord or court may modify the lease by terminating only the perpetrator
- Landlord has limited right to evict the DV victim.

Miscellaneous provisions: The rights granted under this law do not apply when the perpetrator is a child or dependent of any tenant. Landlord may evict a victim who allows an ousted perpetrator to return to the premises.

Texas

Tex. Prop. Code Ann. §§ 92.015, 92.016, 92.0161

- Lease cannot include a waiver of some or all DV rights
- Landlord entitled to proof of DV status
- Early termination right for DV victim
- Lease cannot prohibit calling the police in a DV situation or otherwise penalize DV victim.

Miscellaneous provisions: Tenant who exercises termination rights will be released from any delinquent rent unless the lease includes a clause that specifically describes tenants' rights in domestic violence situations. Landlord may not prohibit or limit a tenant's right to call police or other emergency assistance, based on the tenant's reasonable belief that such help is necessary.

Utah

Utah Code Ann. § 57-22-5.1

- Landlord entitled to proof of DV status
- Early termination right for DV victim
- DV victim has the right to have the locks changed
- Lease cannot prohibit calling the police in a DV situation or otherwise penalize DV victim.

Miscellaneous provisions: When the landlord has rekeyed, a perpetrator who does not receive a key and who is a cotenant but not barred from the rental may ask a court for access and a key or, in the alternative, to be relieved from any further liability under the lease (relief from liability is not available to perpetrators who are found by a court to have committed the underlying act of violence).

Vermont

15 Vt. Stat. Ann. § 1103(c)(2)(B); 9 Vt. Stat. Ann. §§ 4471-4475

- Landlord or court may modify the lease by terminating only the perpetrator
- Landlord entitled to proof of DV status
- Early termination right for DV victim
- DV victim has the right to have the locks changed.

State Laws in Domestic Violence Situations (continued)

Miscellaneous provisions: Protected tenants include victims as well as parents, foster parents, legal guardians, and caretakers with at least partial physical custody of a victim of abuse, sexual assault, or stalking. Landlords with documentation or knowledge of a tenant's status as a domestic violence victim must, with exceptions, keep the information confidential (must not divulge to subsequent landlords) unless authorized by the tenant.

Virginia

Va. Code Ann. §§ 55.1-1203, 55.1-1208, 55.1-1230, 55.1-1236

- Lease cannot include a waiver of some or all DV rights
- Landlord entitled to proof of DV status
- Landlord cannot terminate a victim of DV
- Early termination right for DV victim
- DV victim has the right to have the locks changed
- Perpetrator of DV liable to landlord for resulting damages
- Landlord or court may modify the lease by terminating only the perpetrator

Miscellaneous provisions: Right to change locks extends to "authorized occupants" (persons who occupy with landlord's consent but have not signed a rental agreement and are not responsible for rent). Victim with a restraining order loses the right to continued occupation if the perpetrator reappears and victim fails to notify landlord. (Va. Code Ann. § 55.1-1230.) A landlord must consider evidence of a rental applicant's status as a victim of family abuse to mitigate any adverse affect of an otherwise qualified applicant's low credit score. Statute provides direction on how applicant can show status as a victim. (Va. Code Ann. § 55.1-1203). If an otherwise qualified applicant's status as a domestic violence victim negatively affected the applicant's credit score, landlord must disregard the negative effect (tenant must provide documentation of domestic violence status).

Washington

Wash. Rev. Code Ann. §§ 59.18.130(8)(b)(ii), 59.18.352, 59.18.570, 59.18.575, 59.18.580, 59.18.585

- Landlord entitled to proof of DV status
- Landlord cannot refuse to rent to victim of DV
- Landlord cannot terminate a victim of DV
- Early termination right for DV victim
- DV is an affirmative defense to an eviction lawsuit
- DV victim has the right to have the locks changed.

Miscellaneous provisions: Victim tenants can terminate early, but the request to terminate must occur within 90 days of the reported act of violence that gave rise to a protective order or report to a qualified third party. The law also recognizes the possibility that the landlord might be the perpetrator of violence, and provides special protections for victims of landlord violence and stalking. (Wash. Rev. Code Ann. § 59.28.575(b).)

State Laws in Domestic Violence Situations (continued)

West Virginia

No statute

Wisconsin

Wis. Stat. §§ 106.50, 704.14, 704.16

- Landlord entitled to proof of DV status
- Landlord cannot refuse to rent to victim of DV
- Landlord cannot terminate a victim of DV
- Early termination right for DV victim
- DV is an affirmative defense to an eviction lawsuit
- DV victim has the right to have the locks changed
- Landlord has limited right to evict the DV victim

Wyoming

Wy. Stat. Ann. §§ 1-21-1301 through 1-21-1304

- Lease cannot include a waiver of some or all DV rights
- Landlord entitled to proof of DV status
- Landlord cannot terminate a victim of DV
- Early termination right for DV victim
- DV is an affirmative defense to an eviction lawsuit.

State Laws on Landlord's Access to Rental Property

In all states, even in the absence of a statute, landlords may enter to deal with a true **emergency** (an imminent and serious threat to health, safety, or property) or when the tenant has **abandoned** the property (left for good). Most states specify non-emergency circumstances that justify entry, and some explicitly include abandonment and "extended absence" (temporary but prolonged absence, which allows a landlord to enter when necessary to protect the property). But even when the statute doesn't mention "extended absence," landlords may enter when it's necessary to avert serious property damage (an emergency situation).

				Reasons Landlord May Enter					
State	**State Law Citation**	**Amount of Notice Required in Nonemergency Situations**	**Form of Notice**	**To Deal With an Emergency**	**To Inspect the Premises**	**To Make Repairs, Alterations, or Improvements**	**To Show Property to Prospective Tenants or Purchasers**	**During Tenant's Extended Absence**	**When Tenant has Abandoned the Property**
Alabama	Ala. Code §§ 35-9A-303, 35-9A-423	Two days	Not specified	✓	✓	✓	✓	✓	✓
Alaska	Alaska Stat. §§ 34.03.140, 34.03.230	24 hours	Not specified	✓	✓	✓	✓	✓	✓
Arizona	Ariz. Rev. Stat. Ann. § 33-1343	Two days; notice period does not apply, and tenant's consent is assumed, if entry is pursuant to tenant's request for maintenance as prescribed in Ariz. Rev. Stat. § 33-1341, paragraph 8	Not specified	✓	✓	✓	✓		✓
Arkansas	Ark. Code Ann. § 18-17-602	No notice specified	Not specified		✓	✓	✓		

State Laws on Landlord's Access to Rental Property (continued)

				Reasons Landlord May Enter					
State	State Law Citation	Amount of Notice Required in Nonemergency Situations	Form of Notice	To Deal With an Emergency	To Inspect the Premises	To Make Repairs, Alterations, or Improvements	To Show Property to Prospective Tenants or Purchasers	During Tenant's Extended Absence	When Tenant has Abandoned the Property
California	Cal. Civ. Code §§ 1950.5, 1954	Reasonable notice; 24 hours is presumed reasonable (48 hours for initial move-out inspection)	Written notice required, but oral notice is sufficient if the entry is to show the property to prospective or actual purchasers, but only if the landlord has given written notice within the previous 120 days, telling the tenant that the property is for sale and such oral notice might be given (24 hours' notice is presumed reasonable; landlord must leave a note when leaving).	✓	✓	✓	✓		✓
Colorado	Colo. Rev. Stat. Ann. § 38-12-1004	Notice statute relates only to access for inspecting for or treating a bed bug infestation. 48 hours' notice required unless lease says otherwise.	Not specified, unless the access is related to a possible or actual bed bug infestation, in which case notice must be electronic or written.						

State Laws on Landlord's Access to Rental Property (continued)

State	State Law Citation	Amount of Notice Required in Nonemergency Situations	Form of Notice	Reasons Landlord May Enter: To Deal With an Emergency	To Inspect the Premises	To Make Repairs, Alterations, or Improvements	To Show Property to Prospective Tenants or Purchasers	During Tenant's Extended Absence	When Tenant has Abandoned the Property
Connecticut	Conn. Gen. Stat. Ann. §§ 47a-16 to 47a-16a	Reasonable notice	Written or oral	✓	✓	✓	✓	✓	✓
Delaware	Del. Code Ann. tit. 25, §§ 5113, 5507, 5509, 5510	48 hours	Written, by giving a copy to an adult who resides at the rental unit or at the tenant's usual residence (if it's not the rental) or by mailing via registered or certified mail or first class mail as evidenced by a certificate of mailing postage-prepaid, addressed to the tenant at the rental. The notice can also be posted at the rental unit when it's combined with a return receipt of a certificate of mailing.	✓	✓	✓	✓	✓	

State Laws on Landlord's Access to Rental Property (continued)

				Reasons Landlord May Enter					
State	**State Law Citation**	**Amount of Notice Required in Nonemergency Situations**	**Form of Notice**	**To Deal With an Emergency**	**To Inspect the Premises**	**To Make Repairs, Alterations, or Improvements**	**To Show Property to Prospective Tenants or Purchasers**	**During Tenant's Extended Absence**	**When Tenant has Abandoned the Property**
District of Columbia	D.C. Code Ann. § 42-3505.51	48 hours	Written and electronic (including email and mobile text messaging), but if the tenant doesn't provide an acknowledgement of the electronic notice in writing, the landlord must provide a paper notice.	✓	✓	✓	✓		
Florida	Fla. Stat. Ann. § 83.53	12 hours	Not specified	✓	✓	✓	✓	✓	
Georgia	No statute								
Hawaii	Haw. Rev. Stat. §§ 521-53, 521-70(b)	Two days	Not specified	✓	✓	✓	✓	✓	✓
Idaho	No statute								
Illinois	No statute								
Indiana	Ind. Code Ann. § 32-31-5-6	Reasonable notice	Written or oral	✓	✓	✓	✓		✓

State Laws on Landlord's Access to Rental Property (continued)

				Reasons Landlord May Enter					
State	State Law Citation	Amount of Notice Required in Nonemergency Situations	Form of Notice	To Deal With an Emergency	To Inspect the Premises	To Make Repairs, Alterations, or Improvements	To Show Property to Prospective Tenants or Purchasers	During Tenant's Extended Absence	When Tenant has Abandoned the Property
Iowa	Iowa Code Ann. §§ 562A.19, 562A.28, 562A.29	24 hours	Not specified	✓	✓	✓	✓	✓	✓
Kansas	Kan. Stat. Ann. §§ 58-2557, 58-2565	Reasonable notice	Not specified	✓	✓	✓	✓	✓	✓
Kentucky	Ky. Rev. Stat. Ann. §§ 383.615, 383.670	Two days	Not specified	✓	✓	✓	✓	✓	✓
Louisiana	La. Civ. Code art. 2693	No notice specified	Not specified			✓			
Maine	Me. Rev. Stat. Ann. tit. 14, § 6025	24 hours	Not specified	✓	✓	✓	✓		
Maryland	No statute								
Massachusetts	Mass. Gen. Laws Ann. ch. 186, § 15B(1)(a)	No notice specified	Not specified		✓	✓	✓		✓
Michigan	No statute								
Minnesota	Minn. Stat. Ann. § 504B.211	Reasonable notice	Not specified	✓	✓	✓	✓		

State Laws on Landlord's Access to Rental Property (continued)

State	State Law Citation	Amount of Notice Required in Nonemergency Situations	Form of Notice	Reasons Landlord May Enter: To Deal With an Emergency	To Inspect the Premises	To Make Repairs, Alterations, or Improvements	To Show Property to Prospective Tenants or Purchasers	During Tenant's Extended Absence	When Tenant has Abandoned the Property
Mississippi	Miss. Code Ann. § 89-7-49	When a landlord believes tenant has abandoned property, and the tenant owes rent, the landlord may request the constable of the county to go onto the premises to ascertain abandonment and leave a notice.	Written notice						✓
Missouri	No statute								
Montana	Mont. Code Ann. §§ 70-24-312, 70-24-426	24 hours	Not specified	✓	✓	✓	✓	✓	✓
Nebraska	Neb. Rev. Stat. §§ 76-1423, 76-1432	One day	Not specified	✓	✓	✓	✓	✓	✓
Nevada	Nev. Rev. Stat. Ann. § 118A.330	24 hours	Not specified	✓	✓	✓	✓		✓

State Laws on Landlord's Access to Rental Property (continued)

				Reasons Landlord May Enter					
State	State Law Citation	Amount of Notice Required in Nonemergency Situations	Form of Notice	To Deal With an Emergency	To Inspect the Premises	To Make Repairs, Alterations, or Improvements	To Show Property to Prospective Tenants or Purchasers	During Tenant's Extended Absence	When Tenant has Abandoned the Property
New Hampshire	N.H. Rev. Stat. Ann. § 540-A:3	Notice that is adequate under the circumstances; however, 48 hours' notice when entering after receiving notice of a bed bug infestation in an adjacent unit	Not specified, but 48 hours when entering to evaluate a possible or actual bed bug infestation.	✓	✓	✓	✓		
New Jersey	N.J. Stat. Ann. § 2A:39-1; N.J.A.C. 5:10-5.1 (for buildings with more than one unit)	In buildings with less than three units, landlords can enter only when they have the tenants' permission or a court order. In buildings with three or more units, landlords have a right to access the unit to inspect it, make repairs or perform maintenance, and deal with emergencies, but must give reasonable notice (one day under ordinary circumstances) before entering.	Not specified						

State Laws on Landlord's Access to Rental Property (continued)

				Reasons Landlord May Enter					
State	**State Law Citation**	**Amount of Notice Required in Nonemergency Situations**	**Form of Notice**	**To Deal With an Emergency**	**To Inspect the Premises**	**To Make Repairs, Alterations, or Improvements**	**To Show Property to Prospective Tenants or Purchasers**	**During Tenant's Extended Absence**	**When Tenant has Abandoned the Property**
New Mexico	N.M. Stat. Ann. §§ 47-8-24, 47-8-34	24 hours	Written notice	✓	✓	✓	✓	✓	✓
New York	No statute								
North Carolina	No statute								
North Dakota	N.D. Cent. Code § 47-16-07.3	Reasonable notice	Not specified	✓	✓	✓	✓		✓
Ohio	Ohio Rev. Code Ann. §§ 5321.04(A)(8), 5321.05(B)	24 hours	Not specified	✓	✓	✓	✓		
Oklahoma	Okla. Stat. Ann. tit. 41, § 128	One day	Not specified	✓	✓	✓	✓		✓
Oregon	Or. Rev. Stat. §§ 90.322, 90.410	24 hours	Not specified	✓	✓	✓	✓	✓	✓
Pennsylvania	No statute								
Rhode Island	R.I. Gen. Laws § 34-18-26	Two days	Not specified	✓	✓	✓	✓	✓	✓
South Carolina	S.C. Code Ann. §§ 27-40-530, 27-40-730	24 hours	Not specified	✓	✓	✓	✓		✓

State Laws on Landlord's Access to Rental Property (continued)

				Reasons Landlord May Enter					
State	State Law Citation	Amount of Notice Required in Nonemergency Situations	Form of Notice	To Deal With an Emergency	To Inspect the Premises	To Make Repairs, Alterations, or Improvements	To Show Property to Prospective Tenants or Purchasers	During Tenant's Extended Absence	When Tenant has Abandoned the Property
South Dakota	No statute								
Tennessee	Tenn. Code Ann. §§ 66-28-403, 66-28-507	24 hours (applies only within the final thirty days of the rental agreement term, when landlord intends to show the premises to prospective renters and this right of access is set forth in the rental agreement)	Not specified	✓	✓	✓	✓	✓	✓
Texas	No statute								
Utah	Utah Code Ann. §§ 57-22-4, 57-22-5(2)(c)	24 hours, unless rental agreement specifies otherwise	Not specified			✓			
Vermont	Vt. Stat. Ann. tit. 9, § 4460	48 hours	Not specified	✓	✓	✓	✓		
Virginia	Va. Code Ann. §§ 55. 1-1229, 55.1-1249	For routine maintenance only: 24 hours, but no notice needed if entry follows tenant's request for maintenance	Not specified	✓	✓	✓	✓	✓	✓

State Laws on Landlord's Access to Rental Property (continued)

				Reasons Landlord May Enter					
State	State Law Citation	Amount of Notice Required in Nonemergency Situations	Form of Notice	To Deal With an Emergency	To Inspect the Premises	To Make Repairs, Alterations, or Improvements	To Show Property to Prospective Tenants or Purchasers	During Tenant's Extended Absence	When Tenant has Abandoned the Property
Washington	Wash. Rev. Code Ann. § 59.18.150	Two days; one day to show property to actual or prospective tenants or buyers	Written notice, unless it is impracticable to do so	✓	✓	✓	✓		✓
West Virginia	No statute								
Wisconsin	Wis. Stat. Ann. § 704.05(2)	With advance notice, landlord may enter at reasonable times	Not specified	✓	✓	✓	✓	✓	
Wyoming	No statute								

Landlord's Duty to Rerent

State	Legal authority	Must make reasonable efforts to rerent	Has no duty to look for or rent to a new tenant	Law is unclear or courts are divided on the issue
Alabama	Ala. Code §§ 35-9A-105, 35-9A-423	✓ [1]		
Alaska	Alaska Stat. § 34.03.230(c)	✓		
Arizona	Ariz. Rev. Stat. § 33-1370	✓		
Arkansas	*Grayson v. Mixon*, 5 S.W.2d 312 (Ark. 1928)		✓	
California	Cal. Civ. Code §§ 1951.2, 1951.4	✓	✓ [2]	
Colorado	*Schneiker v. Gordon*, 732 P.2d 603 (Colo. 1987)	✓ [3]		
Connecticut	Conn. Gen. Stat. Ann. § 47a-11a	✓		
Delaware	25 Del. Code Ann. § 5507(d)(2)	✓		
Dist. of Columbia	D.C. Code Ann. § 42-3505.52	✓		
Florida	Fla. Stat. Ann. § 83.595		✓ [4]	
Georgia	Ga. Code Ann. § 44-7-34; *Peterson v. Midas Realty Corp.*, 287 S.E.2d 61 (Ga. Ct. App. 1981)		✓	✓ [5]
Hawaii	Haw. Rev. Stat. § 521-70(d)	✓ [6]		

1 Landlord can prioritize renting other vacant units first. (Alabama)

2 Landlord must make reasonable efforts to rerent. However, landlord may keep the lease in effect and recover rent as it becomes due if landlord has not retaken possession, and the lease states that the tenant has the right to sublet or assign, subject only to landlord's reasonable limitations. (California)

3 Case law favors mitigation. (Colorado)

4 Landlord has the option of rerenting, standing by and doing nothing (tenant remains liable for rent as it comes due), or invoking its right to a liquidated damages, or early termination, provision. Latter remedy is available only if the lease includes a liquidated damages addendum, or addition, that provides for no more than two months' damages and requires tenant to give no more than 60 days' notice. Liquidated damages provision must substantially include specified language in Fla. Stat. Ann. § 83.595. (Florida)

5 Ga. Code Ann. § 44-7-34 states that nothing precludes landlords from retaining the security deposit for rent and other damages provided the landlord attempts to mitigate the actual damages. However, a Georgia court has held that a landlord could keep the rental vacant and sue for rent as it becomes due in spite of this statute. *Kimber v. Towne Hills Dev. Co.*, 274 S.E.2d 620 (Ga. Ct. App. 1980). (Georgia)

6 The statute implies that the landlord has a duty to rerent: When a tenant breaks the lease, the landlord is entitled to the lesser of (1) the entire rent due for the remainder of the term or (2) the amount of rent accrued during the period reasonably necessary to rerent at a fair rent plus the difference between fair rent and the rent under the lease, as well as a commission for the renting of the unit. The landlord is entitled to the lesser of these two even if the landlord doesn't actually rerent the unit. (Hawaii)

Landlord's Duty to Rerent (continued)

State	Legal authority	Must make reasonable efforts to rerent	Has no duty to look for or rent to a new tenant	Law is unclear or courts are divided on the issue
Idaho	*Consol. Ag v. Rangen, Inc.*, 128 Idaho 228 (Idaho 1996)	✓		
Illinois	735 Ill. Comp. Stat. § 5/9-213.1	✓		
Indiana	*Nylen v. Park Doral Apartments*, 535 N.E.2d. 178 (Ind. Ct. App. 1989)	✓		
Iowa	Iowa Code § 562A.29(3)	✓		
Kansas	Kan. Stat. Ann. § 58-2565(c)	✓		
Kentucky	Ky. Rev. Stat. Ann. § 383.670	✓		
Louisiana	La. Civ. Code § 2002; *Easterling v. Halter Marine, Inc.*, 470 So.2d 221 (La. App. 4 Cir. 1985); *Gray v. Kanavel*, 508 So. 2d 970 (La. Ct. App. 1987)	✓		✓
Maine	Me. Rev. Stat. Ann. tit. 14, § 6010-A	✓		
Maryland	Md. Code Ann., [Real Prop.], § 8-207	✓		
Massachusetts	*Edmands v. Rust & Richardson Drug Co.*, 191 Mass. 123, 128 (1906).	✓ [7]		✓ [8]
Michigan	*Fox v. Roethlisberger*, 85 N.W.2d 73 (Mich. 1957)	✓		
Minnesota	*Control Data Corp. v. Metro Office Parks Co.*, 296 Minn. 302 (Minn. 1973)		✓	

7 From www.masslegalhelp.org/housing/lt1-chapter-11-moving-out.pdf: For various statements of the landlord's requirement to mitigate damages, see *Edmands v. Rust & Richardson Drug Co.*, 191 Mass. 123, 128 (1906). The Massachusetts Supreme Court found that the "[landlord] owed to the [tenant] the duty to use reasonable diligence and to make the loss or damage to the [tenant] as light as [the landlord] reasonably could." *Woodbury v. Sparrell Print*, 198 Mass. 1, 8 (1908). See also *Loitherstein v. International Business Mach. Corp.*, 11 Mass. App. Ct. 91, 95 and n. 3 (1980), rev. denied 441 N.E.2d 1042 (1981); *Cantor v. Van Noorden Co.*, 4 Mass App. Ct. 819 (1976). But see *Fifty Assocs. v. Berger Dry Goods Co. Inc.*, 275 Mass. 509, 514 (1931). Note that the Boston Housing Court has at least twice found a clear obligation to mitigate. *Bridges v. Palmer*, Boston Housing Court, 07326 (May 24, 1979); *Grumman v. Barres*, Boston Housing Court, 06334 (March 1, 1979). See also *Gagne v. Kreinest*, Hampden Housing Court, 91SC1569 (December 6, 1991), where the judge found that a landlord who did not advertise a vacant unit in the newspaper had not mitigated her damages. (Massachusetts)

8 Although case law seems to accept a duty to mitigate, there is no definitive statement of the law and the issue remains unsettled. (Massachusetts)

Landlord's Duty to Rerent (continued)

State	Legal authority	Must make reasonable efforts to rerent	Has no duty to look for or rent to a new tenant	Law is unclear or courts are divided on the issue
Mississippi	*Alsup v. Banks*, 9 So. 895 (Miss. 1891)		✓ [9]	
Missouri	*Rhoden Inv. Co. v. Sears, Roebuck & Co.*, 499 S.W.2d 375 (Mo. 1973); Mo. Rev. Stat. § 535.300	✓ [10]		
Montana	Mont. Code Ann. § 70-24-426	✓		
Nebraska	Neb. Rev. Stat. § 76-1432	✓		
Nevada	Nev. Rev. Stat. Ann. § 118.175	✓		
New Hampshire	*Wen v. Arlen's, Inc.*, 103 A.2d 86 (N.H. 1954); *Modular Mfg., Inc. v. Dernham Co.*, 65 B.R. 856 (Bankr. D.N.H. 1986)			✓
New Jersey	*Sommer v. Kridel*, 378 A.2d 767 (N.J. 1977)	✓		
New Mexico	N.M. Stat. Ann. § 47-8-6	✓		
New York	N.Y. Real Prop. Law § 227-e	✓		
North Carolina	*Isbey v. Crews*, 284 S.E.2d 534 (N.C. Ct. App. 1981)	✓		
North Dakota	N.D. Cent. Code § 47-16-13.5	✓		
Ohio	*Stern v. Taft*, 361 N.E.2d 279 (Ct. App. 1976)	✓ [11]		
Oklahoma	Okla. Stat. Ann. tit. 41, § 129	✓		
Oregon	Or. Rev. Stat. § 90.410	✓		
Pennsylvania	*Stonehedge Square Ltd. P'ship v. Movie Merchs.*, 715 A.2d 1082 (Pa. 1998)		✓	

[9] Many Mississippi attorneys believe this old case is not sound authority, and that a trial judge would find a duty to mitigate in spite of it. (Mississippi)

[10] Landlord must mitigate only if intending to use tenant's security deposit to cover future unpaid rent. (Missouri)

[11] Duty to mitigate applies in absence of any clause that purports to relieve the landlord of this duty (courts might enforce such a clause). (Ohio)

Landlord's Duty to Rerent (continued)

State	Legal authority	Must make reasonable efforts to rerent	Has no duty to look for or rent to a new tenant	Law is unclear or courts are divided on the issue
Rhode Island	R.I. Gen. Laws § 34-18-40	✓		
South Carolina	S.C. Code Ann. § 27-40-730(c)	✓		
South Dakota	No cases or statutes in South Dakota discuss this issue			✓ [12]
Tennessee	Tenn. Code Ann. § 66-28-507(c)	✓ [13]		
Texas	Tex. Prop. Code Ann. § 91.006	✓		
Utah	Utah Code Ann. § 78B-6-816; *Reid v. Mutual of Omaha Ins. Co.*, 776 P.2d 896 (Utah 1989)	✓		
Vermont	Vt. Stat. Ann. tit. 9, § 4462		✓	
Virginia	Va. Code Ann. § 55.1-1251	✓		
Washington	Wash. Rev. Code Ann. §§ 59.18.310, 59.18.595	✓ [14]		
West Virginia	W.Va. Code § 37-6-7, *Teller v. McCoy*, 253 S.E.2d 114 (W.Va. 1978)	✓		
Wisconsin	Wis. Stat. Ann. § 704.29	✓		
Wyoming	*Goodwin v. Upper Crust, Inc.*, 624 P.2d 1192 (1981)	✓		

12 However, it is likely that a S.D. court would require a landlord to mitigate damages. The S.D. Supreme Court has found that "[t]he breaching party has the burden of proving damages would have been lessened by the exercise of reasonable diligence on the part of the non-breaching party." *Ducheneaux v. Miller*, 488 N.W.2d 902, 918 (S.D. Sup. Ct. 1992) (South Dakota)

13 Applies only in counties having a population of more than 75,000, according to the 2010 federal census or any subsequent federal census. (See Tenn. Code Ann. § 66-28-102.) (Tennessee)

14 TENANT'S DEATH: Detailed procedures must be followed when premises are vacant due to tenant's death. (See Wash. Rev. Code Ann. § 59.18.595.) (Washington)

State Laws Prohibiting Landlord Retaliation

State	Statute	Tenant's Complaint to Landlord or Government Agency	Tenant's Involvement in Tenants' Organization	Tenant's Exercise of Legal Right	Retaliation Is Presumed If Negative Reaction by Landlord Within Specified Time of Tenant's Act
Alabama	Ala. Code § 35-9A-501	✓	✓		
Alaska	Alaska Stat. § 34.03.310	✓	✓	✓	
Arizona	Ariz. Rev. Stat. Ann. § 33-1381	✓	✓		6 months
Arkansas [1]	Ark. Code Ann. § 20-27-608	✓			
California [2]	Cal. Civ. Code §§ 1940.35, 1942.5	✓	✓	✓	180 days
Colorado [3]	Colo. Rev. Stat. § 38-12-509	✓	✓		
Connecticut	Conn. Gen. Stat. §§ 47a-20, 47a-33	✓	✓	✓	6 months
Delaware	Del. Code Ann. tit. 25, § 5516	✓	✓	✓	90 days
Dist. of Columbia	D.C. Code Ann. §§ 42-3505.02, 42-3505.06	✓	✓	✓	6 months
Florida [4]	Fla. Stat. Ann. § 83.64	✓	✓	✓	
Georgia	Ga. Code Ann. § 44-7-24	✓	✓	✓	3 months
Hawaii	Haw. Rev. Stat. § 521-74	✓		✓	

1 Only prohibits retaliation by landlord who has received notice of lead hazards. (Arkansas)

2 Applies when a retaliatory eviction follows a court case or administrative hearing concerning the tenant's underlying complaint, membership in a tenant organization, or exercise of a legal right. In this situation, a tenant may claim the benefit of the antiretaliation presumption only if the eviction falls within six months of the final determination of the court case or administrative hearing. Landlord cannot disclose or threaten to disclose to any government authority information regarding tenants' or occupants' immigration or citizenship status for the purpose of retaliating. Statute also provides for actual damages, punitive damages and attorneys' fees to the prevailing party upon request. (California)

3 Statute prohibits landlord from retaliating by increasing rent, decreasing services, or threatening eviction. When a landlord illegally retaliates, tenants may terminate rental agreement and recover either three months' rent or three times their actual damages, whichever is greater, plus attorneys' fees and costs. Also specifies that if a landlord replaces an appliance with a substantially similar one (presumably in response to a complaint), there is no presumption of retaliation. (Colorado)

4 Statute lists retaliatory acts as illustrative, not exhaustive, and includes retaliation after the tenant has paid rent to a condominium, cooperative, or homeowners' association after demand from the association in order to pay the landlord's obligation to the association; when the tenant is a servicemember who legally terminates the tenancy; and when the tenant has exercised his or her rights under state, local, or federal fair housing laws. (Florida)

State Laws Prohibiting Landlord Retaliation (continued)

State	Statute	Tenant's Complaint to Landlord or Government Agency	Tenant's Involvement in Tenants' Organization	Tenant's Exercise of Legal Right	Retaliation Is Presumed If Negative Reaction by Landlord Within Specified Time of Tenant's Act
Idaho [5]	No statute				
Illinois	765 Ill. Comp. Stat. § 720/1	✓			
Indiana	No statute				
Iowa	Iowa Code Ann. § 562A.36	✓	✓		1 year
Kansas	Kan. Stat. Ann. § 58-2572	✓	✓		
Kentucky	Ky. Rev. Stat. Ann. § 383.705	✓	✓		1 year
Louisiana	No statute				
Maine [6]	Me. Rev. Stat. Ann. tit. 14, §§ 6001(3)(4), 6021-A	✓	✓	✓	6 months
Maryland [7]	Md. Code Ann. [Real Prop.] §§ 8-208.1, 8-208.2	✓	✓		6 months
Massachusetts [8]	Mass. Ann. Laws ch. 239, § 2A; ch. 186, § 18	✓	✓	✓	6 months
Michigan [9]	Mich. Comp. Laws § 600.5720	✓	✓	✓	90 days

5 No statute, but Idaho courts have recognized retaliation as a defense to evictions. *Wright v. Brady*, 889 P.2d 105 (Idaho App. 1995). (Idaho)

6 Also presumption of retaliation when tenant has complained to a fair housing agency, has informed landlord that the tenant or tenant's child is a victim, or has communicated to the landlord about or has filed a complaint about the landlord's or landlord's agent's act of sexual harassment. Retaliation is also presumed if tenant is served with an eviction notice within 6 months of tenant's exercise of rights regarding bed bug infestations (does not apply to eviction for nonpayment or for causing substantial damage). (Maine)

7 Landlords may not retaliate against tenants who provide information to the landlord regarding the state's lead hazard reduction program. (Maryland)

8 Applies when a retaliatory eviction follows a court case or administrative hearing concerning the tenant's underlying complaint, membership in a tenant organization, or exercise of a legal right. In this situation, a tenant may claim the benefit of the antiretaliation presumption only if the eviction falls within six months of the final determination of the court case or administrative hearing. (Massachusetts)

9 If landlord tries to increase tenant's obligations under the lease as a penalty for asserting rights, and the tenant doesn't perform these additional obligations, the tenant can use the retaliation as a defense against eviction for failure to perform under the lease. (Michigan)

State Laws Prohibiting Landlord Retaliation (continued)

State	Statute	Tenant's Complaint to Landlord or Government Agency	Tenant's Involvement in Tenants' Organization	Tenant's Exercise of Legal Right	Retaliation Is Presumed If Negative Reaction by Landlord Within Specified Time of Tenant's Act
Minnesota	Minn. Stat. Ann. §§ 504B.285, 504B.441	✓		✓	90 days
Mississippi [10]	Miss. Code Ann. §§ 89-8-9, 89-8-17			✓	
Missouri	No statute				
Montana	Mont. Code Ann. § 70-24-431	✓	✓		6 months
Nebraska	Neb. Rev. Stat. § 76-1439	✓	✓		
Nevada [11]	Nev. Rev. Stat. Ann. § 118A.510	✓	✓	✓	
New Hampshire	N.H. Rev. Stat. Ann. §§ 540:13-a, 540:13-b	✓	✓	✓	6 months
New Jersey [12]	N.J. Stat. Ann. §§ 2A: 42-10.10, 2A:42-10.12	✓	✓	✓	
New Mexico	N.M. Stat. Ann. § 47-8-39	✓	✓	✓	6 months
New York [13]	N.Y. Real Prop. Law § 223-b	✓	✓	✓	One year
North Carolina	N.C. Gen. Stat. § 42-37.1	✓	✓	✓	12 months
North Dakota	No statute				
Ohio	Ohio Rev. Code Ann. § 5321.02	✓	✓		

10 Mississippi law specifically requires that landlords exercise good faith when they terminate or don't renew a lease. This could expand the categories of behavior that are considered prohibited retaliation. (Mississippi)

11 Statute protects tenants or tenants' guests who reasonably request emergency assistance. Local government cannot deem the request itself to be a "nuisance." Landlord may, however, take appropriate adverse actions based on information supplied by emergency responders, as can local governments with regard to declaring a nuisance. (Nevada)

12 If a tenant fails to request a renewal of a lease or tenancy within 90 days of the tenancy's expiration (or by the renewal date specified in the lease if longer than 90 days), a landlord may terminate or not renew without a presumption of retaliation. (New Jersey)

13 Landlord also cannot retaliate for tenant's attempt to enforce the warranty of habitability, nor evict when tenant objects to a new lease with an "unreasonable" rent increase. Presumption of retaliation applies to nonpayment evictions as well as holdovers. (New York)

State Laws Prohibiting Landlord Retaliation (continued)

State	Statute	Tenant's Complaint to Landlord or Government Agency	Tenant's Involvement in Tenants' Organization	Tenant's Exercise of Legal Right	Retaliation Is Presumed If Negative Reaction by Landlord Within Specified Time of Tenant's Act
Oklahoma [14]	No statute				
Oregon	Or. Rev. Stat. § 90.385	✓	✓	✓	
Pennsylvania	68 Pa. Cons. Stat. Ann. §§ 250.205, 250.504-A, and 399.11		✓	✓	6 months (for exercise of legal rights connected with utility service)
Rhode Island	R.I. Gen. Laws Ann. §§ 34-18-46, 34-20-10, and 34-20-11	✓	✓	✓	6 months
South Carolina	S.C. Code Ann. § 27-40-910	✓			
South Dakota	S.D. Cod. Laws Ann. §§ 43-32-27, 43-32-28	✓	✓		180 days
Tennessee	Tenn. Code Ann. §§ 66-28-514, 68-111-105	✓		✓	
Texas	Tex. Prop. Code § 92.331	✓	✓	✓	6 months
Utah	*Building Monitoring Sys. v. Paxton*, 905 P.2d 1215 (Utah 1995)	✓			
Vermont [15]	Vt. Stat. Ann. tit. 9, § 4465	✓	✓		90 days
Virginia [16]	Va. Code Ann. §§ 55.1-1258, 55.1-1259	✓	✓	✓	
Washington	Wash. Rev. Code §§ 59.18.240, 59.18.250	✓		✓	90 days

[14] Oklahoma law specifically requires that landlords exercise good faith in their performance under the Oklahoma Residential Landlord and Tenant Act. An argument could perhaps be made that terminating a tenancy or otherwise retaliating against a tenant for taking certain legal measures could be in bad faith. (Oklahoma)

[15] Retaliation presumed only when landlord terminates for reasons other than rent nonpayment, after tenant has filed complaint with a governmental entity alleging noncompliance with health or safety regulations. (Vermont)

[16] Tenants can sue for damages and injunction. (Virginia)

State Laws Prohibiting Landlord Retaliation (continued)

State	Statute	Tenant's Complaint to Landlord or Government Agency	Tenant's Involvement in Tenants' Organization	Tenant's Exercise of Legal Right	Retaliation Is Presumed If Negative Reaction by Landlord Within Specified Time of Tenant's Act
West Virginia	*Imperial Colliery Co. v. Fout,* 373 S.E.2d 489 (1988); *Murphy v. Smallridge,* 468 S.E.2d 167 (W. Va. 1996)	✓		✓	
Wisconsin	Wis. Stat. § 704.45	✓		✓	
Wyoming	No statute				

Index

D

O

P

S

V

W

Z